GOD'S
ADVOCATES

D1376936

List of Contributors

Tina Beattie is Senior Lecturer in Christian Studies at Roehampton University, London.

David Burrell is Hesburgh Professor of Theology and Philosophy at Notre Dame University.

J. Kameron Carter is Assistant Professor of Theology and Black Church Studies at Duke University.

Sarah Coakley is Edward Mallinckrodt Jr Professor of Divinity at Harvard University.

Stanley Hauerwas is Gilbert T. Rowe Professor of Theological Ethics at Duke University.

Christopher J. Insole teaches the philosophy of religion at Cambridge University.

Joan Lockwood O'Donovan is a freelance theologian and lecturer.

Jean-Luc Marion is Professor of Philosophy at the Sorbonne University in Paris, and John Nuveen Professor of the Philosophy of Religion and Theology at the University of Chicago.

David Martin is Emeritus Professor of Sociology at the London School of Economics, and Hon. Professor of Religious Studies at Lancaster University.

Janet Martin Soskice is Reader in Philosophical Theology at Cambridge University.

John Milbank is Professor of Religion, Politics and Ethics at Nottingham University.

Oliver O'Donovan is Regius Professor of Moral and Pastoral Theology at Oxford University.

Simon Oliver is Lecturer in Theology at the University of Wales, Lampeter.

Alvin Plantinga is John A. O'Brien Professor of Philosophy at Notre Dame University.

Christoph Schwöbel is Professor of Systematic Theology and the Philosophy of Religion at Tübingen University.

Miroslav Volf is Henry B. Wright Professor of Systematic Theology at Yale University.

Samuel Wells is Dean of Chapel at Duke University.

Rowan Williams is Archbishop of Canterbury. He was formerly Lady Margaret Professor of Divinity at Oxford University.

GOD'S
ADVOCATES

Christian Thinkers in Conversation

RUPERT SHORTT

DARTON·LONGMAN+TODD

for
GLYN PAFLIN

First published in 2005 by
Darton, Longman and Todd Ltd
1 Spencer Court
140–142 Wandsworth High Street
London SW18 4JJ

© 2005 Rupert Shortt

The right of Rupert Shortt to be identified as the Author
of this work has been asserted in accordance with the
Copyright, Designs and Patents Act 1988.

ISBN 0–232–52545–5

A catalogue record for this book is available from the British Library.

Designed and produced by Sandie Boccacci
Phototypeset in 10/12.5pt Minion
Printed and bound in Great Britain by
Page Bros, Norwich, Norfolk

"Stare into the void and then turn away, and maybe the answer is God."

Janet Martin Soskice

Contents

Acknowledgements

For discussing the philosophy underlying this book with me, I am most grateful to Timothy McDermott, Anthony Kenny and Richard Cross. Advice on theological questions was generously given by John Webster, Jane Williams, Steve Holms, Michael Barnes SJ, Gerald O'Collins SJ and Lionel Wickham. I have also profited from guidance of a general kind from Bernice Martin, José Prado, Arnold Hunt and Alison Shell.

My deepest debt is to the nineteen theologians and philosophers who agreed to be God's advocates, and then provided me with so much stimulus and good company thereafter. (One of their number, Kathryn Tanner, had to withdraw halfway, through pressure of other work. But I hope that her mark can be traced at various points in the pages that follow.)

The labour of transcribing and editing a large body of recorded material was eased by the patience and helpfulness of all concerned, and the invaluable assistance of Sarah Hillman. My burden was further lightened through a grant from the K Blundell Trust. I am obliged to Dorothy Sym of the Society of Authors who administered my application, and to the judges of the 2003 awards: Simon Brett, John Burnside, Anne Chisholm, Susanna Gross and Philip Ziegler.

I am also very thankful to Brendan Walsh of Darton, Longman and Todd for inviting me to undertake the project, and for all the support that he, Helen Porter and their colleagues have provided along the way.

RUPERT SHORTT
London, April 2005

Rupert Shortt

Preface

What is happening at the cutting edge of Christian thought, and why does it matter? Three decades ago the academic-turned-politician Bryan Magee published *Men of Ideas*, drawn from dialogues with fifteen major scholars, 'to introduce a new and wider public to the present state of ... discussion in some of the most interesting areas of philosophy'.[1] Though I would not claim to have Magee's expertise, and consequently take a lower profile during the conversations ahead, my aim in *God's Advocates* is to apply parts of his template to theology. I do so by concentrating specifically on a group of outstanding thinkers – established names and newer voices – in and on the fringes of the anglophone world.

A comprehensive review, including figures from the Eastern Orthodox fold, Latin America, Africa and Asia, would therefore have been beyond my brief. Much interesting work and many distinguished people are omitted. Nonetheless, I hope that this book reflects variety on several levels, and consensus, too: if my collaborators have a premise in common, it is that theology has recovered its nerve notably in recent years, especially in North America and Britain, and this confidence springs from renewed esteem for Christianity's core resources rather than a thirst for simplistic certainties.

At a time of sharp conflict between secularists and religious conservatives on several continents, the noteworthiness of such a starting point hardly needs emphasising. Its tenability also needs to be probed. Cardinal Cormac Murphy-O'Connor, to name only one sympathetic observer, has declared Christianity to be 'almost vanquished' as an influence on political decisions and people's moral lives in Western Europe.[2] For many others, of course, the problem is precisely that faith groups wield too much power. I write as a journalist without settled convictions about many of the subjects discussed; so as well as inviting every interviewee to describe his or her work, I also play Devil's advocate at various points.

The opening chapter, in which Archbishop Rowan Williams defends the credibility of Christian belief and answers some common objections to it, may serve as an aid to orientation. His reading of a significant strand of modern theological history is widely shared, and can be summed up as follows. It was natural that the Church should spend a period on the back foot in reaction to the Enlightenment, when its privileges were challenged for often laudable reasons. During the nineteenth and early twentieth centuries cultural change was shunned by the Roman Catholic hierarchy, with one set of very damaging and widely rehearsed consequences. But some Christians of other backgrounds made the opposite mistake of embracing modernity with too tight a grip. In the Protestant world, the tide turned after the First World War with the writings of Karl Barth. His achievement lay in insisting that theology has its own coherence, and must therefore identify its criteria independently of secular authorisation. His weakness sprang from his strength. Underscoring the centrality of revelation was achieved at the high price of downgrading reason and withdrawing into a fideistic cocoon.

For much of the 1960s and 1970s (so this thesis runs), liberal theology made a well-intentioned attempt to express the Christian message in terms palatable to humanity 'come of age', but often reproduced earlier errors. Time and again my interlocutors identify the ethos of this period as one of the spurs to their evolution along a different path, assisted by the renewal of Catholic thought, among other developments. A fresh estimate of the theological task emerged: to give the full-blooded account of belief desiderated by Barth, but without thereby blowing up bridges to the wider world. The novelty of this conception was relative, of course. Numerous luminaries from the patristic and medieval periods had undertaken a comparable project, and their vision was echoed as recently as the mid-twentieth century by Henri de Lubac and other pioneers of the *nouvelle théologie* in France.

This return to the sources – or *ressourcement* – is to be seen not only in the chapter on Radical Orthodoxy, one of the most significant theological movements in the Christian world today, but also in the revival of trinitarian teaching discussed by Christoph Schwöbel; in J. Kameron Carter's argument that black Christians should unshackle themselves from secular categories in order to express an authentically theological vision; and in the emphasis of both Sarah Coakley and Tina Beattie on the tradition's capacity to nourish thinking about the symbolism of gender. The variety to which I've already referred is reflected in some frank clashes of outlook, especially about the relation between positive and negative statements about God,[3] and the vexed subject of a Christian's right relation to society and the political order. Stanley Hauerwas and Sam Wells commend a radical perspective; David Martin upholds the integrity of Christian realism as conceived by Reinhold Niebuhr. Oliver and Joan O'Donovan see a contradiction at liberalism's heart, on the basis that it spurns a comprehensive vision of the common good. Christopher Insole, on the other hand, sees a theological ground for arguing in liberalism's defence. As I've indicated, it is not my business to take sides or seek to arbitrate in these arguments. I ask my interviewees to defend their positions, and leave readers to make their own minds up about the available alternatives.

That discussions of this kind are far removed from being shop talk should be evident, but in a climate where atheism is often thought to be synonymous with common sense or neutrality, it perhaps needs restating. Secular assumptions are challenged at length in the philosophical chapters, and sceptics (devout or otherwise) might consider starting here – with the case for belief made in different ways by Janet Martin Soskice and Alvin Plantinga, for example; or with David Burrell, who sees parallels between St Thomas Aquinas and postmodernism, and shows him to have been a far less parochial figure than many of his successors, religious or otherwise, in the West. Aquinas' dialogue with Jewish and Islamic thinkers has helped reopen deep channels of communication at the dawn of the twenty-first century, and forms part of the background to a subject pursued by Miroslav Volf, who grew up in Communist Yugoslavia and experienced the Balkan war at first hand before moving to the United States. I have no section specifically devoted to interfaith dialogue, but Volf, among others, erects signposts showing how such an encounter might proceed.

Non-believers sometimes misconstrue the creed they reject. The perils of turning a deaf ear to reputable theology were underlined for me recently when Antony Flew, a British proponent of atheism for half a century, announced a change of heart. For scientific reasons, he now accepted the hypothesis that the universe was created. 'I'm thinking of a God very different from the God of Christianity and far away from the God of Islam,' he added, 'because both are depicted as omnipotent Oriental despots, cosmic Saddam Husseins.'[4] And what of the insistence by theologians over many centuries that God is neither a tyrant nor any other kind of thing? It's hard to say much in defence of Flew's misjudgement, other than that it partly overlaps with the view of some even bigger philosophical names, including those who have professed greater sympathy for religion. Heidegger famously distinguished between beings in the world and the ground of being, or being as such. He held that Western thought, starting with Plato, evolved as a 'history of nihilism',[5] since this radical contrast, known as the ontological differ-ence, had been consistently ignored, thereby reducing God to the status of a superbeing pitched on the same plane as creation. He described this sorry legacy as 'ontotheology'. Christian thought has indeed fallen into this trap at times, with disastrous results, as John Milbank and Jean-Luc Marion contend. But Heidegger was tilting at windmills. Aquinas, among other architects of tradition, equips Christians to conceive of divine being in a far subtler way. He also supplies a vocabulary for talk-ing of creation *ex nihilo*, and addressing the question that is perhaps atheism's Achilles' heel: why there is something rather than nothing.

To say more at this stage would be to anticipate, but two pithy remarks, by Jean-Luc Marion and Janet Martin Soskice respectively, strike me as worth flagging. Marion, who holds chairs in philosophy formerly occupied by Levinas at the Sorbonne and Ricoeur in Chicago, suggests that theology is more of a force to be reckoned with – 'more interesting . . . much more rational' – than even many theologians realise. Soskice's comment forms the epigraph to this book, and arises from the conviction that our lives afford us glimpses of an inexhaustible glory.

All the chapters have been edited for the page, but the conversational flavours of the original transcripts are by and large preserved. I also invited everyone to speak autobiographically if they wished, and varied the format from chapter to chapter. In several cases it seemed appropri-ate for me to give an introductory sketch of the terrain as an aid to readers; in other instances the device was unnecessary. Some people asked to be part of three-way conversations, and this appeared reason-able, given the close working partnerships between the O'Donovans, say, and between Stanley Hauerwas and Sam Wells. Simon Oliver speaks as a former pupil of John Milbank, pondering possible ways forward for Radical Orthodoxy. Alvin Plantinga represents one major approach to the philosophy of religion; Christopher Insole ploughs a different furrow in the same field. Other contributors preferred to be interviewed as individuals. The varied length of the chapters is connected with accessi-bility. Rowan Williams spreads his wings to provide a *tour d'horizon*. Others take up less space, confining themselves to general accounts of sometimes dauntingly technical subjects. I hope that a mixed menu of this kind will prove more appetising.

I
Rowan Williams

Belief and Theology: Some Core Questions

SHORTT: I'd like to cover a fair amount of ground in this discussion – to talk about a few of the commonest objections to Christian belief, and then look briefly at the evolution of your own thought, and at developments on the frontiers of theology over the past few years. But let's begin with what prompts the spiritual impulse in the first place. How would you go about defending your world view to an audience of sceptics?

WILLIAMS: I think theological talk gets off the ground because some profound puzzlement has shaken up frames of reference. You need to find new words to talk about the whole environment, the entire context in which you're living. And that's why the New Testament is so important for looking at how theology works. Something enormous has happened, which has really challenged the categories available, and so I like to say the New Testament is work in progress because it reflects not a uniform, bland final version, but – this is where inspiration comes in – the immediacy of a shock and a realignment of how you talk about God and creation. In a sense, it muddles up the categories, it says you have to start somehow thinking about God as not confined to elsewhere – but in terms of Word or Son or Spirit actually accessible within very material, specific conditions.

SHORTT: Can we spool back a stage in the argument before returning to the New Testament? How would you engage with an atheist who can't make any sense of religious language, and can't see the need for it?

WILLIAMS: Yes. Beyond specifically Christian theology is the question of why religious reference at all is interesting or plausible or convincing. And I've been thinking quite a bit in recent years about the way in which there is something about language itself that poses a question, poses a problem to naked secularism. When we speak, we make a very considerable act of trust. We expect to be understood, we expect to be answered. We expect, in other words, that what we generate from our imagining and remembering plays into something larger, and we do so, of course, because we have been shaped by language. You speak to a child, a speechless child, and over a period of years language emerges. One of the most exciting things for any parents is simply watching how a child starts to speak and how he or she assimilates that world that is language. And you can speak to your cat for as long as you like, and somehow it doesn't happen. At least we'd be very surprised and startled if it did, and, of course, some of the very best fantasy stories are predicated on just that surprise.

But here we go in human relations, making large acts of trust all the time as we speak and communicate with each other, and as language evolves it becomes something much more than simply an exchange of information. Indeed, to put it that way is perhaps misleading. It's not as if you begin with a set of simple directions and then you evolve towards something more imaginative. After all, when you talk to a child you will do considerable damage if all you ever say is 'Don't touch,' or 'The cat sat on the mat.' You sing to children, you tell them stories from the word Go. You progress through these little board books with them that take them into bright and different worlds. It's as if language itself is always trying to bound out of functional and practical limits, as if the very existence of language says, The world is colossal, we will not exhaust it. Now that doesn't say, And so, you've got to believe in God. It *does* say that understanding what human consciousness and human interaction are about is a long process with no obvious cut-off point. It places us in relation to something more than ourselves. And it's that question which seems to me very near the heart of distinctively religious commitment. We are already in relation to something we can't say. To call that God, and I'm deliberately echoing St Thomas Aquinas here, requires quite a bit of stitching together of different bits of experience and history. I'm thinking of those moments in which a sense of newness, or conversion if you like, arises in collective and individual lives, and a connection is made with events, traditions, practices, that have the name God around them. You see the balls falling into the holes, click, click, click, ah yes, there is a way of connecting the something to which we already related with the idea of a reality that is, in some manner, more like the personal than anything else. In other words sensing the something you're already related to as a bestower, a giver, a maker, a lover.

SHORTT: **And moving on to something nearer the Church's proclamation?**

WILLIAMS: As for the coherence of the ideas of Christianity, everything evolves like the oak from the acorn out of that sense of dislocation that comes around the death and the resurrection of Jesus. If Jesus is the one who now and for ever decides, determines, who is in the company of God, who is in the favour of God, who belongs to the people of God, then the authority, the inner solidity of who Jesus is, has to be connected with the very purpose of God, what God is about. Jesus acts as if he has the right to determine who belongs to the people of God. And he does that in welcome, in forgiveness and judgement and all the other things that the Gospels spell out. And therefore, if you take him seriously, you have at some point to make the connection with, as I say, what God is about, what are the purposes of God, the desires of God. And distinctively Christian theology begins to take shape when those two things are brought together: the actions and the words and the sufferings of this particular human being, and the vision of a God whose purpose is unrestricted fellowship with the human beings that he's made.

Inexhaustible resourcefulness in recovering them from their sin and their failure, inexhaustible promise in drawing them into joy. That's where the distinctively Christian picture of God begins, putting those things together, and, furthermore, understanding that the community formed on this basis subsists not just because its members choose to opt in, but because they say, in the basic metaphor of some of the New Testament, The air we breathe, the Spirit, is the life of God. When you're close to the Jesus who died and was raised and vindicated, then the air you breathe is God. And the sort of jargon – Holy Spirit – which trips off the tongue so easily now has in some ways to be, as it were, rendered back into that basic powerful metaphor: Spirit is breath, Spirit is wind, Spirit is the air you breathe. And therefore that's the very climate of life when you are in friendship, proximity, communion, with the Jesus who is not dead.

SHORTT: **Many people who know your writings or preaching will be familiar with the emphasis you lay on the evidence of transformed lives in any account of the faith.**

WILLIAMS: Yes. If I were trying to persuade somebody now of the coherence of Christianity, I'd certainly think there was a task to be done of expounding the doctrinal pattern, but what interests me more and more is, if you like, pointing people towards a Christian life and saying, Now, what are the contours of that life? What's the shape of it? What are the problems it poses? It's almost as if the religious person needs to say to the secularist, there's not only a problem of evil: there's a problem of good. Take a life like that of Dorothy Day, the American Catholic radical pacifist. A long life – she wrote a book about her own life called *The Long Loneliness* – somebody who starts off as a Marxist and social activist in the United States in the post-First World War period, has an abortion, has an illegitimate child, goes in and out of an unsuccessful marriage and several other relationships, then fairly suddenly comes to a point where she says, 'Why am I passionate about people?' And goes into a church, and something connects. After that she simply spends the rest of her very long life being an advocate and a companion for people who have no one else to be an advocate and companion. And she does it because of a sense that the most decisive and fruitful way of being human is to be an advocate and companion in the name of God.

I'm interested in tracing through what pushes a life like that, what gives it energy and shape. And to say to the secularist, Well, can you at least see the connection there between a particular intensely committed attitude to humanity and a belief in God? Now that's the start of a conversation. It's not saying, Oh, you've got to believe in God because Dorothy Day believed in God; or, People are so wonderful: therefore you've got to believe in God. No, it's more, How is it that in a life like that you can carry on in perpetual defeat at some levels, deliberately clinging to a very minority interpretation of Roman Catholicism, if you think of American Catholicism of the twentieth century? Dorothy Day writing about the Cardinal Archbishop of New York in the 1950s is quite an education.

SHORTT: How did they fall out?

WILLIAMS: She was always deeply respectful of church authority and made it absolutely clear she disagreed with the cardinal about everything except the Catholic faith. They clashed over Vietnam and the blessing of the military and all the rest of it. So what is it that holds someone in defeat, in a minority position, through all that? To talk about the coherence of the Christian faith isn't just to lay out a system of doctrine and say, That's what it looks like. It's to look at how lives cohere, how a vision gives shape to a life.

SHORTT: Let's look now at some of the most troublesome objections to Christianity. I know a very bright and thoughtful theological graduate who's a floating voter as far as professions of faith are concerned. He thinks that making a formal commitment would pose too large an intellectual burden, and he instances three stumbling blocks in particular. One is the question of the brain and the mind. Like many others, he feels that Christianity in the end entails some kind of dualism, but that this is precluded by a scientific understanding of the world. Christianity appears to say that the mind and the body can exist independently if God wishes. My friend maintains that, as physical creatures, we *are* our mental process – no brain, no mind – and therefore that death means total extinction. This of course leaves him highly sceptical about the possibility of an afterlife.

WILLIAMS: Certainly, popular religious belief has always swung towards dualism. It sounds easy. There's a bit of us that's solid and a bit of us that's shadowy, smoky, vapoury, the cartoon image of the dead body and the little ghost whizzing up and away. Now I think from the very beginning of Christianity, never mind other faiths, that theologians have been fighting a bit of a rearguard action against this, and I'm very interested by the way in which, for somebody like Aquinas in the Middle Ages, the soul and the body are, whatever else the relation, absolutely not like that. The soul is the form of the body, he says. What we mean by soul is not some little extra bit, but the shape and the sense of the cohesion of this bodily history that is a person in the world. It's rather like, to use a simile that owes a bit to Wittgenstein, the relation between the smile and the face; or it's more like that than the relation between the coffee and the cup. Now that immediately poses the problem that's supposed to be posed by modern science: OK, so what about when the body stops being there? I think there are two kinds of response that can be made. But both depend on the idea that life after death, to use the shorthand, isn't a function of something in us that survives, but something to do with our doctrine of God. So let me try to explain that.

For the Christian, part of the shape and the cohesion of a human material life is bound up with relationship with God, and a belief that God's relation with us is one of commitment. One of the things that's driven Christians to say that you can't just draw a line at physical death, is whether that can be consistent with the nature of God. If God has bound his life in with ours in a material life, when we happen to die, does God say, Oh well, there's a shame, and move on to the next relationship, as it were? 'So I kissed her little sister and forgot my Clementine.' And the answer Christians have given is, No, that isn't what happens, that's counter-intuitive in relation to our doctrine of *God*, not our doctrine of us.

The second theme that comes in is what Christians have talked about in terms of the resurrection of the body. Whatever our relationship is with God on the far side of our material death, it involves God's giving another shape, another carrier, another vehicle, to the (in scientific terms) information complex that is the life we have lived, the memory we have acquired in this physical body. And something has got to be continuous between now and then. Unfortunately we haven't a clue how that works. And that's why I think with talk about eternal life, life after death, we have to be very reticent, and not suppose we've got this sorted. This is why I say it's about our doctrine of God, not trying to locate the bit of us that survives. It's saying, We, in biblical terms, believe in a God who raises the dead, which is a huge claim. But the more that's about the character of God and the less it's an attempt to produce a dualist theory of us, the less vulnerable I think it is to the straight scientific criticism. That still leaves a lot of loose ends, goodness knows. But all these issues about the relation between brain and mind philosophically seem to get more, not less, complex as we go on.

SHORTT: **And not necessarily inimical to religious claims?**

WILLIAMS: No, that's right. I think a lot of theorists in this area get a bit panicky when it's suggested that they're moving in a faintly religious direction. They will say, quite rightly, It's not about that. But I think that a very respectable sector of the philosophical community would say that reductionism – the mind is no more than physical processes – is actually a philosophically inept way of coming at the issue – because 'no more than physical process' is itself an analysis that presupposes other sorts of process than physical process. And you end up caught in a philosophical trap.

SHORTT: **And you find this mistake in the pronouncements of scientists hostile to Christianity such as Richard Dawkins or Peter Atkins or Susan Greenfield?**

WILLIAMS: Yes. I find reading Dawkins and others that there's tremendous analytical sophistication in respect of physical processes, allied to philosophical crudity. What fascinates me about the notions of the selfish gene and the selfish 'meme' is that you need metaphors drawn from highly sophisticated intentional accounts of human interaction to describe supposedly physical processes. That ought to give you pause because it suggests that reductionism collapses on itself. Selfish is a highly loaded, highly sophisticated word. Selfish is a word about motives, not material processes. Selfish is a word that assumes things about purposes, consciousness, and all the rest of it. And you end up with what seems to me an almost comical mythology of little things running around with intentions inside your head or inside your organism. It's what philosophers sometimes call the homunculus problem, the little man who does things. The selfish gene is bad enough. The selfish meme – the mental structure that reproduces itself – I can't make any sense of, philosophically speaking. Come back, A. J. Ayer, I say, on that point.

SHORTT: **The next of my three objections is the old conundrum about divine action and miracles. You know the view: science is so successful at explaining the phenomena of the world, and so talk of miracles flies in the face of that. There's a lack of evidence for miracles, as well as an intrinsic implausibility about them.**

WILLIAMS: It's a very big issue, the question of divine action, and again, I think, it has to be taken in connection with a doctrine of God rather than a very specific examination of any particular claim to start with. Let's put it this way. For a theological believer the relation of God to creation is neither that of the old image of someone who winds up the watch and leaves it, nor is it that of a director in a theatre or, worse, a puppet master who's constantly adjusting what's going on. It's the relation of an eternal activity which moment by moment energises, makes real, makes active, what there is, and I sometimes feel that a lot of our theology has lost that extraordinarily vivid or exhilarating sense of the world penetrated by divine energy in the classical theological terms.

SHORTT: **Augustine's view.**

WILLIAMS: It's in Augustine, it's in Thomas, it's very clearly in the Eastern Orthodox tradition, where you have precisely that sense of what they call the 'divine energy' penetrating creation so everything is in that sense shot through with the grandeur of God, as Gerard Manley Hopkins said.

SHORTT: **'Charged'.**

WILLIAMS: 'Charged with the grandeur of God./It will flame out like shining from shook foil': there we are. And people say Christianity is a bit sniffy about material reality. Well, all right, some of it is, but it does us no harm to remember that other tradition. As the Dominican philosopher Herbert McCabe – God rest him – used to say, God is more deeply involved with any creature than we can imagine, and that's why we don't have to invent stories about God getting involved.

How, then, does that energising work? It works, we believe, according to the rational purpose of God. It works in orderly and cohesive ways. The world that God makes is a world that makes sense, interlocks, balances, works together, and what we mean by natural laws in the theological sense. You relate to that divine rationality, very deeply rooted again in Christian and Jewish and Muslim tradition. So the Jew and the Muslim and the Christian would, I think, then want to add the following question: Can we imagine certain circumstances in which the action of God in relation to one of these coherent bits of the world is, to use a rather weak analogy, that much closer to the surface than it habitually is? We may not be able to understand what the rule of that is, or the regularity of that is, but if what is sustaining every reality is the energy, the action, of God, then is it so difficult to believe that from God's point of view and not ours, there are bits of the universal order where the fabric is thinner, where the coming together of certain conditions makes it possible for the act of God to be a little more transparent? And when we talk of miracle, it's that.

It's not God making a punctiliar intervention – 'Oh, I think I'd better sort that out', leaning down from heaven and adjusting a few nuts and bolts – it's more that the world is such that when certain conditions arise, certain responses are made, and, all right, let's say it, certain prayers are prayed, a door is opened for divine action to act irregularly, to act in a way you would not, from the rest of the picture, have expected. So I think you have to start by trying to get hold of the implication of that picture of a universe in which the glory and energy of God is always pretty near the surface, and in certain circumstances very near the surface.

SHORTT: Perhaps that provides a fitting lead-in to the third objection: the problem of evil and suffering.

WILLIAMS: I think the picture of the universe and God's relation to it that I've sketched provides a way to bring some sense to talk about the problem of evil. Now here, with what's obviously emotionally the greatest barrier for most people to belief, it's very easy to fall into different sorts of caricature. You know: the distant God who's wound up the spring of the universe and gone away; or the interfering God who mysteriously fails to interfere when we really want him to. If you hang on to some sense of God's intimate relation with the world, God's energising, as I say, of what's going on and the consistency and interlocking coherence of that, what you're rejecting is a picture of a God whose mind and will observe the world from a distance deciding whether or not to intervene. We have a God deeply involved in the process of the world, whose control of the world's processes is very unlike that of the puppet master. The world is different from God and yet activated by God. Because it's different from God, it's subject to

possibilities of tension, collision. The way in which laws and regulari-
ties unfold will, from the human point of view, lead to tragedy from
time to time. God's relation to that is not one of either planning it or
resolving it as we normally understand it. God's relation to that is his
own accessibility, the resource that is there in God for any situation
which makes it possible for that situation to be transfigured or taken
forward.

And I think that in traditional Christian discussions about this
subject, especially in St Augustine, what you've got is an attempt to say
that for creation to be different from God it can't be perfect. It unfolds
in time; it unfolds by processes working out their own logic. Now in
a world without conscious creatures that wouldn't be a problem.
Earthquakes on Jupiter are neither here nor there, and you know the
famous philosophic example of the tree falling in the forest un-
observed: does it make a noise? Well, whether or not it does, again it's
neither here nor there: it doesn't fall on anybody. As soon as there is
somebody for a tree to fall on or somebody for an earthquake to
crush, you have a problem. You have the conscious, infinitely valuable
person involved in this. So the real problem of evil, I think, arises
when there are conscious beings who tell stories about suffering,
remember suffering, make connections about it, and I leave open the
question of how far into the animal kingdom that extends, but I suspect it already is a problem as soon as you have sentience, as soon as
you have beings with feeling.

So, as I say, it's not that God is at a distance from which he can
come in and sort things out, because God doesn't sit alongside the
world. But in a world where tragedy happens, God is faithfully
present, able to offer, to give what he is to help us in living through or
living past suffering. It's not a very satisfactory answer: it's an answer
at a rather broad metaphysical level which is not what you talk about
when you're alongside the mother of the child with leukaemia.

SHORTT: You've said in a critique of Professor Marilyn McCord Adams'
discussion of theodicy that you suspect it is more religiously imperative to be worried by evil than to put it into a satisfactory theoretical
or aesthetic context, 'if only because such a worry keeps obstinately
open the perspective of the sufferer, the subject, for whom this is
never a question of aesthetics, however imaginatively and
discriminatingly pursued'.[1] And yet the believer is committed to the
conviction that God will wipe away all tears, as the New Testament
puts it.[2] That traditional view of theodicy does seem to contradict the
models of human love that we have. We speak of God as parent, and

yet if your child were in the path of an oncoming juggernaut and you had just enough time to leap out into the street and rescue him or her, you would do so. It would be a dereliction of your parental duty if you didn't. Yet so many people say that God does have the power in principle, but doesn't use it.

WILLIAMS: 'God is up in heaven and he doesn't do a thing,/With a million angels watching and they never move a wing.' Yes.

SHORTT: Who said that?

WILLIAMS: Sydney Carter in *The Good Friday Song*. 'It's God they ought to crucify instead of you and me', which I remember had a huge impact on me as a teenager. Because it's the good thief saying it to Jesus. 'It's God they ought to crucify instead of you and me,/I said to the carpenter a-hanging on a tree.'

First of all, then, on the parenting image. It is undoubtedly one of those places where that language breaks down. And people rail at God for being a bad parent. The trouble is that the God who has the power to intervene but doesn't, in the way it's usually perceived, suggests the Superman model; that is, God is an agent who can come in and change things in a nice simple manner, pushing the child out of the way: what Superman does in the comics. And you know some of the best Superman fantasies are all about the choices he faces, he can't opt for more than one of these at once; if he does, he or his powers are weakened in particular ways and particular circumstances. There's lots of theology in Superman – not very good theology, but the questions are there. The point I'm making is that whatever the power of God is, it's not quite like that.

God is better characterised in Bill Vanstone's phrase, I think, as the agent who bears everything up. Which means that the instant solution of suffering or avoidance of suffering, if it ever happens, can't happen by the Superman method. It just may be that in some circumstances, in ways we can't see because we don't have that independent perspective, the intensive prayer of somebody may allow God in.

SHORTT: **Because you've spoken of miracles, and Christian tradition is committed to belief in miracles.**

WILLIAMS: That's right, I do believe that that sometimes happens. C. S. Lewis has that extraordinary account, in one of his letters, of praying to experience his wife's suffering in her last illness, and being promptly crippled with the pains in the bone marrow that his wife was going through. Sometimes prayer, it seems, lets God in. To believe in creation at all is, I think, to believe in that sort of relation between God and creation which does not provide a neat distance between

God and us. Total difference and yet not a distance. And the hard thing talking about all this is coming to terms with what it means.

SHORTT: Creation involves contingency and risk – to put it starkly, you're saying that you've got to crack some eggs to make an omelette.

WILLIAMS: Yes, if you want to talk of eggs and omelettes.

SHORTT: One person who picks up on this in blunt terms is the literary critic James Wood. His grasp of theology may not be all that nuanced, but he does encapsulate the common scepticism about whether Christianity provides a convincing account of our experience. You'll recall that at the end of his book *The Broken Estate* he moves from asserting that the problem of pain has no solution to what he sees as its corollary – the business of what possible justification there can be for our earthly life (notionally just the flickering of an eye when measured against eternity), given that our destiny is said to be one of bliss in the company of God. 'I have always found Philip's cry to Jesus in John 14, piercing,' Wood writes: ' "Philip saith unto him, Lord, shew us the Father, and it sufficeth us." But the Lord does not show us the Father. It seems obvious to theologians like Richard Swinburne that a world of limited freedom and absolute transparency of knowledge, in which not one of us is in any doubt about our creator, would be a limited, useless place. But it would not, presumably, be useless to God. It is what heaven would be like; and why, before heaven, must we live? Why must we move through this unhappy, painful rehearsal for heaven, this desperate ante-chamber, this foreword written by an anonymous author, this hard prelude in which so few of us can find our way?'[3]

WILLIAMS: One of the interesting points James Wood makes there is that if we're going to live in bliss with God for ever, why not start now? And leaving aside for a moment the general cosmological question about the nature of creation, I suppose the Christian would have to say, We are such beings that living in bliss with God can never be other than something we *learn*. And that doesn't mean we have to learn through an unnecessarily painful obstacle course: it is simply something that takes time. Growing into fellowship with God is not an instantaneous thing, even in a life relatively light on suffering. Relation with God takes time. Just as in human love you can't rush it, just as in the learning of a language you can't rush it, so this is the kind of thing that just ineluctably takes time.

Why does God create at all, and why, if this is the best of all possible worlds, isn't it better? Ultimately the only answer is that if it's part of the very essence of being creation that it takes time and that it's subject to change and to some extent to conflict, then you're always in a sense looking at possible creations, you're always looking at a choice of imperfections. We can have no idea what multiple-choice universes are like in that sense. Sooner or later, if you believe in creation itself, you're brought back to that fundamental point: it's not God, it's different from God.

God creates so that what is not God will be drawn into the joy of being God. And the constraint here is that whatever is not God is in some way vulnerable. And you could say that the very smoothest imaginable world would, in infinite time, still be vulnerable. C. S. Lewis's science fiction fantasies are fascinating in this respect. Here we are living in the Fall, and there on Venus the Fall hasn't happened, everything is wonderful, but the fall could still occur. In the event it doesn't – whoopee for the Venusians – at least they haven't got some of our problems. But they're still growing into relation with God.

SHORTT: **One of Marilyn Adams' arguments in the exchange you've had with her is that,** *sub specie aeternitatis,* **we will feel that our lives are retrospectively vindicated, justified. Isn't that implicit in Christian belief? Some people might be surprised that you reacted against that so strongly, describing it as flawed, both philosophically and morally.[4]**

WILLIAMS: 'Vindicated': that's where I have the problem. I may look back on an experience of enormous trauma and say, Well, out of that came some understanding for which I thank God. What I can't bring myself to say is that, so to speak, it was all OK. I can't quite cope with the idea that somebody else's suffering was planned for a good purpose.

SHORTT: **But you believe that creation is ultimately a good thing.**

WILLIAMS: I believe that creation is a good thing because of that long-term purpose which is the sharing of fellowship with God, the gift of the divine life and the divine nature to creatures. But to say that creation is good overall, I think, can't commit us to adding, And everything that happens must be for the best. Not only is that often not true; even when we can make the best of a bad situation, that doesn't mean it had to happen or that it was good that it happened. I look here to those who have written out of the very dark places of the modern experience. One thinks of somebody like Etty Hillesum writing from the camps, or on the Christian side Mother Maria Skobtsova, a Russian nun who died in Ravensbruck, and what I understand them to be saying is not, Well, it's all OK, there's a reason for my being here, but, rather, Here is something which for all its utter, unqualified horror, I can by God's grace give a future to, open up to God. And in that sense, I think, the Christian looking back over a life containing suffering and tragedy and trauma can say that it has all been drawn together by grace, rather than that it's all vindicated or justified.

SHORTT: I've referred in my preface to the recovery of nerve in theology over the past few decades. Can you describe your own evolution in that context?

WILLIAMS: Inevitably, my view was shaped mainly by the British scene. I think that probably from the middle sixties onwards there was a sense of some uncertainty, almost some embarrassment, in the British ecclesiastical scene about old-style doctrinal writing. It's an interesting moment, I think, although the war period and the postwar period produced some really remarkable material inspired by the classical tradition, Gregory Dix on the liturgy, Eric Mascall in philosophy, and others.

SHORTT: Austin Farrer?

WILLIAMS: Austin Farrer, who still is a bit of a mountain peak of that generation. But there was also a thinning out of historical theology, reflected, for example, in a work like John Robinson's *Honest to God*. That did lead to a situation where academic theology in the late sixties was marked by a huge concentration on New Testament study, still very much dominated by Bultmann; a certain amount of writing about ethics and philosophical theology; and a rather careful avoidance of the doctrinal heartland, so that continental dogmatic theology was regarded as just too much to cope with; and the average textbook on philosophical theology, let's say, might have a page or two on Barth, telling you why you couldn't be doing with this, and then you'd go on to what was considered the real stuff, and the legacy still at that time of the debates within analytic philosophy over the meaning of religious language.

Now I think a number of us who were growing up as theologians in that generation, people on the whole born between 1945 and 1955, found ourselves frustrated by this. There were big issues there, issues which had to do with the very shape and foundation of the Church's life that were connected with how you worshipped intelligently, both personally and corporately, all these things which seemed not to be entering into the discourse of academic theology. And, in a funny sort of way, it was often fringe writers, for some of us from liberation theology, who brought these themes back in. When I myself decided to do a thesis on Eastern Orthodox theology it was a rather deliberate counter-cultural move. I could think of a number of areas that I could have pursued in New Testament or patristics, and I thought, No, I don't want to do that: I want to go and read something completely different. And it was helped by discovering Vladimir Lossky's *The Mystical Theology of the Eastern Church*.

SHORTT: What did you gain from Lossky?

WILLIAMS: Precisely that sense of the interweaving of doctrine and worship. And also this pervasive apophatic or negative strand that says you will never get it wrapped up, you will never have it completely sorted.

SHORTT: From earlier discussions we've had, I know that you also lay great emphasis on the role of Karl Barth in the turnaround being described, Barth who asked radical questions about the coherence and distinctiveness of theology.

WILLIAMS: Let me get round to Barth in a minute. As I say, Lossky was part of what precipitated me into doing the research I did, and, oddly in a way, it was what got me reading modern Continental dogmatics a bit more as well, some Roman Catholic writing, Rahner particularly. Von Balthasar was just beginning to appear in English, and then Barth. And by the late seventies I was involved with some other theologians in writing about Barth,[5] but also involved in the group that was translating von Balthasar.

SHORTT: It included Stephen Sykes, I think.

WILLIAMS: Stephen Sykes and David Ford and Richard Roberts and myself were working on Barth, and that was a sort of intensive seminar. The book was a very collaborative venture, where we discussed and criticised each other's work quite a lot in a series of meetings.

SHORTT: And your essay was on Barth and the Trinity.

WILLIAMS: Yes, and that was a big eye-opener, which also helped me in later years when I was teaching Barth in Cambridge, and asking myself why he was so interesting. I suppose part of the answer is in Barth's own career under the pressure of a violently anti-Christian, barbarous state apparatus. Barth, you might say, asks what the point is of theology at all? If it's just, as he said, talking about man in a loud voice, if it's just uplift or examination of the religious consciousness, well, frankly you're still trapped, you're still under the net of a deeply oppressive and barbaric political system.

And so you have to have a theology which begins by saying God is God, and not part of any system and only in the light of that do you have a sort of ground from which you can put the questions back and

make the challenges to the barbarism of modern politics. And I sometimes used to say to students that Barth's way of being relevant to
Germany in the 1930s was by being, on the surface, completely
indifferent to Germany in the 1930s. I mean his own life, of course,
consisted of anything but indifference. He took huge risks and suffered for it. But in his dogmatic theology, it's as if he's saying, Look,
I'm absolutely not going to get caught up in the problems of Germany
in the 1930s, because the best way of responding to these problems is
to say God is God, and therefore your agenda can be drawn from
somewhere else than Germany in the 1930s. It's a huge enterprise, and
what caught me and still catches me about Barth is that sense of
exuberant bloody-mindedness, enlarged upon at huge length, the
gusto, the verve of the theology, with all its outrageous misunderstandings of other people and its wonderfully sanctified egotism. It's
a great performance, *The Church Dogmatics*, and Barth enjoys being
Barth and spreading himself like this, and in that enjoyment does
convey, I think, uniquely among twentieth-century theologians, a
sense of the exhilarating otherness of God.

SHORTT: At the same time, as you've mentioned, you became involved
in translating Balthasar's *Herrlichkeit* [The Glory of the Lord], along
with John Saward and ...

WILLIAMS: Andrew Louth, John Riches, Brian McNeil and one or two
other people – this experience was more than just sitting with a text
and a dictionary. And Balthasar and Barth are, I suppose, still for me
the two great poles of twentieth-century Western theology. Absolutely
alike in their commitment to the distinctiveness of theology and the
otherness of God; endlessly fascinatingly different in their assessment
of how you articulate that. Balthasar's immense indirection in coming
to God through what he himself describes as the bridge half-built
from the human sense of the divine and the human sense of beauty,
and then the aspiration to beauty that is in the human mind being
both answered and wholly overturned in the unbeautiful form of the
crucified Christ, which is in one way a very Barthian thing – *senkrecht
von oben*, Barth says: straight down from above comes something you
could never have expected. Barth is, in a sense, happy to leave it there.
Balthasar, as it were, says, But you only see it for what it is if you see
exactly how it both corresponds to and overturns all that you have
ever been thinking and moving towards. And I wrote a bit on
Balthasar and Rahner at the time[6] to try to draw out the difference
between that sense of shock and surprise in Balthasar, and his
apprehension, too, of the tragedy that comes with that, and Rahner's

much more unified sense of moving up out of the intrinsic grace-orientedness of human nature towards receptivity to the concrete grace of Jesus Christ.

So, Lossky, Barth, Balthasar – I think in my twenties those were the people I was absorbing, and it was quite a rich diet. Probably after that, when I was most heavily involved in teaching university theology in my thirties, they were there constantly in the background: but I was also exploring rather more philosophically at that time, reading more of Wittgenstein, tackling some of the issues about reality and reference that arise philosophically, and, towards the end of the period, beginning to absorb a bit more of Hegel.

SHORTT: Will you say something briefly about Hegel? I think his influence is evident in some of the things you said earlier in this conversation.

WILLIAMS: When I was first doing my research on Russian theology I saw Hegel through Russian spectacles, that is, through the spectacles of mostly late-nineteenth-century theologians and philosophers in Russia who were using him as part of their system-building, and I got very impatient with what seemed a vast edifice of speculative metaphysics, where really you could say pretty much anything you liked. And that put me off Hegel, I confess – though I always remembered having read a bit of his writing on tragedy in my early twenties which went quite deep, especially his discussion of *Antigone*. But it took me some time to get back to him after being more interested in Wittgenstein for a long while. The connection, I think, would go something like this. What fascinated me in Wittgenstein was, if you like, the refusal to go behind appearances. Language is language, not an inept substitute for something better. We understand who we are by looking at how our language works, and I don't think that's reductive at all. On the contrary, I think it's a very exciting approach.

But turning to Hegel, I found that, just as for Wittgenstein, you start where you are, you watch how sense is made in practice, so, strangely, for Hegel, you start where you are as a speaker and a thinker, and you look at what the very act of speaking, the very act of thinking, means, and, relating a bit to what I said earlier, you begin to understand how the very act of speaking, the very act of thinking, locate you in something more than just the historical exchange that happens to be going on at the moment.

I owe a lot here to two people. One is my former pupil and great friend Andrew Shanks, who kept on asking me awkward questions about Hegel when I was trying to teach him – I say trying to teach him, because I know he was the one who did most of the teaching – and his superb books on Hegel[7] and related matters have meant a lot to me. And the other was, of course, Gillian Rose, a bit later on, in my late thirties: getting to know Gillian and seeing Hegel through her eyes as anything but a philosopher of closure and system.

SHORTT: **You've spoken of *Honest to God*, and I guess the zenith of that style came with *The Myth of God Incarnate* in 1977. In my book about you, I went into your criticisms of a work that hasn't weathered well. Can you talk about what started to happen in the early eighties? At various times in the past you've spoken about a revived interest in narrative, in community, and the way that anglophone theology became less obviously Protestant, among other things.**

WILLIAMS: When *The Myth of God Incarnate* appeared in 1977, I think many people felt that this was about as far as a particular kind of rational revisionism could go. So it was one of those moments when people did begin to turn towards other sources, and the presence of writers like von Balthasar in the background, the growing profile in the British university scene of some Catholic theologians, Nicholas Lash being a very prominent example, did mean that there was a bit of a turn against a certain kind of very insular Protestantism. A curious thing about *The Myth of God Incarnate* is that there is barely one reference to anybody outside the anglophone liberal Protestant world. Barth doesn't feature. I think there is one reference to Pannenberg, and that's it. The rest of theology might not have existed. And there is an awful insularity about the book in that way. Now, getting us away from that insularity was, I think, part of the important agenda of the years that followed. Balthasar was making an impact, as I've said. Nicholas Lash was doing a lot. Donald MacKinnon, of course, whom I haven't talked much about, but who is clearly a huge presence in the background of all this: Donald who was interested in Barth, was interested in Balthasar, and pushed him at us, and was interested in philosophers such as Paul Ricoeur and Hans-Georg Gadamer.

SHORTT: **MacKinnon was your greatest teacher, I think.**

WILLIAMS: My greatest teacher without any doubt, yes. And of many of my colleagues and peers. It meant that by the early eighties there was a bit of a sense of the tide having turned. And I can remember conversations with contemporaries like Angela Tilby and Sarah Coakley and others whom I'd known for a long time. We shared a sense that we needed to get ourselves out of this rather narrow and oddly cosy liberal environment into a slightly intellectually more rigorous, spiritually more challenging – and even alarming – world. So, yes, there is a move away from what I think of as that rather pale liberal Protestant consensus. It felt like and still feels like a rather more multicoloured world. And, of course, out of this then came during the eighties the beginnings of John Milbank's work and Radical Orthodoxy.

SHORTT: You're sometimes described as the father of Radical Orthodoxy. The movement will be discussed in detail in a later chapter, but could you say a quick word about it now?

WILLIAMS: Yes. A number of the Radical Orthodoxy people, above all John Milbank, were very close to me either as pupils or friends of pupils: people whose work I sat alongside and discussed. So I do feel some sense of involvement in the history of Radical Orthodoxy; and the enormous stimulus and constant mental stretching that I've had from conversations with John Milbank is a big part of my life. I've expressed some of my reservations about the project from time to time. Basically, though, I think it's on the right lines.

SHORTT: Let's move on, again quite sketchily, to some other recent developments. It's part of the rationale of this book that anglophone theology is at the cutting edge of the subject these days, and one could also argue that Anglican theologians have played an especially distinguished role in bringing this about.

WILLIAMS: It would be nice to think so. I think the array of Anglican theologians in the past decade has been extraordinary. We Anglicans have perhaps been able to be a bit more free with the Catholic tradition than some Roman Catholics in an era when the control of Catholic theology has been rather stepped up and the levels of anxiety among Roman Catholic theologians are a bit higher than they used to be or than they need be. It's as if, to take von Balthasar as an example, an Anglican can come at him without a political agenda of the kind that almost inevitably hangs around his name in the Roman Catholic Church. I think that helps a bit.

SHORTT: Because he's associated with a highly conservative agenda.

WILLIAMS: For a Roman Catholic to be interested in von Balthasar is very often part of a package which is powerfully conservative. It doesn't work quite like that for his Anglican interpreters.

SHORTT: You don't have to be against the ordination of women, for example.

WILLIAMS: No. Indeed, the people who have written most extensively on Balthasar in the Anglican world have supported the ordination of women. So there has been a grateful but critical reception of traditional theology. And because, like it or not, the anglophone world tends to set quite a lot of cultural trends, it may not be an accident that it's in that environment that some of the innovative material arises.

SHORTT: The chapters that follow will flesh out this and other points you've made, but before we round off it would be good to narrow the focus a bit to give a concrete instance of the sort of thing you've been working on in the interstices of life as a bishop and archbishop. An example judged especially interesting by several observers was your 2001 Aquinas Lecture on St Thomas and the Trinity, 'What Does Love Know?',[8] where you defend the integrity and value of Thomas' picture. Can you pull together a few of the threads from that address?

WILLIAMS: One of the things I was trying to say in the lecture was that I think the whole of Aquinas' discussion of the Trinity[9] takes off from the springboard of his immediately preceding discussion of whether God enjoys himself. That's a strange way of putting it, but he's been discussing the bliss of God, and by establishing that to make any sense of the biblical God you've got to think of a God who is not only loving and intelligent, but who is wholly in love with his own loving and intelligence, because it's the supremely delightful and wonderful reality that can be conceived. And I think the way I put it was that it's as you unpack that sense of a joyful God – an intelligent, joyful God – that the Trinity comes into focus. And that's why, when Aquinas talks about subsistent relations in God – that very complicated, very technical discussion whose distant roots are in Augustine – what you have to think of is a God in whom there is nothing that is not intelligence and joy.

There is nothing that as it were stays at home while bits of the godhead go out to understand things and enjoy and love things and all the rest of it. The whole process of the divine life is that bestowal and outpouring in another. So I used the analogy of a Moebius strip:[10] you go round and round and round Aquinas' language trying to understand how God understands his act of understanding and loves his act of loving, and all the rest of it. And it can sound very abstract, but then you keep having to go back, I think, to that basic point – it's about joy. And having done that basic work on how you characterise the God of the Bible and begun to sort out the hugely complicated matters of terminology in regard to describing this life as the life which is totally involved in relation, then and only then do you begin to see what it is for us to be creatures summoned into that action of understanding and loving. How, if you like, the rationale of being human is somehow rooted in the nature of loving and joyful consciousness which is God. And to be in God's image, to be God's conscious creature, means to be bound up in that bliss. That gives you a kind of springboard once again into the doctrine of redemption. What could redemption mean except having everything taken away which gets in the way of your entry into the blissful self-awareness of God which for us is the blissful self-awareness crafted and realised in community?

So I ended[11] by making a few remarks about how understanding the world and changing the world are not quite as different as Marx thought they were, because if in St Thomas the act of understanding and of loving are relationally inseparable, this is the model on which we are made and the context into which we grow. It gives us the critical leverage to respond to where we are in the human world.

SHORTT: **I know that you were invited to speak about the Trinity to a group of eminent Islamic scholars in Cairo in 2004, so this might be an appropriate moment to raise the question of theological relations between Muslims and Christians, especially in the aftermath of September 11, 2001.**

WILLIAMS: One of the questions that people most often ask us here is: Are Christians and Muslims talking about the same God? It seems to me that actually the history we share is a very considerable thing, both the pre-history, as you might say, of Christianity and Islam – the history of the Jewish narrative, the Abrahamic narrative – but also the later history, the medieval history of intellectual exchange and the painful definitions of common ground and the marking out of boundaries in that context which comes in the exchanges of the great medievals: St Thomas, Ibn Sena [Avicenna, in the Latin form], Maimonides.

What I think emerges from that medieval discussion is something like this. Jews, Muslims and Christians can agree about a very great deal concerning the definition of what it's like to be God. God is not an item in the world. God is not confined by the agency of others. God's will and God's being coincide. God is wholly free to express what God is without interruption, without frustration. That's what we mean by God. Christians, Jews and Muslims agree absolutely about that. And the consequential question, then, is why is it that the three faith traditions see the actual life of God and the work of God in history differently. Part of what, for example, St Thomas is trying to do in the *Summa* is to show that if you really mean what you say about the definition of God, then talking of God as Trinity makes perfect sense. If God really is the freedom of self-bestowal, or however you want to put it, then the Trinity is where it cashes out, but he's not naive enough to think that you can just pull in an appeal to revelation to sort it out as between Christians and Muslims. You have a lot of harder work to do. You can only have that conversation, though, if you can mark out some common territory where you know you're talking about the same sort of reality.

Now I think that's often overlooked in contemporary Christian–Muslim dialogue at a rather simple level. We've forgotten that once we knew how to talk to each other about God, and so we tend to do what St Thomas and other medievals don't do, and just reach for our revelations rather quickly, and say, If you're a Muslim, the revelation given to Muhammad is the last in time, and therefore the most comprehensive and most authoritative, or, if we're Christians, we say the revelation of Jesus Christ witnessed to in Scripture is the revelation of the divine person in human flesh, and therefore trumps all others. Christians and Muslims will go on saying those things, and rightly so. But there is a stage, a depth if you like, of the dialogue, which we've omitted, and where we need to be. We need to acquire a new literacy. Back to St Thomas, Ibn Sena, Maimonides: What's this God we're talking about?

So the question, 'Do Christians and Muslims believe in the same God?' turns out to be quite an interesting one, quite a complicated one. The answer is, Yes and no. Do we mean the same thing by God? In significant measure, we do. Neither the Muslim nor the Christian, nor the Jew for that matter, believes in a God who is just a heavenly individual who is possessed of more power than earthly individuals. We all believe in a God whose being is elusive of any kind of formal definition because it exceeds what we can say. But then we don't believe in the same God, because we encounter that divine life concretely and specifically in different ways, and in different ways that shape something of what we then say more precisely about the definition of God. So it becomes a real dialogue. There is difference, there is convergence. And so it should be. But I do think we need to take seriously that ground-clearing exercise.

SHORTT: **Would you also say something about the work that you've been involved with behind the scenes to strengthen links between Christians and Muslims?**

WILLIAMS: One of the things that I inherited here at Lambeth was the very important work my predecessor set in motion to boost ties between Christian and Muslim theologians, and that's now an annual

Building Bridges Seminar which draws together Christian and Muslim scholars from across the world. We've met in the Middle East, we've met in the United States. We're meeting in Sarajevo next. And the idea is that we sit down primarily with each other's sacred texts and we listen to each other talking about Scripture and asking questions, not talking primarily about the politics of Christianity and Islam, but watching how the meanings of God are made real in a text, and how thinking about it prompts the large questions of metaphysics and cosmology. It's been, I think, for all of us a stretching experience, and a very constructive one. We want to move on to talking about the public good and shared visions of human value which we haven't tackled in such depth before.

So that's an international initiative. Meanwhile, in Britain, for the last few years, we've had a group travelling around doing a sort of listening exercise with local Christian and Muslim communities in the wake of which we're now setting up a sort of standing national Christian–Muslim advisory body to try to keep the discussions going at local level.

SHORTT: I'd like to finish this overview of the territory with a quick look at your thoughts on contemporary religious art. This has exercised you at intervals over the past few decades, and it's probably an area where you are especially likely to make an impact on people at the edges of the Church or outside it.

WILLIAMS: Yes. I find myself coming back quite a lot to the question of how you craft a responsible, plausible Christian art, whether in the novel, the poem, the visual work and the piece of music. In a cultural environment where Christian images are not very accessible, how do you express the differentness of Christ? In moving towards an answer to that, you somehow have to create the visual or the textual or imaginative space in which you can see how a difference shaped by grace appears, and that means that very often the most effective depictions of God and grace and Christ these days are going to be sideways on and a bit different.

And I discussed this some years ago when I was working with Michael Symmons Roberts and James Macmillan on the chamber opera *Parthenogenesis*. We were looking at how to raise fundamental theological questions by indirection in this little work. Recently I've re-read the short stories of Flannery O'Connor, and she, of course, addresses this question head on, saying: In a world where people don't know what the images are, you've got to write stories about grace that are deeply shocking. And that's why she essentially writes tales about grotesque and horrible and comic moments. It's the deepest pitch-black humour at times, but very often the stories move towards a moment of epiphany, negative or positive – the old woman in *A Good Man is Hard to Find* who, just at the moment when she is about to be shot by an escaped convict, says, for no particular reason: 'You're one of my children.' And it comes almost from nowhere, but that terrible moment is also, in the story, horribly comic in its own way. You have this appalling, squabbling, selfish, middle-class family going off on a holiday which suddenly turns into a nightmare when they are hijacked; yet the ordeal becomes a means of grace. Now Flannery O'Connor sets out to shock, no doubt about it, but she's doing it in order to ask, What is grace like in a world where grace doesn't just sit around in the conventional images and forms?

So all of that does interest me a lot, and it relates to one of the things that I'd quite like to do, given a bit more time, which is to write something longer on how you characterise, describe, the religious life in our day, what it's really like to be religious. So many people think they know what it means: they think it means having a certain code of sexual ethics, they think it means signing up to certain beliefs. But neither of these tells you anything about the feel of a religious life. And given a bit of time, I wouldn't mind sitting down with a few biographies, an activist like Dorothy Day, a writer like Flannery O'Connor, people like that, and asking, What's the religious element here? How, by looking at a life like that, do you get a sense of what God meant? I don't quite know how to do it yet, but I'd like to have a go.

2
Janet Martin Soskice

Philosophical Theology

SHORTT: Your first book, *Metaphor and Religious Language*,[1] was a widely praised defence of philosophical realism, and you are soon to publish another landmark work, on naming God.[2] Much of your recent output has consisted of scholarly essays on subjects that also relate to our discussion, including theological anthropology and feminist re-readings of Scripture. I'd like to look at this material later, but to begin by asking about your early life. You grew up in pretty secular surroundings, becoming a convinced Christian in adulthood over a period of years. And the process of your conversion was advanced by a formative personal experience, as well as by intellectual considerations.

MARTIN SOSKICE: Yes. I certainly didn't believe in God when I went up to university, not because belief was unfashionable – though it was certainly that – but simply because God had no part to play in my universe. I was raised a nominal Anglican in western Canada. We lived in a ski town, and most of my winter was taken up with skiing. My friends and I certainly didn't make a dent in that to go to church on Sunday. I was nevertheless confirmed in the Anglican Church. The priest instructing me must have thought I had some disposition towards theology because he got me reading Tillich. I couldn't make anything of it, other than to think that maybe there was something more to explore. But my puerile conclusion from all this was that if God was so great, so loving and wonderful, then God wouldn't hold it against anyone who didn't know they believed in him – and so what difference did it make?

Looking back on it, I had very condescending attitudes towards religious believers. I assumed that they were all people who needed some kind of emotional or social crutch and couldn't manage on their own – which is, of course, precisely true. What changes when you become religious is that you realise you're one of those people, and that Promethean heroic autonomy is a bit of a flight of fancy. So that was the situation when I went to Cornell to read English. I then changed to philosophy and intellectual history.

I'm somewhat timid about saying this, but I am one of those people who then had quite a dramatic religious experience which led to conversion. It didn't seem to come from anywhere – I hadn't been talking to anyone or knowingly thinking about it – but it seemed to me powerfully that it was an experience of God. Afterwards many of my friends, all of them still agnostics or atheists, came up to me with their explanations. One said, 'Well, you know, the time when you had that experience, you were very sad.' Another said, 'The time when you had that experience, you were very happy.' They all had different explanations of why this should have occurred. I don't know why it happened to me, but it did. In response, my first plan was to have a wonderful gathering of all God's greatest hits, as it were. This was the 1970s; so I rushed out and bought *The Tibetan Book of the Dead* and *The Upanishads*, as well as the Bible. And I just kept reading the Bible because it spoke to me, and at that stage I thought this was because the Christian Scriptures were so embedded in the English literature I'd been reading. This was at least partly true. But gradually over time it dawned on me that I was a Christian. It took a couple of years.

SHORTT: How would you describe this dramatic religious experience?

MARTIN SOSKICE: It was like being wrapped in an enormous loving mystery: I had a terrific sense of presence and of mystery, but a presence to whom I could speak. We have a notion, we learn it from Bible stories in our children's illustrated Bibles, that God speaks to people, but what's startling is feeling you're in the presence of a God to whom you need to speak back. But it wasn't with words. I didn't hear words. I didn't see anything. I don't want to compare my experience to that of Moses, since I was only called to open my heart, but I find the scriptural account moving in that when Moses first notices the burning bush – a moment we have come to think of as a great theophany – the impression given by the text is more humdrum. Moses notices a bush that is burning and not consumed, and he is curious, rather like you might see a cookery display at the end of the supermarket aisle. What's going on? It's only when Moses takes some steps forward and is addressed by name – 'Moses, Moses. Take off your shoes. The place you are standing is holy ground' – that things fall into place. Not, as I say, that I had the experience of being called by name, but somehow the sense of being addressed was very strong and something to which I felt I could respond.

SHORTT: **Let's return to your time at university.**

MARTIN SOSKICE: I continued studying philosophy. When I became a Christian, I was a bit hesitant about becoming aligned with various Christian groups, because I was a bit worried that other Christians might put me off Christianity. This was a genuine worry, because of the standard of undergraduate evangelism. People would come to your room in pairs and say things like, 'I love Johnny, and we're going to be married, but I love God even more than Johnny.' And you felt like saying, 'Well, what about strawberries? Are they above Johnny and below God?' Their approach just didn't seem right. I didn't doubt that these people were Christians, but there was something unsatisfying about what they said.

Nonetheless, I started going regularly to services. At the Anglican chaplaincy there was great excitement about the fact that the congregation included the philosopher Norman Malcolm, one of Wittgenstein's former students. So we all marvelled over this, much as you might marvel over an elephant standing on a washbucket. Here was the greatest philosopher at the university, and he was a Christian. How did this work? The regnant assumption was that only idiots or the completely socially depraved believed in that sort of thing. His presence was naturally quite encouraging to me: I thought it vital at this stage to find intelligent people who were both Christian and literate: Christians who'd read Proust, that sort of thing. It sounds so awful now, but that's the way it felt at the time. I didn't dare speak to the great man, although I did write my first piece on metaphor, and its treatment in Wittgenstein's *Blue* and *Brown Books*, for his course at this time.

I didn't plan to be a theologian. I'd hardly heard of theologians, and I certainly didn't think there were such things as women theologians. I hoped to study cultural anthropology, and got a place to do research on religious metaphor. I even did a summer's field work in northern Brazil, where I planned to study poor migrants coming from the rural areas into the big city. They favoured a syncretic religious cult called Condomble that fuses African, indigenous, Catholic and Muslim elements, somewhat like voodoo but more benign. I found that work very interesting, and would gladly have pursued it. But having admitted to myself by this time that I was a Christian, I thought I should apply myself to theology first. In studying Christian thought, I realised that I was mainly interested in metaphor and symbolism. I came to England, initially to do a Master's in biblical studies, and to work with Anthony Thiselton, who was interested in Wittgenstein. After this I pursued the linguistic philosophy by doing a doctorate at Oxford.

SHORTT: **You became a Roman Catholic at this time. Why was that?**

MARTIN SOSKICE: To me it feels as though I discovered that I was a Catholic. I gradually began to see that Christianity is not about solitary seekers after truth who just get together once in a while for a chat: other people are very much part of the divine scheme of things – even Scripture has come down to us through the agency of other people. I spent a year after my first degree working as a waitress and studying at a Plymouth Brethren college in Vancouver. The people were wonderful, but it was more Catholic material that really inspired me – the Metaphysical poets, C. S. Lewis' *The Great Divorce*, and the works of Gerald Vann OP. Malcolm Muggeridge, a friend of our Principal, visited and spoke about how he had become a Catholic. Some found this very shocking, but I did not. I picked up an old Everyman edition of Newman's *Apologia pro vita sua* in a second-hand bookshop, and, reading it, discovered that there was a beautiful and spiritual rationale for Catholic sacramental theology. I felt ashamed of my previous dismissiveness and set out to educate myself, without an eye to conversion.

At about the same time, however, I began to be exercised by church structure. It was the time of Watergate, and Nixon's prayer breakfasts, and I became worried about religion's being too closely aligned with just one national or political agenda. Then, shortly after arriving in England, I met a number of young Catholics who impressed me with their faith and aliveness to the world. I felt I had to ask, given the numerical and historical strength of the Catholic Communion, what was keeping me out; and in the end the pros outweighed the cons.

SHORTT: **Just before we pursue your philosophy, there's an obvious question to ask about what you would say to people who haven't been privy to the special spiritual experience you've described. How would you advise the enquirer who isn't starting from the same place?**

MARTIN SOSKICE: I don't want to make too much of my experience, not because it's unimportant to me, but because I've met many better Christians than myself who've never had any such deep feeling or intuition. Part of me feels this must be dispositional – some are more given to this kind of phenomenon than others. Some who have this experience go no further with it. (Bertrand Russell apparently had some form of spiritual experience near the end of his life, but felt it was too late to change his mind about religion.) Some who have no experience like this become great saints. Some of the greatest saints – Teresa of Avila, for example – have years of darkness with no feeling of the presence of God at all. Some grow up with a quiet faith which they never have cause to doubt.

What, then, of those whose way is different? I think my message would echo that of Pascal: read Scripture, pray, go to church, become involved with this world of faith and with people who believe, and see if things don't click into place. That's how it felt to me once I believed in God: things clicked into place. Maybe I suffered too much the disorientating effects of Camus and Sartre as an undergraduate; but I do feel that it becomes possible to see the presence of the world and its orderliness in a new way when you believe it to be a gift – literally gratuitous – and a gift from a Giver.

SHORTT: **That we're creatures.**

MARTIN SOSKICE: Yes. Now that isn't to pretend for a minute that everything's right and there's no evil. Nor do I want to give the impression that my own life was wholly untouched by sadness. It's just that I do believe that the world fits together only if you believe there's a God, and I'm evangelical enough about this to want to urge people to give it a try.

SHORTT: **And here you're touching on a popular but questionable myth mentioned in my preface to this book: that atheism provides the neutral, common-sense view of the world, while religion is pie in the sky. It would be truer to hold that the existence of the world poses awe-inspiring questions to atheists, as well as to believers.**

MARTIN SOSKICE: Definitely. And atheism is neither obvious nor obviously true. The big question for which there is no answer by reason alone is, of course, why there is something rather than nothing. I was once invited to take part in a radio programme about miracles, and asked whether I believed in them. 'Yes, of course,' I said. And the researcher replied that she had recruited a leading humanist to put the contrary case. 'What would you say to him?' I answered, 'Why is there something rather than nothing?' There followed a baffled silence at the other end of the line, and in the end they asked a priest in charge of the Shrine at Knock to engage with the humanist instead of me.

This was a big question for the ancients as well. The reason why Aristotle thought the universe was eternal (in his sense meaning without beginning and end) is because he thought that nothing can come

from nothing: *ex nihilo nihil fit*. Because if there really was *nothing* –
no space or time – how could anything have come into being? That's
still a big problem, and believe me cosmology hasn't answered it,
astrophysics hasn't answered it. It isn't any more logical to say that the
universe has simply always existed, as did Aristotle, than it is to say
that there's a Creator. Bertrand Russell's reply to Copleston – that
there's no answer to this question – doesn't seem terribly satisfactory
either.

SHORTT: So theology is to some extent a well-kept secret?

MARTIN SOSKICE: Yes, and theologians are indeed partly responsible
for that. At the same time, there's something perverse in the way the
modern academy has sidelined theology. I've been told by colleagues
in medieval languages, and even in Dante studies, that it is not done
to be interested in theology. How can you study medieval texts *without* being informed by theology? Political theorists write gamely
about natural law in the sixteenth century without feeling the need to
enquire into its religious foundations. There seems to be an assumption that, because we are wise and atheists, anyone in the past whom
we admire cannot have been too much affected by religion – that their
faith is just a cultural appurtenance of as little importance to understanding their thought as their hairstyle. This isn't objectivity: it's a
prejudice. The study of theology is immensely broadening – bringing
together ethics, politics, metaphysics, aesthetics – even if you can't
serve up neat and tidy answers.

SHORTT: Returning to *Metaphor and Religious Language*: people
who've read the book will recall that it draws some putatively conservative conclusions on the basis of vigorous arguments. Can you
summarise what you were saying?

MARTIN SOSKICE: Having discovered Christianity as an adult, I had a
particularly vivid sense of its being so wonderful and important and
true. That's not to say, I hope, that I'd ever be dismissive of other faith
traditions, but nevertheless, when I started my graduate studies it was
sobering to meet Anglican divines of the *Myth of God Incarnate*
generation who were coming out with what seemed to me a rather
mildewy liberalism, combined with debates about the invisible
gardener and ethics.[3] It just didn't sing. I thought, No. It's either more
than this, or nothing.

The book was indeed conservative in many ways, and I'm proud of
the label. But on the other hand, my focus was on metaphor, symbolic
language and the philosophy of language. I was interested in moving
the arguments about the reasonableness of belief a step sideways, and

arguing that a religious person is not someone who has a few bizarre beliefs tacked on to what normal people believe, but someone who is informed by certain symbols, who inhabits certain sacred texts and narratives. My question was, How do metaphors and symbols work? Can they be referential? Can they be truth-bearing? I wanted to locate these questions within a realist philosophical perspective because the prevailing dogma was that metaphor was incidental, ornamental and insubstantial. This line had prevailed since Locke, who had aligned metaphor with rhetoric (in this context considered negatively) and put both on the side of the ornamental or incidental. Neither, then, was to be considered integral or substantive. If this was right, and metaphor could never be 'load bearing' if not reducible at some level to literal speech, then religious rationality would have to be consigned to the dustheap.

SHORTT: **You wanted to argue that this couldn't be true, but not simply to respond with a kind of leaden literalism – God really is in his heaven and really sits on a throne.**

MARTIN SOSKICE: That's right. On the contrary, the important thing was to open up a new and more imaginative way of being a religious realist. I was surprised and delighted that the book was a success with conservatives, but I hope their reaction amounted to more than just recognising someone else who believes that God is real, end of story. At the same time, some wrote to me to say they were glad to have a way opened up in which you could say you really do believe in God and God's presence in your life, and the disclosure of God to Israel, without feeling that this realism commits you to believing everything is nailed down in precise terms. Faithful knowing must also be unknowing, for the wonder of God exceeds our frail brains.

SHORTT: **Let's rehearse in a bit more detail your argument that metaphors can be reality-depicting. After discussing what metaphor was and aligning it in various figures of speech, you tried to show the manner in which metaphorical language can be referential by means of a parallel with the philosophy of science. For instance, in modelling the activity of electricity on that of water (with a flow, a current, and so on), the scientist holds that the nature of electricity genuinely informs the discussion, without presuming that the language borrowed from the behaviour of water maps onto everything to do with electricity directly. That, in essence, is what you mean by critical realism.**

MARTIN SOSKICE: Yes, and then there was a final stage of the argument on how metaphors can have a life that runs through traditions and texts. This is true of religious texts and traditions, but equally of some purely literary ones, like Japanese court poetry. Fewer readers picked up on this, although to me it was almost the most important part of the book. In recent years far more people have become engaged by what we might call the changing life of a metaphor. What does it mean, for instance, when Jesus compares his body to the Temple? We have very good reason to believe he did so, by the way, since it was a charge at his trial and clearly an offensive claim. But why was it offensive? Most of us are so removed from the world of first-century Judaism that the comparison seems innocuous – a little vainglorious, perhaps, to compare your body to an important building, to the Albert Hall or Westminster Abbey, in today's terms.

But for a first-century Jew to compare one's body to the Temple is far more extraordinary, far more offensive than that. The Temple was not just a big or a holy building: it was the very place of God's dwelling with Israel, the very place of the harbouring of the *Shekinah*, the divine presence. The Temple was built, according to the Jewish Scriptures, to house the Ark of the Covenant. Therefore Jesus' words bring back a whole tradition of God's presence with the Israelites in the desert, in the Exodus, in the Ark of the Covenant, by the cloud and the fire, and also the distinctive conviction that, on the one hand, Israel's God is in no place, yet this God can also be present to the people as God chooses – in the desert, in the Ark, in the Temple. If you want to know the fire and fuel of a religious mind, you have to see that there are layers of imagery running through the texts and practices of a given tradition, and that these encode the story of God's being with his people. It's an unfolding narrative. And in many ways subsequent work I've done has picked up on aspects of all those different things.

SHORTT: The emerging picture suggests that you've been campaigning on two fronts: against the limitations of secular reasoning, but also against the unacknowledged secularity common in modern Christian thought. The *Myth of God Incarnate* generation has already been mentioned. But you've also taken a stand against people who base their allegiance more on the philosophy of religion than on philosophical theology. These subjects are deceptively similar. Can you explain why they differ, and why the difference matters?

MARTIN SOSKICE: I wouldn't express it as strongly as that. It's true that although I've spent a lot of time teaching straight philosophy of religion and going through the proofs for the existence of God and so on, they've never really been existentially real to me. In my case, God became indubitable. But to give you a more theological answer, although I value philosophy of religion in the analytic tradition and have found my own training here invaluable, I'd say that I'm always somewhat dispirited by the tendency to answer criticisms about the coherence of religious belief with a sort of watertight defence of its rationality. It just doesn't seem to do justice to the sort of evidence as to how people believe and why. Conversely, you can know all the reasons and still not believe.

A certain model of rationality can be a Procrustean bed. As a graduate student I found it depressing to find people defending philosophical realism by saying that God causes the world to come into being in much the same way as I cause this pencil to drop onto the table. There's always this kind of argument: God causes the world to come into being except with some modest provisos such as that God, unlike us, creates outside of space and outside of time. But these aren't modest provisos. Once you've inserted those qualifications, then divine creation becomes something radically different. Philosophy of religion in the analytic tradition has been haunted by a deism in which God becomes a big thing, at the opposite end of the spectrum from a neutrino. But God can't be like that. If you really take on board the idea that God created all that is, including space and time, God's otherness must be absolute. Now for the three major monotheistic traditions, the fascination of the otherness of God does not imply God's total absence. No: it is the reason we can speak of God's total *presence* to the world. This is a lesson I learned from Herbert McCabe and other wonderful Dominicans like Fergus Kerr who effected a kind of marriage between Wittgenstein and Aquinas during the second half of the twentieth century.

The lesson goes back at least as far as Augustine's *Confessions*. You'll remember the sequence: in the early days his mother is a Christian; he hasn't yet been baptised. He reads her Bible and thinks that it's not written in very good Latin: it's not as good as Cicero. It's not very morally edifying, and who are the Jews? They're some provincial people no one's really heard about. Yet when he accepts Christ in the mysterious moment in the Milan garden, he comes to see that this God of the Bible who is present to Israel need not be incompatible with the Neoplatonism which still attracts him. The Christian God is still eternal, as was Plato's god, but that doesn't mean that God has no relation to our temporal order, but is at every time present to it. God's omnipresence doesn't mean God is nowhere, but everywhere – nearer to you than anything can be. Two 'things' can only be so near – but God is not a thing. The non-thingness of God means, as Augustine says, that God can be nearer to me than I am to my own self. And it's this combination of the ultimacy of God with the intimacy of God that undergirds a lot of my work at the moment.

Let me return to the matter of philosophy of religion and philosophical theology. Some problems have always presented themselves to the Western reflective mind – Is there a God? Are the gods one or many? Why is there suffering? These were already problems for the ancient Greeks, for which they had both mythological and philosophical answers. In the eighteenth century there was a resurgence of this chaste classical style of philosophy of religion. Hume deliberately sets his *Dialogues Concerning Natural Religion* in some atemporal polis of reason, and his dialogists have names like Philo and Cleanthes. This ostensibly neutral philosophy of religion is well suited to the modern academy as a branch of philosophy which raises questions about deity or deities. But there are also questions which arise from the Sturm and Drang of religious belief and practice, from the way readers use texts, from the kinds of things the faithful in a particular tradition want to say, and the wish to make what they say compatible with the claims of reason – for instance, how can it be that in Christian teaching one has a Father and a Son, and yet the Father is not superior to the Son? This was the debate Gregory of Nyssa had with Eunomius,[4] and these disputants were highly skilled in philosophy.

So as someone whose way into philosophy of religion was through philosophy of language, I became aware that many earlier debates revolved around what we would call philosophy of language, and it's from there that I've taken my cue. It's 'both/and' for me – philosophy of religion and philosophical theology.

SHORTT: As I mentioned at the start, your writings also offer scope for tracing paths from psychology towards spirituality. I have in mind, for example, an essay you've written called 'Love and Attention', inspired by figures such as Simone Weil and Iris Murdoch, in which you suggest that 'morality, religion and mysticism are of a piece'.[5]

MARTIN SOSKICE: To go back to Augustine again, I've long liked his comment on the dominical teaching: the sum of the law and the prophets is to love God and to love your neighbour as yourself. Augustine observes that this doesn't seem to give guidance on how you're meant to love yourself, but you're meant to love yourself as in the image of God. So we have to love God fully, but we can't love God fully without loving our neighbour fully, and without loving ourselves in the image of God fully. Those things go together.

This is why I object to any account of God's nature which leaves
other people out of the picture. We are here together with other
human beings, with all their virtues and foibles. We become ourselves,
as infants, by learning to love and to speak, and we have language in
particular as a gift from other people. None of us invents it for ourselves (this is true of sign language, too, of course). With language we
move into the social world, and with language we praise, pray and
promise. We characteristically move in language – we ask questions,
we call out to people, we name things, we ask someone to pass us
butter or bricks, we create metaphors, we make puns. This is why
Wittgenstein is so important: he never lets us forget that language,
whatever else it may be, is a practice. Religion in many ways is a practice too: it's intensely social. I believe that God has made us to be
intensely social. We come from each other. We would not be, but for
our parents. We've learned languages from one another. This is another
great Augustinian theme. In *De Doctrina Christiana* he says that
although God could have taught us all individually and immediately
by means of angels, it was part of God's good plan that we should
learn from one another, that we are tied to one another by the
ligatures of love.

SHORTT: Could you address the apologetic potential of all this? I
wonder, for example, how much of a correspondence there is
between your thinking and that of someone like Gillian Rose, who
was baptised as an Anglican just before her death in 1995. As far as I
know she didn't have an enormously moving personal experience,
but came to faith through reflecting on the implications of her
ethical and political commitments, and her work as a Hegelian
philosopher.

MARTIN SOSKICE: I've never been influenced by Hegel – only angry at
his dismissive treatment of Schleiermacher and his anti-Judaism. I
would say that my feeling about the connection between ethics and
theology and spirituality comes more from people like Gregory of
Nyssa. When you set out as a Christian it's not a matter of getting all
the answers to all the questions – it's a path, and in some ways you lose
the answers. This is the beautiful thing about Augustine's *Confessions*.
After the first, autobiographical section, which culminates in his
conversion and the death of his mother, and just when you think he
might settle back into a great paean of praise about being once lost
and now found, comes a chapter about memory and identity, which
seems to upset that particular apple cart. He swirls himself and his
reader into a vortex of confusion: Am I the same person when I'm

asleep as when I'm awake? What happens when I'm dreaming? And so on. The resolution of all of this is not, 'Thank heavens, now *I* know who I am' – in fact, Augustine remains a mystery to himself, especially as a sinner – but, rather, *God* knows who I am, and that's all that matters. I know that I am known by God, and on this basis I can carry on. In another place Augustine notes St Paul's remark that a man who loves will be known by God. How wise it is, Augustine adds, that Paul does not say that a man who loves, knows God, because how God is in Godself, we can never know. But we can know who God is for us, that we are known by God – and this is what we need to carry on.

Knowing who God is for oneself means that you are on a path of discovering who you are and who other people are which is always in a sense leading you deeper and deeper into mystery. This is not because you're continually more baffled, but because you're aware of an ever-greater plenitude of being which is beyond our conceiving. You are led deeper and deeper into this, but what matters is not your comprehensive understanding, but the fact you are a follower.

There's a beautiful expression of this at the end of Gregory of Nyssa's *Life of Moses*,[6] a book in which the law-giver is held up as a template of the ideal Christian life. That's wonderful: Moses wasn't even a Christian. But Moses is a follower of God, a man who spoke to God, whom God loved above all others. He's a follower and a leader – a leader because he is a follower. Towards the end of the book Gregory is musing about Moses' request to see God's face. God denies this request and says, I will put you in a cleft of rock, and I will cover you with my hand until I have passed by, then [rather rudely] I will take away my hand, and you shall see my back parts (Exodus 33:21–3). Gregory thinks it's a pity that even so great a friend of God as Moses was not allowed to see God's face, but then observes that, after all, our Lord did not say, 'If anyone wants to be my disciple let him go ahead of me,' but, rather, 'If anyone wants to be my disciple, let him follow me,' and when you see someone's back you know you are following them. I think that's lovely. That catches it, and it's this bringing together of the ethical and the object of our religious understanding. Progress in religion is not about being able to delineate God. It's to be drawn on in a relationship of love which one hopes is ever broadening – and it's to follow. It's to follow the Christian way.

There I think we need to be reminded that the antique world out of which Christianity emerged was a fusion of Jewish and Greek influences. To become a philosopher in one of the ancient schools was to have a discipline that sometimes involved even your clothing, your hairstyle, what you ate, because it was to be schooled in the virtues and to follow a way of life. To its Gentile converts Christianity must have seemed like that, in a sense – a whole way of bending one's life towards God. But, of course, what Christians believe, unlike the Neoplatonists with whom Augustine was familiar, is that this is not a Promethean undertaking. We are not just doing it all alone. We are following someone, and we are enabled by grace.

SHORTT: I hope what you've just said will be of particular interest to people who don't feel very sure about what to make of Christianity. Let's talk further now about how your insights can enrich the texture of theology itself.

MARTIN SOSKICE: In my view theologians need to get beyond questions of what I've elsewhere called 'etiolated orthodoxy'. Take the doctrine of the resurrection. You get the impression in some quarters that to believe in the resurrection all you need to accept are two things: the tomb was empty and we'll go up in the end. But when you look at the New Testament and at Paul, the resurrection faith is far more than this. The resurrection is a sign that Jesus was who he was. It's a fulfilment of the end times promised by the prophets. It's a sign of an introduction of a new kingdom, a kingdom of justice and peace – a much deeper thing.

The men of Paul's generation were not as impressed as we are by mere violations of laws of nature (the term is anachronistic applied to Paul's time, of course, since they did not think in terms of 'laws of nature'). A mere empty tomb was surprising, but not the be all and end all. We project a later set of assumptions onto the biblical text. We see this in some of the early healing stories. Half those who witness the healings acknowledge Jesus to be the Messiah, and the other half denounce him to the authorities, presumably as a wizard or wonder-worker of some sort. None of them doubts that the miracle happened; they just vary in what they make of it. Jesus' contemporaries were exercised not just about what he did but who he was, under what authority he did what he did. Another example is the calming of the storm in Luke 8. A modern congregation may well just think that this story shows that Jesus is able to 'violate the laws of nature'. But the disciples in the boat ask: 'Who is this that even the winds and the seas obey him?' and that is almost a direct quote from Psalm 107. The answer given by the psalm is that it's the Creator whom the wind and waves obey.

SHORTT: In other words, a very high Christology is implied in this narrative from an early part of the tradition.

MARTIN SOSKICE: I think so. This Jesus is being identified with the Creator, with the one who made heaven and earth. And that is shocking. That's happening all the time in the Gospels when you begin to see it. Paul does it too. When he identifies Jesus in 2 Corinthians with the Lord who 'Let light shine out of darkness' (2 Corinthians 4:5–6), Paul uses epithets which the devout Jew of his day would recognise as appropriately applied only to the God who created heaven and earth.

SHORTT: So the process of digging deeper to uncover Jesus' Jewish roots can prompt conclusions that seem at once fresh and surprisingly orthodox – at least to those schooled in the theory that the creeds represent a Hellenistic contamination of the original Jewish message.

MARTIN SOSKICE: It has certainly been very exciting to observe the rediscovery of Christian origins by both Jewish and Christian scholars over the past thirty or forty years, and to see how very Jewish Christianity is. Part of this excitement lies with its unexpectedness and in the challenge it makes to both religious communities to be honest about our shared past. Christianity has often portrayed itself as a new faith in total opposition to its Jewish heritage. And on the Jewish side, too, there's been a tendency to see Christianity as a wholly aberrant and heretical rupture. It now seems that both Christians and Jews will have to admit to far more continuity of emphasis and concern than that.

Partly prompted by the Shoah, but working with straight academic integrity, scholars have shown that most of Jesus' teaching is deeply Jewish. Surprisingly, perhaps, even the doctrine of the incarnation has Jewish roots. John's Gospel would never have begun with a proclamation that the Word became flesh and dwelt among us if John did not have before him the Exodus narrative in which God is described precisely as dwelling, or tabernacling, among his people. This capacity of the Holy One of Israel to be with his people while at the same time being the Lord of all is a deeply Jewish idea. From a Jewish perspective, of course, this is taken too far in Christian doctrine, but its origins are Jewish nonetheless. It certainly didn't come from Greek philosophy.

In the nineteenth century an influential school of German biblical scholars argued that the metaphysical material in the Gospels had to be late. Their reasoning, driven more by Hegelianism than by their ancient sources, was that the earliest forms of Christianity must have been those of simple Semitic carpenters and fishermen which, as you've said, got muddied with Greek ideas. On this reasoning John's

Gospel, which has always been acknowledged to be more Hellenistic
and metaphysical than the other three, would have to be late. This
thesis is not borne out by the facts. The earliest Gospel manuscript
which we possess is a fragment of John, a papyrus dated about AD 130.
The Gospel was not late. The Jewish milieu of Paul was already
Hellenised, and Christianity took root in the Hellenised Jewish
communities.

SHORTT: **This is one source, I think, of the importance of Philo, a
Jewish contemporary of Paul living in Alexandria. Philo apparently
didn't know anything about Paul or Jesus or the new Christian movement, yet many of the things he says about God's power, and God's
action in the world, have parallels in the Christian texts.**

MARTIN SOSKICE: Yes. It's all exciting and very challenging. One more
example: the baptism of Jesus, and the words 'This is my beloved
Son.' Try to think what that would mean to Jewish ears. There had
been a whole history of 'beloved sons' in the Jewish Scripture – the
younger son, the chosen son. There was Joseph, sold by his brothers
into Egypt; there was Isaac, the beloved son whom Abraham was
asked to sacrifice (but fortunately did not have to). So at his baptism,
Jesus is located among and identified with these other 'beloved sons'
who've carried forward the history of Israel. There's a wonderful book
about all this by Jon Levenson, a Jewish scholar at Harvard, called *The
Death and Resurrection of the Beloved Son*.

Let me develop this in conjunction with what I was saying earlier
about the significance of the Temple, because it fits in with my interest
in metaphor. After his baptism, Jesus goes into the desert. He's there
for forty days, which recalls Moses' forty years in the desert, and is
tempted. Satan tempts Jesus with three things, and the order varies
from Gospel to Gospel. In Luke's account [Luke 4:1–13] Jesus is first
asked to turn the stones into bread and says, 'Man shall not live by
bread alone.' Next he's tempted to rule the kingdoms of the world. He
refuses that power, but the final temptation is to throw himself off the
pinnacle of the Temple. Assuming these temptations represent a
crescendo, I have always thought that this last temptation wasn't
terribly tempting. You might want bread, and you might want (if you
were very foolish) to rule the kingdoms of the world, but why would
you want to throw yourself off the pinnacle of the Temple? But
following the Chronicles, Jews believed that the Temple was built at
the place where Abraham was to have sacrificed Isaac: it was supposed
to be the location of the sacrifice of the beloved son. So the devil is
saying, 'You're the beloved son. God declared this at your baptism. He

saved this other "beloved son" Isaac at this spot. If you're the beloved, then throw yourself down and the angels will come and save you.' It's the connection between the beloved Son, the Temple and God's dwelling with Israel. The more we find out, the more we realise that Christianity is deeply and resonantly Jewish.

Similarly, although the doctrine of the Trinity is only fully formulated in the third century, I like to think it's one of Christianity's most Jewish doctrines in this sense – that it would have been very easy for Christians to say that they worship two gods, a father god and a son god, or to have gone a polytheistic route by saying that they worshipped three gods. Counter-intuitively, they insisted that although they prayed to the Father and the Son, and through the Spirit, they were monotheists nevertheless. The architectonics of the doctrine of the Trinity were worked out to enable Christians to stand firm in their conviction that they are monotheistic.

There's a further dimension here that I think should be mentioned. It's that much of the hostility in nineteenth-century German Protestant scholarship towards the allegedly legalistic and priest-ridden cult of the Jews was a deflected form of anti-Catholicism. I don't want in any sense to say that the whole Lutheran tradition is tarnished in this way, but Lutheran scholars themselves have exposed Luther's belief that just as Jesus (and Paul's preaching of Jesus) broke with a priest-ridden and cultic Judaism, so, in the sixteenth century, the Reformers were introducing a more spiritual religion by abolishing the priestcraft and trappings of the medieval Church. In the nineteenth century this was echoed by Hegel and many influenced by him, some of whom, like Feuerbach, argued that they were developing an even freer and more spiritual religion by getting rid of God altogether.

SHORTT: Scriptural scholarship is one of the areas not covered in detail by this book, so it's good to have a sample of the important work that's being done. Can you pull some of these threads together in the time remaining – your position as a philosophical theologian, your particular interests, including feminism and the naming of God, and your obvious sense of a new confidence in the circles you move between?

MARTIN SOSKICE: As I've said, I continue to read and value analytic philosophy and philosophy of language. I'm back to Kaplan and Kripke for some parts of the book on naming God. Philosophy is like a toolkit. You don't pick up a hammer when you want a screwdriver, and for some kinds of problem one needs guidance from an analytic philosopher. But to solve another problem I might look elsewhere.

Much depends on what you're trying to think about – the integrity of the subject matter – whether it's a question of aesthetics, whether it's science and religion, religious rationality, or gender and religion. These are all quite different, and you may need different equipment to approach them.

But it's worth noting that some issues won't even present themselves as questions within certain parameters. Here's an example. During the early 1980s I wanted to organise a series of talks on the way in which ideas about women were treated as a topic in historical theology. I was told by a kindly Oxford professor (and he *was* kindly) that although he would be in favour of it, a number of others might wonder if this was a topic for serious academic theology. I pointed out that there was a special series of lectures being run at the time on the theology of horses (admittedly in Oriental Studies). It's a natural thing that, as a woman of my generation, I should have become interested in feminism and gender; yet I am puzzled by those who think that my interests here are somehow different from, or even antithetical to, my interest in philosophy of language (and I have met both philosophers, on the one hand, and feminist theologians, on the other, who assume this is the case). It's been a common assumption that Gregory of Nyssa's *Life of Moses*, a later work, is mystical and not philosophical, and that his earlier 'Against Eunomius' is philosophical and not mystical. No: it's one person doing the whole thing. If you're profoundly interested in religion, religious language and symbolism (as was Gregory, for that matter), then gender symbolism is going to present some of the most interesting questions in the biblical litera-ture. There are questions about audience and subjectivity, about the universality of what was until recently called in most theology courses 'the Christian doctrine of man', and is now more neutrally entitled 'Christian anthropology'.

Another example: I was struck once while reading an essay by a dis-tinguished French Catholic theologian of an older generation about the duty that a theologian owes to his Church. It was the text of an address given at a seminary. Addressing the seminarians, who were naturally all male, the theologian spoke throughout of the Church as female. This, too, is altogether conventional biblical typology – the Church as the female bride of Christ, the theologian a loyal son of mother Church. All fine. But at a certain stage the lecturer began to develop this metaphor in highly detailed ways, and to remind his audience of how we relate to and look after our mothers – and what a loyal son does to protect his mother. At this point I began to feel almost dizzy with dissonance. The talk depended so much on how a *son* would relate to a mother – a daughter, however loyal, would not speak in such a way. This example is in one sense trivial, but, on the other hand, here is a central image in ecclesiology – the Church as female, as bride – to which men and women might actually relate quite differently. If they do so, is this not important? Perhaps not; but this seems doubtful. After all, in other areas, such as the Vatican's insistence that priests be male, we are told the gender symbolism is decisive and ontological.

SHORTT: And what of the fatherhood of God?

MARTIN SOSKICE: That's even more central. Let's leave to the side for the moment those feminists who have difficulties with the fatherhood of God. Even where women are positive about the fatherhood of God, is it the same thing for a woman to address God as father, and to think of God in paternal imagery, as it is for a man? These are at least questions that a philosopher should be interested in, especially if we ask, following Wittgenstein, not just for meaning but for use. How does the language work? All manner of things come in here: philosophy of language, Christian anthropology, Christology, liturgy and ecclesiology – and a philosophical theologian has to be concerned with all these things. Philosophy's problems don't lie neatly like tennis balls on the lawns of the world: you have to hunt around in the bushes for the ones that are lost.

SHORTT: Would it be right to place your work under the category of what's known in the Catholic world as fundamental theology?

MARTIN SOSKICE: I think so. In Catholic theological faculties fundamental theologians do pretty much what I do, which is philosophy of language, philosophy of science, hermeneutics, apologetics, and that really is what philosophical theology is about. When I read historical theology, although I try to keep informed by what patristics scholars, medievalists or early modernists do, I am reading as a contemporary philosophical theologian. That's where I feel most at home.

SHORTT: What about your pantheon?

MARTIN SOSKICE: It shifts. As you'll have seen, I come back constantly to figures such as Augustine and Gregory of Nyssa. At the moment I'm also reading quite a lot of Philo, Aquinas, Buber and Rosensweig, and Julian of Norwich.

SHORTT: Is Charles Taylor, among living Christian thinkers, there as well?

MARTIN SOSKICE: At certain stages, yes. It is rain water that's gone a long way into the soil. Taylor's book *Sources of the Self*, with its diagnosis of the Cartesian self, what he calls 'the punctual self', spoke to me powerfully. This is his analysis of the self of early modernity, which continued through right to our own time – a completely self-contained and self-sustaining, languageless, cultureless, willing agent. Taylor's puncturing of that particular notion was immensely helpful. Of course, other people had done it before him, or at the same time. Iris Murdoch took this 'Kantian Man', as she called him, apart marvellously in *The Sovereignty of Good*. Luce Irigaray debunked it highly effectively in a different way, in *Speculum of the Other Woman*, as did Alasdair MacIntyre in *After Virtue*. This has been a very important philosophical moment, not just for theologians of my generation, but for philosophers as well.

I think that what has emboldened theologians like John Milbank and others who locate themselves as critics of modernity is the intuition that the best way out of modernity's crisis vis-à-vis the self might be God. Because once we've got rid of the punctual self, a comforting if delusionally Promethean notion from the past few centuries, we need to ask what self we are left with. The offerings given to us by philosophy are not inspiring. Who is going to be happy with a dissipated self that is pushed hither and yon by powerful contesting rhetorics, or advertising, or whatever? The self cannot be all-powerful and all-knowing – cannot, as Augustine knew well, claim to know itself. But is it to be nothing at all? In the face of the death, not only of God but, as Nietzsche foresaw, of all absolute values – of ethics, aesthetics, politics, or painting and beauty – I think theology shows us another way. We are 'bare forked animals', but called to the divine. Theologians are tired of sitting on the sidelines of the academy and asking, 'Please, sir, may we say something?' On the contrary, many are looking around the academy and finding high levels of intellectual bankruptcy. In reply we want to say, 'Think about what we can offer with this God business. Stare into the void and then turn away, and maybe the answer is God.'

3
Alvin Plantinga and Christopher J. Insole

The Philosophy of Religion

SHORTT: If an imminent resurgence in the philosophy of religion had been forecast in the 1960s and 1970s, many people would have thought that this was far more likely to happen in the Continental than the analytic sphere. But in the event it is analytic philosophers who have made much of the running in recent decades, among them Nicholas Wolterstorff and Peter van Inwagen in the United States, and Richard Swinburne and John Haldane in Britain.

Alvin, I don't think anyone is more associated with this trend than you. We'll shortly discuss several of the topics at the heart of your large body of work, including epistemic warrant, the free-will defence to the problem of evil, and your evolutionary argument against naturalism – the intriguing thesis that atheism is fatally undermined by science itself. Another point worth stressing at the outset is that you take Christian objections to natural theology very seriously, in part, perhaps, because of your Reformed background. You therefore see the relation between spirituality and the philosophy of religion as a delicate one, and I'd be grateful if you could address this question as well, after starting with your background.

PLANTINGA: I was brought up as a Christian, and would say that Christianity and philosophy have been the most important forces in my life. Apart from having some youthful doubts, as many people do, I've always believed the faith that was passed on to me in childhood. As a freshman at Harvard in the early 1950s, I encountered for the first time really serious and substantial opposition to Christian and theistic belief: people of high intelligence who thought Christianity was nonsense and had nothing but contempt for either Christianity or theism.

But then something remarkable happened. I was coming back from the university dining hall one miserable November evening, and suddenly felt as if the heavens had lit up and opened. I heard music of the most incredible beauty and sweetness (Mozart – Barth thought that there would be a lot of Mozart in heaven). There weren't any voices or anything like that: it just felt like a kind of confirmation of what I'd thought all along. It wasn't as if I could literally see into heaven, but it felt somewhat as though I could. The experience was in that general neighbourhood. And after that, I still took part in discussions about whether there is such a person as God or not, but they didn't have the same existential force. It was more like arguing about whether there's an external world out there, or whether there are other persons. It's also very hard to give a proof for the existence of other persons, other centres of consciousness, other beings who think and feel and believe as you yourself do, or an argument demonstrating that past events actually occurred – Bertrand Russell, for example, once said that the world could have come into existence five minutes ago, with all the crumbling mountains and wrinkled faces and all the vestiges of history, all the mouldering books in the libraries, and so on. One can have fun arguing about this suggestion, but it, too, lacks existential force. I don't really wonder whether you and Chris Insole are other persons, whether you are actually conscious and listening to what I say. And after the experience I've just recounted, that's the way it was with me and belief in God, along with the central lineaments of Christianity.

Nevertheless, I was very struck by the many objections to Christian and theistic belief thrown up by serious people elsewhere in academia, and I found myself strongly inclined to investigate these objections to see whether they really had the substance that many people imagined. And that's fundamentally one of the things I've been doing ever since.

SHORTT: Who supplied the music? Can we be clear that you believe you had a mystical experience?

PLANTINGA: There weren't any actual orchestras around, as far as I know, at the time. Whether other people could have heard it had they been there, I can't say. But that's the way it seemed to me.

SHORTT: This puts you in the same camp as Janet Martin Soskice, who also reports an exceptional experience that established her religious beliefs on the firmest of footings. It forms a useful springboard for discussing your claim that belief in God is 'properly basic'. Among other things you're renowned for staking out the middle ground between fideists such as Barth, who deny any place for 'unaided' reason in the search for God, and the rationalistic philosophy that used to be standard fare in Roman Catholic apologetics, where students started from purportedly neutral premises, and ended up with something akin to the creeds. I think it's broadly right to say that your own position entails a restatement, with greater philosophical sophistication, of an argument of Cardinal Newman in *A Grammar of Assent*,[1] namely that some of the beliefs we hold with the greatest confidence have not been reached by argument, and can't even necessarily be defended by argument. His examples are that Great Britain is an island, and that you and I will die some day; and he shows how futile it would be to try to set out premises from which these beliefs would follow as conclusions, because we believe them more strongly than we believe any of the bits of evidence that we might adduce in terms of atlases or mortality figures, and so forth. But there are clearly lots of people who'd deny that belief in God is properly basic in these senses. Could you detail your thesis and then outline your reply to the counter-arguments?

PLANTINGA: Roughly speaking, between the Enlightenment and the middle of the twentieth century the idea was that one could properly believe in God only if one had an argument, only if one had evidence in the sense of propositional evidence, some sort of argument from other propositions that one believed. If you didn't have such arguments, then the idea was that belief in God wasn't appropriate. So philosophy of religion courses in the 1950s and early 1960s would generally entail study of the classical arguments for the existence of God – the ontological argument, the teleological argument, the causal argument, maybe one or two more, like the moral argument, and generally people would judge that these arguments really aren't conclusive, and the inference would be that it's intellectually irresponsible to affirm the existence of God, let alone belief in the whole panoply of Christian doctrine.

But there's an enormous assumption there. Why does one think there have to be arguments of that sort in order for it to be proper, reasonable and justified to believe in God? There are lots of other things, some of the very things I was mentioning a moment ago, which one can't justify on the basis of other propositions that one believes. From time to time foundationalist epistemology has actually attempted to give some kind of argument for other minds. Take, for example, the analogical argument for other minds. Those who propose this argument say that I note that when I'm happy, let's say, my body is behaving in a certain way; so when I see some other body functioning in that way I form the hypothesis that there is a self connected with that body who's happy, just as I am. This seems to me to be an extremely weak sort of argument. In the first place, one doesn't really know what one looks like when one is happy. We don't carry around mirrors to observe our faces and see what they look like when we're happy and when we're sad. And in any event, it's an argument from one case alone. Nobody would really set much store by an argument as flimsy as that, but we all nevertheless believe that there are indeed other persons, and we believe this with certainty. We take it utterly for granted. It's not a mere hypothesis, like, say, the Copenhagen interpretation of quantum mechanics.

Why couldn't it be the same with respect to belief in God? Why think that there has to be deductive or inductive argument? The first serious book I wrote was called *God and Other Minds*,[2] in which I argued that there was a kind of detailed epistemological analogy between belief in other minds and belief in God. My claim was that if one of these is rational, so is the other.

SHORTT: Would you say a bit more about what you mean by basicality?

PLANTINGA: There I was thinking of basicality as being within one's intellectual rights, hence the term 'properly basic'. This issue can be understood in at least three ways. There is being justified, that is, not being irresponsible. There is being rational, which, in the basic Aristotelian meaning, is about having properly functioning cognitive faculties – you're not insane, not in the grip of some great passion that clouds your reason, and so on. And then there is warrant, which would be the property a true belief has when it's knowledge, so that warrant plus truth, a belief that's both warranted and true, would be knowledge.

Now the question is, with respect to various kinds of belief, belief in other minds, belief in the past: are they properly basic in the justified sense? Are they properly basic in the rational sense? And are they properly basic in the warrant sense? In *God and Other Minds* I was thinking just about justification, but more recently I've also thought about these other two epistemic desiderata. And as far as I can see, there aren't any decent philosophical grounds for denying that Christian belief – not just theistic belief, but Christian belief – is properly basic in all three of those ways. So that if I believe there is such a person as God, even if I don't have any evidence, don't have an argument or don't believe on the basis of evidence, nonetheless my belief might be perfectly justified. I might be perfectly well within my rights. I don't have to be insane or blinded by fear of death, or anything like that. And it seems to me it could also be that if Christian teaching is true, my belief could also be warranted, so that as a matter of fact, I don't merely believe these things, but know them. That's the way I've been thinking.

SHORTT: Your critics sometimes pick up on this and complain that you don't seem so much interested in persuading people as defending your ground and demonstrating that you're within your intellectual rights to think as you do.

PLANTINGA: My whole life has been spent in a dialogue with people who hold views very different from my own – people who think that Christian belief is foolish or irrational. But it's true that what I'm doing is a necessary but not sufficient ground for persuading people to accept Christian belief. Persuasion of that kind would be a different project entirely: it's a worthy enterprise, but it's not the only thing one can do. If I work on one project, I can leave another one to an exponent of natural theology such as Richard Swinburne, for example. I myself don't think that the arguments from natural theology persuade very many people either to become believers in God, or to become Christians. It seems to me that this ordinarily happens more through preaching, the presentation of the Word of God. That's what occurs, in my view, when we come to be serious Christians, or maybe serious Muslims or Jews too, for that matter. So I accept your point, but don't think it calls for an apology on my part.

SHORTT: A distinct instance of this might be the work you've done on recasting the ontological argument, the theistic 'proof' stating that God must exist because he has maximal greatness by definition, and a deity who existed only in the human mind, and not also in actuality, would be less than maximally great. I'm not sure that we should go over this ground in detail, because it involves technical moves in modal logic and some equally intricate discussion about the metaphysical status of possible worlds.[3] But the bottom line, for you, is that a sound argument is not necessarily a strong argument.

PLANTINGA: Yes. That's what I think about the ontological argument. An argument is sound if it has true premises and the conclusion follows from the premises. Here's a very simple argument:

> Either God exists, or seven plus five does not equal twelve.
> Seven plus five does equal twelve, therefore God exists.

Since I believe that there is such a person as God, I think the premises of this argument are true; it is also obviously valid, so it's sound. But it's not a strong argument. And the ontological argument is a little bit like that. Once you get clear about exactly what's involved in it, then you will certainly either accept both the premise and the conclusion, or not accept either one, but it's unlikely to convert you to belief in God.

SHORTT: Chris, how does this strike you, as someone who's been fairly evenly immersed in several philosophical currents, and recently thought a good deal about the territory bordering philosophy and politics?

INSOLE: I first came across your work, Alvin, when I was an undergraduate at Oxford studying philosophy and theology. It was like a breath of fresh air, a world away from the slightly over-rehearsed business of either picking or plugging in holes in arguments for the existence of God. One of the things I've found most intriguing and attractive about your approach is that it seems to challenge some of the usual distinctions between Continental and analytic philosophy. I have in mind the way that you tackle the sceptical problem about the external world or other minds. It has at least some resonances with aspects of the thought of Heidegger, for instance. You are keen to emphasise that our primary attitude to the world is not that of theory builders inferring from sense data to the existence of persons and a world. Similarly, Heidegger saw our involvement with the world as being always already practical, committed and immersed. The world discloses itself in certain ways to us which are more fundamental than our theory. Theory is derivative on practice, rather than practice derivative on theory. So I wonder if you see some perhaps surprising allies in Continental philosophy or in the work of someone like Heidegger.

PLANTINGA: I can't really say that I have, but that's basically out of ignorance. I haven't studied Heidegger very carefully. I have made attempts to do so and then found myself getting hopelessly bogged down. Sometimes it appears that he's devoting a lot of space to saying something fairly banal, or, if not banal, then quite mysterious. I don't say this to denigrate Heidegger or Continental philosophy. There just may be a difference between people along these lines. And maybe Continental philosophers aren't trying to do the very same thing that analytic philosophers are trying to do. Maybe Continental philosophers are trying to produce something that isn't just an answer to certain questions, but has a certain kind of beauty to it, a certain structure or emotional resonance, and it's deliberately framed in opposition to the rather dry exposition one finds, for instance, in Thomas Aquinas – and I would count Thomas as a prime example of an analytic philosopher. Continental philosophers often claim that analytic philosophy is boring, but also trivial. And analytic philosophers return the compliment by saying that Continental philosophy is completely opaque. There is some truth in both of these claims. And I think part of the problem is that it's not exactly the same things that are aimed at in these two schools of philosophy. There are different criteria of what success would be.

But whether or not the questions I'm interested in chime with Continental philosophy, they certainly have a very long pedigree. They go back to Plato and even before Plato, and I'm interested in approaching them in roughly the way the great tradition has done, the tradition that encompasses Plato and Aristotle, Augustine and Aquinas, Scotus and Ockham, Descartes, Locke, Berkeley, Leibnitz and so on, all the way up to, say, Kant. After Kant, starting perhaps with Hegel or Nietzsche, there seems to me to be a kind of sharp off-shoot from the great tradition where things develop in a way that I don't really understand.

INSOLE: Would it be fair to say that your work aspires towards an almost democratic spirit, because there is no resort to authority? I have in mind the way in which all the premises, moves in argument and conclusions are supposed to be visible and transparent – even if the argument developed is that reason should assent to its own limitations, by denying the need for intellectual and rational adjudication of evidence. Continental philosophy, by contrast, can be much more authoritarian. Depending on the position of the author, one is frequently told that certain statements or propositions are no longer possible 'after Kant', 'after Wittgenstein' or 'after Foucault'. But you, along with analytic philosophy more generally, give your reasoning, and display a more individualist spirit.

PLANTINGA: Well, that's the hope anyway.

SHORTT: I hope we'll return to this territory later when Chris talks more about his own work. In the meantime, let's move on to a dimension of Alvin's thought that does have strong existential resonances in the broader sense, and that's the free-will defence in response to the problem of evil.

PLANTINGA: It runs as follows. If God creates free creatures, he has to let them decide whether they do what's right or what's wrong. That's what it is for them to be free. Perhaps God can't create a world in which there are free creatures who always do what is right. It just may not be possible for him to do that. Consider the example of Adam and

Eve in the garden. Maybe what God knew in advance was that if he were to create them and leave them free, they would, in fact, freely go wrong. Well, if that's the way things are, then God can't create a possible world in which Adam and Eve are in that very same situation, and freely do what's right. There's no way God can do that, because what he sees in advance is that they would in fact go wrong. So there are lots of possible worlds, possible states of affairs, that are in fact genuinely possible but that God can't cause to be actual, even though he's omnipotent. He has to depend in part on the co-operation of his creatures. And he can't enforce the free co-operation of his creatures. That's really the heart of the free-will defence.

When I started off in philosophy, the problem of evil was always presented as entailing a logical conflict between believing in God's love for us and God's omnipotence.

SHORTT: Hume's challenge.

PLANTINGA: Hume's challenge, restated by many others, including John Mackie:[4] that it's just not logically possible that these propositions should both be true: that God is omnipotent, omniscient and good; and that there is evil. And I countered that these propositions are not contradictory. It could be that God can't create a world in which there is moral good, that is, good which is done by free creatures, without also creating one in which there is evil. Our own world is like that: there is moral good and moral evil. And the reason would be that these counter-factuals of freedom – these truths about what various free creatures would do if they were in various different sets of circumstances – are so arranged, their truth values are such that in all the very good worlds, there are free creatures who also do what's wrong.

SHORTT: I can see that your argument is solid on its own terms, and that it gives many people an adequate answer to their difficulties. Others, though, may reply that the problem remains intractable in another way or at another level. How about suffering, as opposed to evil, for example? What you've said doesn't answer the objection put into the mouth of Ivan Karamazov by Dostoevsky, that if the price of our enjoying immortal bliss were that a single child be torn limb from limb by wild beast, then the cost would be too high.

Orthodox Christianity commits one to belief in miracles, and this points to a further consideration. In his contribution to this book Rowan Williams has already described how miracles are understood in classical Christian thought, and he mentions the example of C. S. Lewis's prayer that the pain of his wife's cancer be transferred to him.[5] I won't express a view on whether Joy Davidman's cancer was miraculously relieved, although those symptoms were softened for a time, to the great surprise of observers. But it does make an awful lot of people wonder why God doesn't perform other miracles that avert suffering on much larger scales. If God can act in the case of one woman's cancer, or one man's withered arm, why can't he act in the case of an earthquake that kills hundreds of thousands of people?

PLANTINGA: But if God *has* averted some colossal horrors, then, of course, we might not know about that, because the colossal horrors haven't taken place. It seems to me, first of all, that it's very hard for us to answer the questions, 'Why would God do this?' or 'Why wouldn't God do that?' His knowledge of the whole situation is obviously vastly greater than ours. There might be all sorts of creatures involved in our history – for example, angels, and Satan and his minions, as many Christians have thought over the centuries – about which we know very little, maybe many about which we know nothing whatever. And God's dealings aren't simply with the human race. Maybe he has dealings with angels and other beings, and we may not have any idea why God permits evils to occur in a given case, because God's reasons for permitting that evil have to do with these other creatures.

This is the proper message of the Book of Job. Job is suffering and he can't figure out why. The book begins with a transaction between God and Satan, a transaction Job never finds out about. So the reason for Job's suffering is outside his field of knowledge. He has no idea what the reason for his suffering is, and if God were to tell him, he might not be able to understand it. At the end of the book, he complains about this. He says something like the following: 'I'm no worse than Eliphaz the Temanite, Bilbad the Shuhite and Zophar the Naamathite. They keep insisting that the reason I suffer must be that I'm a bad person, but I'm no worse than they are.' And he wants to go to court with God. He gets angry, he wants to rebel against God, but then he realises he's not going to get anywhere doing that, because if he went to court with God, God would be the judge and the jury and the executioner, all rolled into one, so he wouldn't have much of a chance. But then at the end of the book, God comes to Job and Job actually experiences God's greatness and power, his loveliness and beauty, and he says to himself, I don't know why God permitted this, but being God, he would have a very good reason, even if I don't know what it is, so I'll trust him.

That, it seems to me, is the sort of attitude one can properly take with respect to evil. It's not that if one recognises suffering and evil in the world, even appallingly awful suffering and evil, then one's got some reason for rejecting belief in God. No, if you've got a proper grasp of God's greatness and presence, his beauty and the like, what you've got is a reason for thinking that there are things here you simply don't understand.

INSOLE: And pursuing the line you drew earlier between your work and Richard Swinburne's, should we also distinguish here between the free-will defence and a fully fledged theodicy?

PLANTINGA: Yes. In a defence, you don't claim to know the answer to the question, 'Why does God do so-and-so?' But you do claim to be able to show that there isn't any contradiction in there being such a person as God who is wholly good, wholly powerful, wholly know-ledgeable on the one hand, and evil on the other hand. In a theodicy, you try to say what God's reasons for evil might in fact be. So, for example, Swinburne and various other people offer theodicies. I've always thought that theodicies are a bit presumptuous in that the chances are very good that we don't have the faintest idea what God's reasons for permitting evil might be.

But here's another suggestion about theodicy that goes back deep into Christian thought. Let's say God wanted to create a very good possible world. What is it that makes one world better than another world? I mean, he's got all these worlds laid out before him, you might say, and he sees that one is very good and one isn't so good. What is it that makes the very good one a better world than the one that isn't so good? Well, there would be various things – human beings or other rational creatures who love God and worship him in the one world, maybe there aren't any in the other, something like that – but one thing that would make a possible world enormously good would be what has actually taken place in this one, according to the Christian understanding, namely, the first being of the universe, God himself, creates creatures who then rebel against him, turn their backs on him. Rather than destroy these ingrates, however, the Creator arranges a way – a way involving enormous suffering and pain on his own part – whereby humanity can be redeemed. What could be a more impressive property than that?

So maybe all the best possible worlds contain something like in-carnation and atonement, or, at any rate, atonement. But if they do, of course, then all the best possible worlds also contain sin, evil and suffering, and presumably quite a bit of it. If there were incarnation and atonement in a world in which, say, the total amount of evil amounted to one peccadillo on the part of an otherwise admirably disposed angel, then the process would involve enormous overkill. So maybe it's the case that in all the good worlds there is a large amount of suffering and evil, for just the reasons I've been suggesting. I've no idea really whether that's the reason God permits evil and suffering, but it's a possibility.

SHORTT: **Another point springing from your free-will defence, and that's linked to your spirituality, is that it appears to ally you with a Catholic or Arminian rejection of predestination. On the face of it this is paradoxical, given your Calvinist allegiances, and the fact that Arminianism was condemned by your Church at the Synod of Dort in 1618–19.**

PLANTINGA: That's substantially right. As far as Catholicism goes, however, Thomas Aquinas was probably an even stronger pre-destinarian than Calvin. I don't know that there's such a Catholic–Protestant difference here. There might be an internal Catholic difference between the Dominican and Jesuit orders. So you've got Molina on the one hand and Báñez on the other, the latter being a Dominican, a strong predestinarian, the former believing in human freedom. As for my view of the Synod of Dort, I think that the Arminians should also be thought of as Calvinists. They thought of themselves as Calvinists. The synod declared that they weren't, but this was probably a mistake on the part of the Reformed or Calvinist community.

In any case, the free-will defence has to do merely with what's possible. So it would work perfectly well even if as a matter of fact people didn't really have freedom. The free-will defence is not an answer to the questions, Why is there evil? or, What actually explains the existence of evil? It's an attempt to show that a certain proposition, There is evil, is logically consistent with another proposition, God is almighty and all-knowing and wholly good. And it can do that by virtue of proposing this other possible hypothesis about freedom.

INSOLE: You don't say that it's impossible for God to create a world where people are significantly free, but always choose the good. You say it is possible that it is impossible.

PLANTINGA: Yes. It might be that he can't do it.

INSOLE: But it's still possible that he could.

PLANTINGA: That's true too.

INSOLE: I was struck by your earlier observation that, after your religious experience at Harvard, doubting the existence of God had an unreal status in your mind, similar to doubting the existence of other minds or the external world. Given this, it is understandable that your defences of religious belief tend to go along the lines that they are just 'not logically impossible'. But someone who has not had such a powerful religious experience, and occupies more of a twilight zone between faith and unbelief, is going to want to be persuaded by considerations that are more than 'not logically impossible'. They will be looking for arguments that are plausible and compelling. Would it be unfair to say that your sense that doubting God's existence is as unreal as doubting other minds, is reflected in your willingness to accept rather unreal solutions: 'Satan and his minions', for instance, when discussing the problem of evil?

PLANTINGA: Well, the first question I was looking into there was just the logical compatibility of these propositions. John Mackie, as I've mentioned, argued that they're logically incompatible. Those wanting to get into the detail of my rebuttal of this argument can read it elsewhere.[6] My main point is that if you propose a hypothesis that reconciles the two propositions, all it has to be is logically possible. It doesn't have to be plausible at all. And if it isn't plausible, that doesn't make any difference. You're not claiming that it's true, or probable, or possible; you're claiming only that it's logically possible. As for the other part of your question, like other Christians, I, too, have had my doubts, of course. It's just that for the most part I've been interested in responding to objections to Christian belief, responding to claims that it's irrational or that it's not justified or that it couldn't constitute knowledge even if it were true. Producing reasons for people to accept it is not part of that project.

The free-will defence – or for that matter, theodicy – is not much of a reason to accept Christian belief, although the project can take us some of the way. There are strong arguments for the existence of God. I've got an unpublished paper called 'Two Dozen or So Good Theistic Arguments'. These are good arguments, but I doubt that they are strong enough to support the degree of firmness with which Christians actually hold these beliefs.

SHORTT: **Which brings us again to the theology behind your philo-sophy. Lest people think that you're uniquely privileged in having had your special experience, it should be emphasised that you think we're all endowed with a sense or intuition of the divine – the *sensus divinitatis*.**

PLANTINGA: Yes, I think lots and lots of people have had similar experiences to mine, or experiences that go way beyond mine, or experiences of a slightly different sort. You go out on a beautiful June morning, you see the trees, the beauty of the sky, the sun, and you get the sort of sudden upwelling of a feeling of gratitude. You feel that you've got to be grateful to somebody for this, and the only real candidate is God. Or you find yourself in danger, and praying. Even if you're not normally inclined to go to church at all, you might find yourself praying, and this would presuppose that you think God is there, and could help if he wanted to. There are a whole range of experiences, it seems to me, that call forth belief in God. It's not as if belief in God is a kind of hypothesis that someone uses in order to explain what the world is like: it's more, as with the existence of other minds and the past, something that on certain occasions and given certain experiences just seems right, just seems inevitable.

SHORTT: This might strike many people as reflecting a more common-sensical approach than the hardline rejection of natural theology we find in Barth, for example. Perhaps his position is questionable at a deeper level as well, because if we do have the *sensus divinitatis*, then the relentless abasement of human insight or effort appears contradictory, or at least in need of heavy qualification. One would need to stop thinking only of a transcendent deity at an infinite remove from creatures, and think also about God's outreach to human beings, who are themselves equipped with a divine spark. Now I don't suppose that Barth would deny this. But it's certainly possible to ask questions about his slant.

PLANTINGA: It seems to me that the right way to think about this is as follows. You don't need arguments from natural theology in order to have justified, rational or warranted belief in God, but that's not to say there aren't any, or that they aren't of any use, or that you've got to denounce anybody that recommends them. It's perfectly possible that there should be such good arguments. It's just that they're not necessary. There aren't any good arguments for other minds; but perhaps there could have been. If there had been good arguments, it wouldn't be that just because you don't believe in other minds on the basis of these arguments, you ought to be angry about anybody who wants to produce them. If people like Richard Swinburne come up with good arguments, that's terrific. But with Barth, I say: you don't need them in order to have all these epistemic virtues such as being rational, being justified and being warranted.

SHORTT: Let's turn now to one of the major positive arguments for theistic belief you've developed in recent years, namely the evolutionary argument against naturalism. The main idea here is that there isn't any conflict between Christian belief and science, but there is a conflict between philosophical naturalism and science. Since naturalism is very much like a religion, we might say that there is indeed a religion–science conflict, but it's between naturalism and science, not Christian belief and science.

Even though you've developed the argument in far more complex ways, its premise can be simply stated. This involves a distinction between adaptive behaviour and having true beliefs: your claim is that evolution can explain the former, but not the latter. I should explain at the outset that you express the argument formally as a conditional probability:

$$P\ (R/(N\&E))$$

where R stands for the thesis that our cognitive faculties are reliable, and N and E for the claims that naturalism and evolution are true. And your conclusion is that the probability P of R on N and E is low.

PLANTINGA: Right. Examples of naturalists would be biologists like Richard Dawkins, and philosophers like Daniel Dennett and Bertrand Russell, in his famous article 'The Free Man's Worship'. These people champion the view not only that there isn't a God: there isn't anything even like God. It's not as if theism gets fairly close to the truth. It's a long way from the truth.

And with respect to the first part of my thesis, that there's no real conflict between Christian belief and science, one thing you can think about is whether or not science precludes miracles. It seems to me that science clearly doesn't preclude miracles. If you take the classical science deriving from Newton, and the great laws on the conservation of momentum: these laws are stated for closed systems, systems which are such that there isn't any causal influence on them from outside. But if God were actually to perform a miracle in the world – raise someone from the dead, cause water to change into wine, heal someone miraculously, work in someone's heart via the internal testimony of the Holy Spirit that Calvin speaks of, or the internal instigation of the Holy Spirit that Aquinas speaks of – then the universe on these occasions would not be a closed system, and the laws of classical science wouldn't apply at all.

So the laws of classical science are in no way incompatible with God's performing miracles. And as far as contemporary science goes, since the quantum mechanical revolution, the principal laws have been stated probabilistically, so that quantum mechanics, for a given initial configuration of a set of particles, assigns various probabilities to different outcomes arising from that configuration. It doesn't say that there will be just this outcome or just that one. And it's therefore hard to break the laws of quantum mechanics, so to speak, or to think of some event that might do so. It's compatible with quantum mechanics that, for example, the statue of Lord Nelson in Trafalgar Square should get down off its pedestal and walk around. And, of course, it's also compatible with quantum mechanics that someone should rise from the dead. These things are or would be extremely improbable, but miracles are extremely improbable anyway. We already know that.

The other side, about how there's a conflict between naturalism and science, is harder to explain briefly and simply, but I'll do my best. Suppose you consider these two propositions: that naturalism is true and that we have come to be by virtue of the sorts of processes we are taught in evolutionary theory, namely natural selection winnowing or working on random genetic mutation. There are other processes people evoke, but these are considered to be the main ones. So let's consider the propositions N and E that you've spelt out – N for naturalism is true, and E for the theory that we've come to be by virtue of evolutionary processes. If we've come to be that way, then, of course, so have our cognitive faculties: memory and perception, insight, rational intuition whereby we know mathematics, and sympathy, whereby we understand what other people are thinking and feeling. And if this is true, then the purpose or job of our cognitive faculties is not, as it is under Christian theism, to provide us with true beliefs, but to provide us with beliefs that are useful in a certain way, that promote or enhance reproductive fitness.

So then you have to ask the following question: What's the probability that our cognitive faculties would be reliable, given that they are not aimed at true beliefs? What's the probability that our cognitive faculties would be reliable given that N and E are true? And now we can look into this in more detail, and I've written about this elsewhere. You can break up N and E into four kinds of sub-cases and look at the probability of R on each of them. What you wind up with is that R, our cognitive faculties' being reliable, is improbable on N and E. The probability of R on N and E is low.

Consider some other creatures and some other part of the universe, and suppose naturalism is true for them. Suppose also that they came to be by virtue of natural selection working on random genetic mutation, so that the purpose of their cognitive faculties is to promote reproductive fitness, not to provide them with true beliefs. Ask what the probability of R on N and E for them would be, and you'd conclude, I think, that that probability is low.

SHORTT: And the next step of the argument is that if the probability of R on N and E is low, and if you see that while still believing N and E to be true, then you have a defeater for R, that is, grounds for disbelieving R.

PLANTINGA: Yes. If you believe that both naturalism and evolution are true, then you've got a good reason to reject the belief that your cognitive faculties are in fact reliable – a reason to believe its denial or else just to be agnostic about it. And if you've got a defeater for R, for the proposition that your cognitive faculties are reliable, then you also have a defeater for any belief that's produced by your cognitive faculties. Of course, that's all of your beliefs. All of your beliefs are produced by your cognitive faculties. I mean, where else would they come from?

SHORTT: I've several times heard Dawkins say that he thinks intelligent life in the universe is rare. Supposing he were just to say, Well, that's just how things are. It's improbable, but R and N and E all happen to be true.

PLANTINGA: That would be rather like your convincing me that the probability of God's existence, given the extent of evil, is very low, and my saying, OK, it's very low but nonetheless that's the way it is. That's not much of a response.

SHORTT: Isn't that what some people do say? And isn't it in fact a simplified version of what you yourself have said?

PLANTINGA: But I might think that in the case of belief in God, I have other evidence. Dawkins, however, doesn't have other evidence. If the question is whether your cognitive faculties are reliable, you can't try to settle that question by acquiring evidence, because the very process of acquiring evidence presupposes that your faculties are reliable. He has no get-out. He can't go, say, to the MIT Cognitive Science Laboratory, and get himself tested to see whether his faculties are reliable or not. That's not going to help him, because he's relying on his cognitive faculties to tell him that there is such a thing as that laboratory, for the scientists' having told him that his faculties are, in fact, reliable.

SHORTT: For the premises of the argument, as well as for the link between the premises and the conclusion.

PLANTINGA: Yes. And if you have a defeater for R, it follows that belief in N and E is self-referentially incoherent. It provides a defeater for itself. My conclusion is that you can't sensibly believe N and E. And since E is such an important part of contemporary science, what you've got is a conflict between naturalism and science.

SHORTT: There is a whole book devoted to your argument called *Naturalism Defeated?*[7] It includes reaction from a group of other philosophers, and a long section at the end in which you reply to each in turn. Again, the discussion is very technical, and we only have space to glance at it. But perhaps you could address one objection that occurred to me, as well as to some of your other interlocutors. It's your assumption that the generation of reliable belief-producing mechanisms should not itself be part of evolutionary adaptation. Why can't the naturalist just say that our brains have reached a certain level of complexity through evolution, and are such as to sprout true beliefs by dint of that complexity?

PLANTINGA: Well, I guess the naturalist *can* say that, but as I've indicated, I think it's improbable, on N and E, that our brains 'sprout' mainly true beliefs. At the start of *Naturalism Defeated* I use the example of a prehistoric hominoid, whom I call Paul, escaping from a hungry tiger; and I argue that there are many ways in which Paul's beliefs could be for the most part false, but adaptive. Furthermore, I add, we need not restrict ourselves to merely possible examples. Most of mankind has endorsed supernatural beliefs of one kind or another; according to the naturalist, such beliefs are adaptive though false. Readers wishing to do so can pursue the argument in detail.[8]

But you're asking another question too, which is whether I'm not simply falling for 'God of the gaps' thinking. No; I'm not raising the question whether my cognitive faculties are reliable, and then arguing, like Descartes, that they must be by appealing to God. An argument like that couldn't work anyway, because if you have a defeater for R, you have a defeater for the conclusion of any argument you might come up with. Giving an argument for R already and foolishly presupposes that R is true. But I wasn't giving any such argument. We all begin, perfectly sensibly, by assuming that R is true; we could say that belief in R is properly basic. Nevertheless, even though it is properly basic, it is possible to get a defeater for R – as you would if you thought, for example, that you had mad cow disease, or, as in the *Matrix* movies, that you were a brain in a vat – or if you accepted N and E, and saw that $P(R/(N\&E))$ is low. The theist does not have this defeater for R, because it is not improbable, given theism and evolution, that R should be true.

INSOLE: This does seem different from some of your earlier arguments, since it looks like it's pushing more towards something like a persuasive positive case for theism. But I wonder if you could just say what you think the continuities are, say, between proper basicality and your argument against naturalism.

PLANTINGA: I think the connection is something like this. I said earlier that I think there are two dozen or so good theistic arguments. Another sort of argument of a different sort altogether would be to refute the main alternatives, and naturalism is one of the two main alternatives, the other one being something like postmodern anti-realism. So it does have that kind of connection. It's not a direct argument for theistic belief, because all it really does is say that you can't sensibly be a naturalist. You could sensibly be an agnostic. You could just say, I really don't know what the truth of the matter is here. But what I do think is important and interesting is that there's a powerful argument for thinking you can't sensibly accept evolution and naturalism in the way Dawkins, Dennett, and many others do.

SHORTT: Thank you. Now for a change of focus. Chris, we've concentrated on Alvin so far, not least because his work as an analytic philosopher differs markedly from that of the philosophical theologians interviewed elsewhere in this book. As I've mentioned, though, you have a pretty eclectic philosophical background, and my aim is to report on new names in the field, as well as more established ones. In what remains of this chapter, I wonder if you could say more about your very different context, and a bit about where you think the torch is likely to be carried over the years ahead.

INSOLE: I'm glad you put it like that: if there is a torch to be carried anywhere, it is only because of figures of Alvin's stature. It seems to me that there is an outstanding generation of analytic philosophers – William Alston and Richard Swinburne, as well as Alvin – who really did manage to change the contours of what's acceptable to think about and defend in a secular British or American university. I'm sure that analytic approaches to philosophy of religion – evaluating the meaning and justification of religious beliefs using the full rigour of logic and conceptual clarity – should always have an honoured place in the academy. At the same time, I might say that such a project perhaps looks less urgent than it would have done in the 1960s or 1970s. This is partly because it has been done so well by the people I've mentioned, that it's now considered rather retro for an analytic philosopher to assume a 'methodological atheism', or to not look to religious philosophers for insights on a whole range of issues.

Academics are usually motivated by being unhappy: that is to say, one is provoked into researching, thinking about and writing on a topic from a sense of reading what else has been said, caring about the questions, and feeling that such-and-such is not right, or more complicated, or, if right, not adequately justified. I dare say that had I received my education in a British or American university in the 1960s or 1970s, I would have been considerably provoked by the way in which the fundamental principles of theism ('there is a God') were ridiculed by scientistically minded philosophers; but I find the most provoking feature of the present context to be the way that some theologians and philosophers pronounce polemically on a range of cultural and political issues.

SHORTT: **What provokes you in your book** *The Politics of Human Frailty* **is a characterisation of liberalism as hubristic, individualistic and relativist. You write that critics of liberalism, such as Oliver and Joan O'Donovan or John Milbank, are 'not wrong about liberalism', but that they 'are not right either'.**[9] **Could you explain what you mean by this?**

INSOLE: Yes, I am thinking of a broad claim about liberalism that it starts with the unfettered individual will, self-possessed and self-interested, and attempts to construct a society using the notion of a 'contract', that is construed as being manipulative and transcendence-denying. Now there are strands of liberalism that fit this description – those that trace an ancestry to Hobbes, perhaps – but it should also be said that there is a liberal tradition that would oppose all the objectionable features that supposedly characterise liberalism. I would argue that political liberalism is concerned most of all with the preservation of the liberties of the individual within a pluralistic (not secular or atheist) framework, precisely because of a sense of our fallen condition, characterised by frailty, sin and complexity.

When you can read, for instance, one of the greatest nineteenth-century *liberals*, Lord Acton, write that 'the Gospel fastens the sense of evil upon the mind; a Christian is enlightened, hardened, sharpened, as to evil, he sees it where others do not,'[10] I find it incredible that the accusation should be made so frequently and easily that liberals are motivated by a hubristic notion of the self that does not own its own frailty or the need for redemption. This is emphatically not so for thinkers such as Acton or Edmund Burke. It is quite the opposite. It is because of a sense of the vulnerability and falleness of individuals, whether they are acting individually or collectively; just because individuals club together to act in communities does not mean that they act well or virtuously. This simple truth, I think, is sometimes forgotten in the rather naive enthusiasm for 'participatory community' that can follow an onslaught on liberal individualism. The individual needs to be the unit of reflection about justice precisely because individuals are precious, fallen and vulnerable.

I'm convinced that there's a forgotten tradition of liberalism motivated by a sense of our createdness, our solidarity in sin with others, and the pride entailed by judging our neighbour when judgement belongs to God alone. Elements of this forgotten tradition can be found in Hooker, Locke, Burke and Acton; one of the aims of my book is to uncover this theologically informed and motivated liberal tradition.

SHORTT: **To what extent would such a claim be a merely historical caveat? Would it necessarily have any implications for how a contemporary theologian should now regard liberalism, especially if Oliver O'Donovan is correct that the Christian legacy of early modern liberalism has by now more or less exhausted itself?**

INSOLE: A theological defence of liberalism would have both a conceptual and a historical dimension, although the two are to an extent inseparable. Attacks on liberalism involve historical claims as part of their onslaught. So there is usually some sort of narrative revolving around the 'modern turn', supposed to come to fruition around the seventeenth century, but presaged and prepared for by thinkers such as William of Ockham, Duns Scotus and Marsilius of Padua in the late Middle Ages. The modern turn, the story goes, evacuates the universe of divine order and meaning, and places all meaning and order in the constructive human subject. On this point, thinkers such as the O'Donovans and John Milbank are more or less in agreement, and it heavily influences their critique of liberalism, which is thought to be on the wrong side of this modern turn, and to an extent irredeemably contaminated by it.

This history is false or over-simplified, in my view. It misconstrues much of what is written before the alleged modern turn in the medieval period, and is needlessly suspicious and selective when attending to liberal thinkers from the seventeenth century to the present day. I've already suggested that a liberal thinker such as Acton has been misinterpreted. Locke forms another important example. The foundation of liberal government is not, for Locke, a contract, as is almost universally asserted in theological treatments of the subject. Society is a contract (and here his main target is a patriarchal, royalist and absolutist conception of political power), but *government* is a trust, held between the people and those who are entrusted with power – the trustees, we might say, who at a fundamental theological level are equal with the people, because they are created equal in the sight of God.[11] This means that the relationship between government and people is not a manipulative one, where two self-interested parties seek to get something from each other at minimum expense to themselves. It is a trusting relationship based on a sense of our createdness.

In *The Politics of Human Frailty* I attempt to introduce some nuance and complexity to the story of what happens after 'the modern turn', showing that even in an avowedly non-religious thinker such as John Rawls there are elements that the Christian can own and celebrate – for instance, his emphasis on the importance of reciprocity, the withholding of coercive power and the difficulty of making moral judgements given the complexity of the shared human condition. In my future work I hope to turn my attention more to the medieval period, to suggest that many of the elements of contemporary political liberalism – such as a conception of the individual, the role of law, and the importance of decentralising power in a constitutional framework – have an honourable theological pedigree going back to the twelfth century at least.

SHORTT: I hope readers will find it helpful to compare your views with those of John Milbank and the O'Donovans, and then make up their own minds. You've just spoken of future work, but you've recently published another book, *The Realist Hope*.[12] It sounds like a very different sort of project – would that be right?

INSOLE: Yes and no. The main thrust of *The Realist Hope* is that anti-realism – the view that truth is exhausted by a community's beliefs about truth – tends towards absolutism and hubris. I argue that only a conception of truth as non-relative, non-constructed and accessible can guarantee the very humility, sense of fallibility and sensitivity to difference that the anti-realist rightly values. I think that there's a suggestive if non-rigorous relationship between liberalism and realism, and between anti-realism and communitarianism, and I indicate as much in the book. Both liberalism and realism have, it seems to me, a humility before truth, and a sense that a whole community or discourse could be wrong about something in such a way that protects and values the individual (as a citizen or truth-seeker). Similarly, anti-realism and communitarianism can tend to insist that there is no conceptual space for doubting the beliefs of a discourse or a community; in other words, they are too keen to celebrate the ability of communities, over individuals, to define what truth is. On both approaches, dissent from the 'ideal community' is made almost impossible. But as I say, the connection between the two is suggestive, and would not necessarily hold in every case. The nature of the link between realism and liberalism is something that I would like to explore more in the future.

SHORTT: This would suggest that you do not think of yourself as having turned away from analytic approaches to philosophy, even if you are now exploring issues in the history of ideas and political theology.

INSOLE: That's right. The interest in the history of ideas is motivated ultimately by the question of what certain religious and political ideas mean, and what sort of justification is available for them. Analytical clarity and rigour are vital parts of this exploration, but only a part. When thinking about the relationship between salvation, religion and politics, clear rigorous thinking is not possible without attending to the history of a debate going back at least as far as St Augustine. This is still, in my view, 'philosophy of religion', in that it is the exploration of the meaning, justification and ethical implications of religious beliefs, whilst understanding 'religion' in a really full-blooded sense, as being more than an abstracted philosophical theism – although I'm clear that this, too, can be a legitimate and faithful expression of Christianity. To approach such issues effectively one needs an equal respect and dedication to analytic philosophy, systematic theology and history.

An example of the importance of history would be the narrative told by the Radical Orthodoxy movement, whereby fourteenth-century nominalists such as William of Ockham are found guilty of evacuating the universe of divine order and so paving the way for it to be replaced with a nihilistic relativism, whereby the only reality is the will of the individual. Although Ockham is not named, it is this narrative that John Milbank has in mind, in this book, when he comments on the pernicious effects of the 'voluntarism of late scholasticism'.[13] We are told that this voluntarism involves a vision of the 'absolutely autonomous free individual as the ultimate norm' who imposes 'arbitrary formal rules' requiring 'unbounded power'.[14] This is a grave accusation, especially as medieval voluntarism is even blamed for the 'subtle growth of a totalitarian politics' (of which political liberalism is judged to be a variety).

This 'waning of the Middle Ages' story originates from a mid-twentieth-century French school of history, represented by Michel Villey and George de Lagarde. Its reading of history was taken up by the Chicago political philosopher Leo Strauss, and subsequently became widely influential amongst English-speaking theologians – an influence that remains undimmed to this day. As far as I know the Radical Orthodoxy movement has not yet seriously engaged with the fact that, for decades, this historical narrative has been heavily and persuasively rebutted by *historians* such as Quentin Skinner, Brian Tierney, Richard Tuck, Jeremy Waldron, A. S. McGrade and Annabel Brett. It has, in my view, been persuasively demonstrated that there are so-called 'voluntaristic' and 'non-voluntaristic' elements complexly intermingled before and after the late Middle Ages, and even in a thinker such as Ockham.

The actual history of ideas – rather than a theological story told to support a wider contemporary agenda – is so nuanced and complex that I'm not sure that it is even possible to sustain the more modest claim articulated by Simon Oliver that Radical Orthodoxy tries to 'identify moments when broad, long-lasting and complex trends reach some kind of clear articulation',[15] rather than 'singular moments when the rot sets in'. When I say that 'I'm not sure', I really mean that: it may be that such broad sweeping claims can be made in a qualified way, but Radical Orthodoxy would need to engage *much* more with historians ('secular' scholarship if you like) in order to make the case. I am heartened by John Milbank's comment that the Radical Orthodoxy movement might need to be more hesitant in some ways. This story about the demise of the Middle Ages – central to the Radical Orthodoxy project – might be one of the places where some hesitation and qualification would be a good idea.

SHORTT: But isn't it right that theologians and Christian thinkers should have a distinctive and confident voice, even when working in the academy? Certainly many of the contributors to this book have introduced a renewed vitality in the discipline by being willing to profess a robust Christian stance.

INSOLE: Of course, and I should say that the contribution of Radical Orthodoxy has been extraordinary, and in lots of ways quite wonderful, in terms of enlivening debates in the theological academy on a whole range of issues from medieval theology, to aesthetics, literature and politics. Nonetheless, sometimes I worry that a tendency to laud ambitious, unapologetic theological approaches can lead to inattentive scholarship – strong on flair, style and commitment, but lacking both philosophical and historical rigour – which ultimately will do the theological academy and the Church no favours at all. What one learns from the way in which philosophy of religion has become respectable in the last twenty years or so, is that respect is earned by Christian philosophers who do philosophy as well as, or better than, non-Christians. Similarly, if Christian theologians are to command respect among political philosophers and intellectual historians, they have to earn it by doing these subjects at an appropriate level of competence, courtesy and integrity, not simply making pronouncements to the 'secular' academy. That would be my vision of where the torch, as you say, should be carried.

4
Sarah Coakley

Fresh Paths in Systematic Theology

SHORTT: Claims about a recovery of nerve among Christian thinkers seem especially interesting in your case: Anglicans have traditionally shied away from elaborating a comprehensive theological vision at any length, but you're currently at work on a four-volume systematic theology.[1] You initially did research on Ernst Troeltsch (1865–1923), the German liberal Protestant, but your more recent sources of inspiration extend from the Church Fathers to contemporary gender theory. Could you sketch the main phases of your development?

COAKLEY: My theological formation was rather idiosyncratic. I do remember that when I was quite young, even as young as twelve, I think, I decided I wanted to be a theologian. Of course this was an immature fantasy at the time. But it caused me to start rummaging through my parents' house looking for books about theology, of which there were only very few in a home that was otherwise full of books. Perhaps that was what made the subject enticing. Looking back, the two early strands of theological influence that were already significant in my adolescence were what you might call the 'mystical' and the 'critical/rational'. On the one hand, the first alluring theologians I read were modern spiritual directors or 'mystical theologians' such as Evelyn Underhill (she was the very first theologian I encountered, because her work happened to be in the house). Her letters absolutely fascinated me – although I also found their upper-middle-class fussiness and self-absorption quite abhorrent in some ways. And then in the same category there was Simone Weil – especially her essay on 'attention', which somehow attracted me enormously when I was immersed in the early stages of Latin and Greek at school. Reading her argument about how the slog of paying attention in undertaking a

Latin prose composition could ultimately lead to the fullest attention
possible that you might give to someone at the moment of death had
a profound impact on me, even then.

On the other hand, the other influence which came to bear at this
early adolescent stage was the great *bête noire* of 1963, Bishop John
Robinson and his *Honest to God.* The furore over the book was
especially interesting to people in south London, where I was brought
up, because he was our own bishop, and his daughters happened to be
at school with me; I suppose that was why the book found its way into
our house. And I found Robinson's fearless engagement with
historical–critical materials, and his attraction towards Tillich and
Bonhoeffer and existentialist philosophy, enormously intriguing and
exciting as well. Among other things *Honest to God* seemed a good,
rational antidote to the more irritating aspects of the Anglo-
Catholicism in which I was brought up – the tendency to invoke
'mystery' when you couldn't be bothered to think any further.

I was still trying to negotiate these two strands – a kind of
Platonistic Anglo-Catholicism, and so-called South Bank religion –
when I was at Cambridge as an undergraduate in the early 1970s and
taught by John Robinson himself (by then Dean of Trinity). What was
so releasing about being his pupil – and in general he wasn't popular
or admired in Cambridge at all – was his willingness, in effect, to let
his students teach themselves, and to explicate, if they wished, a
fearlessly radical approach. At the same time (with Don Cupitt) I
began to read some analytic philosophy of religion, and for similar
reasons was immediately attracted by its ferocious clarity, its willingness to face hard philosophical questions, which might or might not
cause the tradition to remain unchanged. Here I felt very different
from fellow students at Cambridge like Rowan Williams and David
Ford (Rowan was two years ahead of me, David one), who seemed to
live much more easily within a realm of piety, and were also very
drawn to the 'narrative theology' of the emerging Yale School (subsequently baptised 'post-liberal'), which linked happily with Barthian
authority. I myself was too busy, then, rationally critiquing the
tradition to be able to step happily inside the magic circle of Barth's
world. My appreciation of Barth has really only come about in very
recent years.

SHORTT: It's perhaps worth noting how people often think that other
points of view are stronger or more regnant than their own. The kind
of liberalism that you describe at Cambridge sounds like the
orthodoxy of the period. I know from conversations with people

like Rowan Williams that orthodoxy in the usual sense seemed subversive at the time.

COAKLEY: You're quite right; but then for me the Cambridge Divinity School wasn't nearly liberal (or, rather, critical) enough. To be sure, it wasn't marked by a strong commitment to dogmatic authoritarianism; but for me it was itself too smug about the possibility of keeping even the form of 'liberal' Christianity that it propounded safely on the rails. My frustration with it, therefore, was precisely the opposite of Rowan Williams' at that time.

I think that's really why I came to a great fascination, at the end of my undergraduate days, with Troeltsch. This was because he, in a very compelling way, was facing already at the end of the nineteenth century the critical questions that you might say Anglican liberalism finally got around to in earnest in the 1970s. You might even see *The Myth of God Incarnate* (1977) as a kind of 'Troeltsch *redivivus*' event. I admired Troeltsch because he brought together the two strands I've just described: a great fascination with 'mysticism' (he knew William James, he was profoundly influenced by Baron von Hügel – they were great friends – and he was drawn towards what he called the 'mystic type' within Christianity); but also a fearless liberal critique of forms of German Lutheran orthodoxy, which he felt just couldn't measure up to the challenges of the contemporary world. And so I found in Troeltsch a kind of conversation partner who, I sensed, would put to the test my unresolved question about whether these two components of tradition could coalesce in some way, especially when applied to the critical question of the status and place of Christ.

SHORTT: What was the answer?

COAKLEY: The answer was that nothing much *was* left, and so this for me was an important cathartic undertaking. I wanted to analyse what factors led him to the kind of reductive liberalism that he ended with. I did this in my first book.[2] For cumulative reasons he felt unable to assert, for instance, the full divinity of Christ. It was a very useful exercise for me to parse out exactly what those reasons were, and how many of them still seemed convincing. Some did, but some, frankly, didn't. The latter were tied to neo-Hegelian metaphysical assumptions that now appeared question-begging or outdated.

But there was another strand of Troeltsch's argument which I then tried to rescue creatively. For the Troeltsch who wrote *The Social Teaching of the Christian Churches* saw that doctrine is always profoundly entangled with social and cultural forms, with particular social and political locations. And therefore it's no good talking about

Christology in general; always you have to ask where, exactly, this Christological enterprise is being undertaken. How is it informed by, or entangled with, the political location, the cultural formations, or the psychological commitments of those who express it? It need not be done in a reductive manner; in fact, it can greatly enrich the Christological task to ask these questions. This way we can see how variously 'Christ' language is used in the tradition, and how many different elements of spiritual life it brings together.

And in this side of Troeltsch I saw a possibility for a rescue and a new way out of the kind of Christological dilemma that he himself had enunciated. Troeltsch never satisfactorily brought together the 'historical Jesus' and what he called 'Christ mysticism'. The latter is a rich but elusive theme in his thought, interestingly related to his *Social Teaching* material; but it's the former that he allows to pin him into the corner, as far as de-absoluting 'Christ' is concerned. He therefore falsely puts himself into the same empiricist bind that so frustrated me in my Cambridge biblical teachers (though they were less honest in their conclusions): one couldn't flat-footedly move from historical investigation to Christological affirmation. I began to glimpse that our approach to 'Christ' really can't be restricted by this sort of historical positivism: it must be that 'Christ' is available in other ways. But what could those other ways be, without succumbing to special pleading or self-affirming fantasy? There's just a hint of this dilemma at the end of my Troeltsch book, since – as I came to the end of my thesis – I myself had reached a new crisis, existentially and spiritually, about where to go with the two strands I've described. In fact, it was at this time that I had started on an adventure in prayer that was turning me inside out and upside down.

SHORTT: **So spirituality came to inform your theology to a far greater extent. How did this process unfold?**

COAKLEY: I don't want to speak of this at length, but I shall have to say a bit in order to explain how my whole understanding of 'systematics' has subsequently developed, an understanding that is founded on the practice of prayer, especially the prayer of silence. To begin with, this undertaking was very frightening for me: it was an embracing of a practice which is by no means (as anyone who does this will know) a soft option. However, it was also uniquely alluring and magnetizing, as if all the fragmented pieces of my life were being lined up and drawn inexorably in one direction. Not only is one subject to bombardments from one's own 'unconscious' in such prayer, but there also comes a profound acknowledgement of the incapacity of the self to speak about God any longer as part of the furniture of the universe. But let me get back to my immediate Christological point here, which is identified in your question. It was a very dark and difficult passage for me to get Christology back into the picture by this apparently indirect route. What I discovered as a result of time on my knees was that my earlier dismantling of doctrines such as the incarnation and Trinity was itself being challenged and recast.

This provides one of the central themes for my entire project as a systematic theologian. It is important, first, to underscore that I am not here appealing to 'experience' in a naively empiricist way, as if some particular 'experience' could offset deficiencies in what is otherwise provided by Scripture or tradition or 'reason'. Rather, the regular undertaking of an intentional form of what I term 'dispossession' underwrites and progressively transforms all that one goes on receiving from those other sources: it sets them in a progressively new light. The practice of silence is, as I've said, a very disconcerting one, for what has to be abandoned here first, and never without difficulty, is any sense of mastery. (I shall hope to explain later how such a loss of mastery is not inimical to feminist empowerment, but – paradoxically – is its very condition.) In a Christian context you then get linked back into that element in Christianity that Paul coins in Romans 8, when he speaks about prayer that is 'with sighs too deep for words', and in which you don't even know rightly what to ask for. You are being led by the Spirit beyond conventional modes of rationality.

I had therefore to rediscover a vibrant and distinct sense of the Spirit, starting on my knees, before I could return to those lost strands of Christology and Trinity that I seemed to have utterly dismantled in my Troeltschian 'liberal' quest. First, one has to go through this passage of handing over the reins of control to the Spirit; only then does one begin to see that the theologian who tries to speak of God – stammeringly – is always already engaged in a divine process that is going on all the time.

SHORTT: To know Christ is to know his benefits?

COAKLEY: Not quite. That's too quick. It took me a while to make the link to 'Christ'. Rather, the intuition was that there's always a conversation going on, if you want to put it this way, between what has traditionally been called the 'Father' (the ultimate source in God), and what in Christianity is called the 'Spirit'; and that the process of prayer is, strictly speaking, not done by us but by God. We allow ourselves to become a little bit more conscious of this process, frightening as it is, if we just give attention to it in a regular and disciplined way. I became much clearer first about the Spirit than I did about 'Christ'. But of course I think the answer to this conundrum is implicitly already given in Romans 8:14ff., in which Paul describes how what we do when we pray in this way is to be drawn into the orbit of 'the glorious liberty of the children of God'. In other words the pray-er, in fact, is the 'Christ' figure in this model. The one praying is the one who is being drawn into the life of 'Christ'; he or she is standing alongside Jesus in the cry to the 'Father' that is enunciated in the garden, or on the cross, and doing so every time one steps into that posture of surrender to the source of all being.

So although this seemed like a very roundabout route, you could say that I had to 'reinvent' the Trinity, through my own wayward wanderings, before I could come back to doctrinal questions with a completely new perspective. When I did come back I realised that the questions I'd been asking about 'Christ' had been far too narrowly conceived; I had come back to classic Christology and trinitarianism through the back door, so to speak. In so doing I had realised how these two doctrines stand and fall together.

SHORTT: And you were in your late twenties and thirties at this stage, I think?

COAKLEY: Yes, I was. I was appointed to a lectureship at Lancaster in 1976 (when I was still rather young – twenty-four), and the process I've been describing occurred between that year, when I first started to pray silently, and the late eighties. Among other things it led me back to the patristic authors now with a completely new set of questions. I had assumed, in modernistic mode, that my theology wouldn't have a great deal to do with the Fathers. The lectures I'd been to on the Fathers as an undergraduate I'd found, I'm afraid, fairly deadly – intellectually quite intriguing, but seemingly not representing any live, contemporary options. Now I started reading the Fathers for my own spiritual nourishment, not initially to teach them, but coming at them through what they wrote *de oratione* ('on prayer') rather than first through their more directly doctrinal teaching.

SHORTT: This, presumably, was a revelation, given the atomistic way in which the Fathers have often been taught – a style reflected in many of the textbooks themselves.

COAKLEY: I think so. Students still tend to read only Origen's *De principiis* to see what he had to say about the Trinity, but they tend not to read his *De oratione*, or indeed his commentaries, to see how all that relates to life and prayer. But actually it's much more significant and interesting to come in from the side of spiritual practice. So I found myself at this stage re-foraging in the patristic and medieval resources with these particular sets of interests in mind, and then beginning to incorporate such inputs into my teaching. Finally I was also forced to rethink the classic textbook accounts of the development of the doctrine of the Trinity in the light of this re-reading.

SHORTT: How would you respond to the charge that this approach to systematic theology through the lens of prayer is tainted by subjectivism?

COAKLEY: I would respond rather sharply. Let me make three immediate points in riposte. First, as I've already stressed, this approach does not involve a naive appeal to 'subjective experience' as if that were somehow distinct from the exercise of biblical exegesis or of reasoned theological exposition. Rather, the practice of prayer provides the context in which silence *expands* the potential to respond to the realm of Word and reason. Second, as I hope to explain shortly, this leads to a vision of systematics in which the task of 'justification' of truth claims is actively embraced rather than avoided – albeit in a way that takes on the complication of states in which the mind is 'darkened' first in order to relate to God more intimately and accurately. Third, the kind of feminist epistemology I propose here involves – as I'll show – a much wider range of evidences than is normally employed by systematicians; and I would claim that that contributes to an expanded 'objectivity' rather than to an intensified 'subjectivity'.

SHORTT: Was your particular brand of feminism forged at this same time, then?

COAKLEY: Yes. I'd always believed, from my childhood almost, in a sort of egalitarian feminism; I'd taken for granted the sorts of thing that John Stuart Mill believed in: that women are mentally equal if they're given the right opportunities in education. I hadn't confronted until this time, I think, the peculiar nexus of problems that the Christian tradition throws up to us about the relationship between different dimensions of *eros* – that is, what the connection is between sexual desire and desire for God.

And you might not think that that's immediately anything to do with 'feminism'; especially since – as you may have noticed – I am not the sort of Christian feminist who sees it as her chief goal to obliterate all 'Father' language from the tradition. I want to do some excavating beneath the obvious problem of 'naming', lest mere repression of certain forms of language simply drives the problem deeper. If you begin to read the early Fathers on prayer (Origen, again, or Tertullian) and look at their problematic discussions of how sexual desire for the 'other', usually a woman, to them seemingly impedes the quest for God, you'll see this deep vein of difficulty that runs through the entire Christian tradition and with which we are still struggling: witness the current debates in the Churches about celibacy, homosexuality and feminism. All the conflicted theological questions of the late twentieth and twenty-first centuries require, as I see it, a re-examination of this nexus of difficulty about *eros*; and if you spend any time praying, especially in silence, it is impossible to avoid this nexus because the unconscious – including, of course, powerful sexual material – just floods into the prayer arena very fast and cannot be pushed away. And if you then begin to read the great spiritual authors of the Christian tradition reflecting on this theme, you will see how it is again a result of a mingling of two crucial influences: one comes out of the biblical material on sexuality, and is mediated into the life of prayer, as the early rabbis reflect on the spiritual meaning of the Song of Songs; and the other strand comes out of Plato, and particularly out of the analysis of the nature of 'desire' in the *Symposium* (intriguingly enunciated there by a woman – Diotima – to Socrates). And these two strands meet right at the time when traditions of 'mystical theology' come to be forged, and the early Christian commentaries on the Song of Songs start to be written – in the third and fourth centuries. We cannot of course merely return to that period without critique, including robust feminist critique; but at the same time I believe there is much neglected 'erotic' wisdom there which our post-Freudian culture has simply overlooked.

SHORTT: There's plenty more to say, but I think we've got a distinct outline of your thinking. Could you now explain how the various elements fit into your systematics project?

COAKLEY: The first volume, to which we've already referred, is on the Trinity: God encountered in prayer and found to be ineluctably triune. The second volume is on the first half of the anthropology. It's on what you might call the 'positive' side of the anthropology, that is, on what the human is created ultimately to enjoy – humanity en route to the enjoyment of God, or the beatific vision, or the 'contemplative life'. And so at the same time it covers religious epistemology – how we come to know God, and whether we can 'justify' this 'knowledge'. It's here that I take on certain aspects of current analytic philosophy of religion, though not without significant feminist critique; and here too – you might think oddly – that I look at the subject of race, for I see racism as fundamentally an epistemic problem, especially for white people – a blockage in the very capacity to see. The third volume is on the 'negative' side of the anthropology and on its resolution: 'sin' and 'atonement', in classical terms. It's here that I plan to look at how institutions of hospital and prison are engaged at the state level in these processes. I examine problems of punishment and healing in the public domain. And the fourth volume will come to Christology. You notice that Christology has always been for me the most mysterious aspect of theology, not – as many people presume – the easiest point to get at, but rather the heart of the mystery of how humanity and divinity intersect. And this last volume I plan to write from the perspective of eucharistic theology, coming at my Christology through ritual 'performance'.

What I've been doing is starting to write bits of all of these volumes, and although the first volume is effectively finished now, I expect it will take quite a long time for them all to be brought out – at least ten years, I imagine, for all four, if not more. And if people wonder how the various traditional loci of systematic theology (that is, categories such as creation, atonement, ecclesiology, Christology, sacraments, eschatology, etc.) are all going to be brought into these four volumes, the answer is that I have a rather different way of approaching this from plodding through the subjects one by one, in traditional mode. Instead I'm superimposing various classical loci on one another in these four basic moves, and indeed also introducing new themes, as we've noted, such as desire, gender, race and class. I'm not doing this to be politically correct, but because I believe that our generation has rightly seen that we cannot express theological truth without taking account of these factors. To ignore them is a form of wilful blindness.

SHORTT: **So methodologically your accent is on being strongly interdisciplinary, but without reductiveness.**

COAKLEY: That's the aspiration. It's not that theology can be *reduced*, or turned into, one or more other disciplines, but rather that theology must, to be fruitful, endlessly renegotiate its porous boundaries with philosophy, sociology, anthropology, ritual theory, musicology, art history, gender theory, and so on, whilst carefully maintaining its distinctive voice in speaking of *God*. Secondly, therefore, I call my method '*théologie totale*' (with playful allusion to the French Annales school's *l'histoire totale*), because it attempts to provide an excavation of theology as it is expressed and lived at every level. 'Theology', it follows, is not just 'high' academic discourse in constant interaction with philosophy (vital as that is), but is also 'lived' at prayer, in wor-

ship, in pastoral ministry, in the politics of the state, in science and
technology, in art and poetry, music and film – 'high' and 'low' – and
in the bodily negotiations of everyday life. 'Systematic' theology, to be
truly 'systematic', then, must reflect this 'total' perspective, and gather
up previously neglected fragments; it must work not just through
biblical and doctrinal and philosophical exposition, but through
studies based on field work of how that 'doctrine' is purveyed locally
and politically, through an acute account of the *sui generis* bodily
workings of ritual and sacrament, and through an analysis of how the
arts throw what Lacan would call an extra 'semiotic' light on doctrinal
expression. And thirdly, then, *théologie totale* cannot avoid telling us
how intellect, 'affect' and body are conjoined, and how the fundamental apparatus of human desire is formed, disformed, and transformed
in relationship to God and others.

SHORTT: Let's deal at this point with why the very practice of
'systematics' is so contentious today. As well as the traditional
Anglican coyness about the subject, I think one could cite at least
three grounds for suspicion of your enterprise from a postmodern
standpoint. Firstly, the sense that systematics is necessarily
ontotheological, to use Heidegger's term – that it's sewing God up,
and neglecting the corrective supplied by apophatic theology. Then
there are the critics who look at 'power/knowledge', in Foucault's language, and argue that systematic theology must by definition be
'hegemonic' because it's again attempting to give a comprehensive
account of God and humanity, and so wield specious human
authority. Thirdly, one could cite the assault from Continental –
post-Lacanian – feminist theory. This would allege that systematic
theology in the Christian tradition has always been 'phallocentric': it
has tended to order theology in a linear way that represses the
distinctively 'feminine' contribution.

COAKLEY: Well, recovering from all these major blows when there
isn't even a very strong tradition of systematic theology within
Anglicanism to start with is hard, to say the least. But many people are
trying to get over the objections for a very good reason, I think: that
at its best systematic theology is an attempt to enunciate a coherent
vision, where the pieces all fit together. And if ever we needed people
enunciating coherent visions of Christianity, we need them today.
Moreover, the three objections to systematics you've just outlined can
be overcome, as long as the right safeguards are in place – as long as
systematics is undergirded by the disciplined 'practice' of non-
mastery, such that theology itself is always *in via*, always undergoing

its own apophatic displacement. So it's not for nothing that Anglican theologians worldwide are suddenly seeing that this is a moment of opportunity for the right kind of systematic thinking to occur, and any number of us are starting to engage in the undertaking.

SHORTT: The list of recent or contemporary systematicians is remarkable: Colin Gunton, on the Reformed side, completed a curtain-raiser on a proposed multi-volume project before his death in 2003; then in the States there's Robert Jenson, a leading Lutheran thinker, and Episcopalians such as Kathryn Tanner and Miroslav Volf.[3]

COAKLEY: Yes: they are all important contributors. And then among other Anglican writers, John Milbank has described his book *Being Reconciled* as the beginning of a systematic theology, and Rowan Williams is working on a book on the Trinity which – whether he'll call it part of a systematics – I think will be seen as that; and, interestingly, Mark MacIntosh is gathering together a group of us across worldwide Anglicanism who are going to produce a volume of Anglican systematics as a joint endeavour. So systematics is now a marked new feature of contemporary Anglican theology.

SHORTT: You've just instanced feminism as a challenge to systematic theology. The subject is of course pursued in depth by Tina Beattie in chapter 11, but it's evidently central to your thinking as well. Could you comment a bit more about this, and develop what you've already said about desire?

COAKLEY: The two certainly go together in my view. Many people, including most of the theologians we've mentioned so far, have very little time for feminist theology, and don't think of gender as being a significant category in their systematic endeavours. I wish to distinguish what I'm doing from two other dominant forms of gender theory that remain in problematic relationship in secular American and European thought. On the one hand, one can talk about American pragmatist gender theoreticians such as Judith Butler, who aim to take us beyond the accepted binary of 'masculinity' and 'femininity', and the stereotypes that are normative in 'heterosexist' culture.[4] Judith Butler sets before us a possibility of destabilising repressive binaries through acts of 'performative' dissent – by 'queer protest', as it were; and that kind of approach to gender is very vibrant at the moment. But it has very little time for the kind of transformations that arise out of patient practices of vulnerability before God. It tends to take such practices as merely re-enshrining forms of subjugation.

On the other hand we have an extremely interesting and fruitful debate that is associated with the French feminists Luce Irigaray, Hélène Cixous and Julia Kristeva (all very different figures, actually, but they tend to get lumped together in the American discussion), who, far from wishing to overcome the gender binary *tout court*, are fascinated by a slightly different, psychoanalytic binary in their post-Lacanian discussion between 'phallocentric' thought (associated with the Lacanian category of the male 'symbolic', and order and language), and 'semiotic' material (associated with 'femininity' and the maternal). For Irigaray, for example, this binary is so basic that the only way for women to go forward is to re-create a new image of the divine on the 'feminine' side of the disjunct, which will simply leave behind what are seen as the dominating phallocentric categories of standard Christian tradition.[5]

SHORTT: Could you call that a post-feminist approach in shorthand?

COAKLEY: It depends on how you're defining 'feminism' to start with, and unfortunately many people still think 'feminism' is to be associated with a particular kind of victimology and/or an aggressive, even essentialist, rejection of all male forms of association. But the trouble is, depending on what your definition of feminism is to start with, you may or may not want to say that we're now post-feminist. Personally I think it's dangerous to give up the term 'feminism' too quickly, when many people still haven't even woken up to the basic questions.

So I do acknowledge the continuing importance of the original feminist impetus to transform Christian tradition out of its distorted, 'patriarchal' manifestations. I also feel a certain attraction to both the wings of gender theory that I've mentioned above. The French feminist form is especially insightful about the unconscious forces we negotiate in the area of gender, and the Butlerian approach draws attention to the capacity of gender to be changed by 'performative' action. But I find neither of these two approaches completely adequate in confronting what we learn about gender in the light of the divine: there is a spiritual transformation that has to occur for both men and women in the light of a re-examination of the nature of desire (both divine and human) within Christianity. That is the central problem.

SHORTT: Because desire, for you, is an even more fundamental category than gender. What does this mean?

COAKLEY: It means that I see 'desire' as the category that fundamentally explains our connection with the divine. I see God as a desiring God who implants in our created nature a sexual desire that is the clue knit into our nature to remind us of our deep dependence on God. In contrast I see 'gender' as a relatively malleable and fluid categorisation, which in those deeply committed to prayer is found, strangely, always to be being renegotiated. So if you look at some of the great mystical theologians of the tradition, such as Gregory of Nyssa, you'll see that he rightly perceives that it's the relatively immature Christian who is most concerned to keep a clear boundary between 'masculinity' and 'femininity'. As Christians advance in maturity they will realise that these clear boundaries, which were consoling to begin with, are start-ing to disappear under their feet.[6] That's not to say that the play of 'otherness' has gone; the erotic call of the desired to the one who desires continues; but the negotiation continues as the pray-er – the believer – continues to puzzle about the relationship between the humanly desirable one (of whatever sex and orientation) and the ultimate, *divinely* desirable One.

So 'gender' is always in renegotiation, in my view, and it's desire – but not, note, in the Freudian sense – that fuels the whole engage-ment. In the light of this, I further want to suggest that a distinctively theological view of gender should not merely borrow from secular gender theory and then use that theory to beat the tradition. Rather, we should examine the deep heart of the central doctrines of Christianity – incarnation and Trinity – and see what they tell us about desire and gender.

The argument about incarnation and gender has only recently started to dawn on me as a result of my priestly ordination in 2001. But one of the most fascinating things about being in some sense *in persona Christi* at the altar is that one finds oneself at some points in the service (especially when celebrating in the east-facing tradition, which I'm required to do in my parish in Littlemore, Oxford, because the altar cannot be moved) kneeling on behalf of the laity – and thus *qua* 'feminine' in the terms of the traditional nuptial heart of the eucharist (see Ephesians 5:21ff.) – and so representing the Church. But then when one turns to bless or to absolve or to offer the elements to the people, one's crossing the liminal boundary to the divine side of things: now one is standing in the realm of Christ as the divine lover, *qua* 'masculine'. One is symbolically moving from one theologi-cal gender pole to another, and so implicitly 'destabilising' these poles at the same time.

SHORTT: **Are you also saying that there's something about crossing this threshold liturgically which makes the priestly aura an erotic one?**

COAKLEY: Yes. Or perhaps we should call it 'proto-erotic', as it comes from God. What I think it shows us is that the tradition in the Church of the eucharistic act as itself 'nuptial', indeed the tradition in the Church that represents the whole Christian life as that of coming to be the lover of Christ – all this points to the deep heart of incarnational doctrine. It tells us about how gender both has to be played with and, at the same time, renegotiated in the light of the erotic embrace of Christ. It puts gender under the judgement, if you like, of Christic transformation. In other words, I think there's something about the hypostatic union which is itself a transgression of the view that so-called masculinity can be safely tidied up into the divine arena; the incarnation itself questions the stereotypical view of the gender binary.

SHORTT: Is this liturgical insight particularly suggestive for a woman? I'm just wondering what a male priest would make of it.

COAKLEY: So far, in trying out this argument, I've been told by many heterosexual male priests that they have no idea what I'm talking about. But I've also been told by virtually every gay priest that I've talked to that they know exactly what I'm talking about. It would seem that the very idea of gender 'fluidity' causes some straight men a good deal of anxiety – no surprises here.

SHORTT: Elizabeth Stuart, in her book on queer theology,[7] argues that a fair amount of Christian doctrine is queer, in her terms.

COAKLEY: Yes, you could put it that way. And there are some parallels here, which I've already spoken about, with Judith Butler's work. But what I'm saying is vitally different from Butler in the sense that one isn't performing this liturgical act as a 'queer protest' to sanction various forms of previously unacceptable pleasure. Rather, what's happening here is a transformation of the self within the realm of *God's* desire. So this is the basic idea: that in co-operating with the fundamental logic of God's desire, one is following Christ, as it were, into this stepping backwards and forwards across the bride/bridegroom duality.

SHORTT: Where does the layperson fit in?

COAKLEY: The layperson is vital here precisely because this view of what's going on in the eucharist (which is much more clearly evidenced in late medieval theology than in the theology of Trent, let alone in contemporary Roman Catholic theology of the eucharist) has the priest as much as a 'layperson' in this role as a Christic person. The current state of affairs in Roman Catholicism (and indeed also in Protestantism) is that the priest now becomes fixed, west-facing, behind the altar, with the danger that the priest will be seen as somehow 'play-acting' Christ, instead of stepping into the orbit of Christ whilst also kneeling before Christ as representative of the (Marian/'feminine') laity. Does that make sense?

SHORTT: I think so; but I'm just thinking about the layperson who doesn't shift back and forth between one way of facing and the other.

COAKLEY: What I'm saying is that the layperson is being brought into that orbit precisely through the priest's shifting. The priest acts *in persona Ecclesiae* in acting also *in persona Christi*. And I think that the current form of eucharistic theology which has the priest representing Jesus behind the altar, and the people in front of the altar, and doesn't adjust that symbolic and liturgical placing, is in much greater danger of reinstantiating a sense of passive subordination amongst the laity, and amongst women, than this labile, fluid perception of what is happening in the eucharistic act.

SHORTT: The idea of sacramental activity as a reworking of desire would naturally form a stiff challenge to the large numbers of people who find services, or their memories of them, unexciting at best.

COAKLEY: I'm not going to say what or whom I would blame for that! It could also be that the eucharist, as a special and intense form of prayer, cannot be fully enlivened for us unless we are also leading individually a life of disciplined and regular prayer. Without such prayer one is unlikely to respond to the idea that Christian life is not a suppression of desire, but a reformulation – and even intensification – of it. That's a message that needs to be reheard. It's a hard path, but ultimately it's also the most delightful one that you could imagine.

SHORTT: You've spoken about gender theory in relation to Christology. Let's turn to the Trinity.

COAKLEY: I talked earlier about what I called the 'Romans 8' approach to prayer in the first volume of my systematics, namely participating in the life of the Trinity through the practices of prayer as a way of not only reinvigorating your sense of the doctrine in general, but also changing your notions about gender in the light of the doctrine. This is a correlative approach to the one I've just enunciated in terms of sacraments and Christology, but with a different nuance. In the prayer in which one surrenders control to the Spirit, there is, I think, a kind of giving up of all 'certainties', including the certainty of a clear gender binary. That's part of the 'apophatic' displacement of being willing to give oneself into the conversation between Source and Spirit. You might say that the irreducible threeness of the Trinity is crucial here: the Spirit cracks open our hearts to the breaking of the 'certainty' of the gender binary, and brings us into the orbit of the Father/Son relation; but the Spirit is also that which conjoins, and yet keeps distinct, the love between 'Father' and 'Son' *within* the Trinity. It breaks open the love between 'two' so that even mutual narcissism is displaced; divine love, as Richard of St Victor argued, must always be love between (at least) three.

In the first volume of my systematics, utilising the tools of *théologie totale* as outlined above, I not only explore these intrinsic gender evocations in the doctrine of the Trinity, but I approach classic texts on the doctrine to show that patristic authors themselves tend to relate the Trinity (perfect-relations-in-God) to discussions of 're-lationship' at other levels, including gender, sexual relations, celibacy and prayer. When you read these authors in this way, it causes you to see much greater commonalities in them than you might expect. So my approach has tied in with other recent work on Augustine and the Cappadocians which is questioning the supposed disjunction between them – a thesis that can be traced back to a late nineteenth-century textbook tradition.

SHORTT: **Augustine as a monist and the Cappadocians as tritheists?**

COAKLEY: Exactly. Such oversimplifications collapse; and although I didn't know, when I set out on rethinking the Trinity through this lens of prayer and sexuality, that it would contribute to the current rethinking of these two traditions, as a matter of fact it has done so. So a great part of my undertaking as a systematician, in each volume, is to take really crucial, but often neglected, material from the patris-tic or medieval or Reformation or Counter-Reformation traditions, and re-read it with new questions that come out of my interest in the renegotiations of gender. And this *isn't* a distortion of what is in the text, but rather a recovery of nexuses of association that have always been there, but have been curiously ignored or sidelined in modern readings.

SHORTT: **Having done this preliminary work with texts, you will go on in each of your volumes to examine a concrete setting in which the doctrine can be seen in operation. People might find this idea sur-prising at first sight; but you maintain that it is possible to do field work among contemporary Christians in a way that illuminates how they are implicitly responding to a doctrinal heritage, and maybe showing things about it which you couldn't tell simply from doing textual work. Can you give an example?**

COAKLEY: For the first volume, I did fieldwork in Lancaster during the early 1990s, looking at how Anglican Charismatics were working out, in the process of 'renewal', a new understanding of the doctrine of the

Spirit which ultimately was pushing them towards explicitly trini-tarian thinking. In contrast, a 'control group' of independent Charismatics whom I also interviewed, and who'd rejected the Anglican Charismatic fold, were in a more strictly 'sectarian' manifes-tation, and were coming up with a quite different kind of pneuma-tology. You might think this has nothing much to do with my view of the Trinity. But I show in the book that the question of how you're relating to the Spirit in prayer has everything to do with the way you think about the Trinity, and this in turn interestingly relates to how you view the powers of women (and men) and how you reflect on the 'erotic' power of worship.

So I'm trying not only to read classic doctrinal texts afresh, but also to ask really tough questions about how 'doctrine' actually relates to current church practice, and how different people in slightly different social and political and class circumstances work out these things on the ground, and what the correlations are here.

SHORTT: Did you have any other differences between the two Charismatic congregations to report?

COAKLEY: What was fascinating here was that I happened to catch the Anglican Charismatics at a moment of implicit doctrinal decision. The members of the congregation had been 'renewed' for about ten years, and during this time their prayer had deepened a great deal, and they had also run into the problem of seeming failure in prayer. In other words they might often pray for the recovery of someone's depression or bad back, and yet the Spirit wasn't always co-operating (apparently) with these desires. Here, then, they struck at the heart of the question of how our desires relate to divine desires – and as a result of finding that they couldn't always predict or control whether their prayers would be answered, they were forced up against a hard theological question. Was the Holy Spirit going off duty when they weren't getting what they wanted, or was it that the Holy Spirit was driving them, so to speak, into Gethsemane so as to chasten and transform their desires? By wondering about this (and the initiative came from them: I didn't impose it), they were asking an implicitly 'trinitarian' question about whether Spirit and Son were 'of one sub-stance' with one another. Thus, they were asking a question about whether the activity of the Holy Spirit in sustained prayer actually leads one to a point where one's desires have to be transformed – a place of Christic transformation in the face of apparent failure.

SHORTT: And the independent group?

COAKLEY: The independents had split away from the Anglicans and accused them of too easily giving up when they didn't get what they wanted in prayer. They felt that the Anglicans were lacking in faith, and their use of tongues had died down, and this suggested a loss of commitment and verve. So the more sectarian groups were much more ardent in their use of tongues, and in their insistence that all properly requested prayers would be answered according to their desires. So there was much less perception that human desire in the Spirit might have to undergo some kind of checking and chastening. That was at the moment I caught them. I'm not saying that that didn't change thereafter. But it was a very interesting snapshot of how what appears to be an abstruse patristic-dominated discussion about the origins of the doctrine of the Trinity could have practical implications for theological choices now. And this is part of what I'm trying to do in overcoming a false disjunct between 'practical' theology and 'high' academic theology, by showing how this 're-asking of the Fathers', in a way that is alert to questions of desire, can then be actually investigated in the contemporary pastoral field in a way that brings doctrinal matters alive.

SHORTT: I understand that each volume of your systematics is also to contain an element on an aesthetic tradition relating to a given doctrine.

COAKLEY: I'm using art specifically in the first volume, because the history of the way in which the Trinity has been painted is fantastically revealing in certain ways that the history of texts can't be. It shows not only a different set of developments over time in consciousness about how you relate the three to the one, but also that the doctrine of the Trinity, when painted or sculpted, very obviously reflects people's gender and power arrangements in society in many different ways. And this makes it visually obvious that the critique of patriarchy in the tradition is an absolutely necessary one. In other words, when you see a painting of three men representing the Trinity, and arranged in such a way that a female worshipping public is clearly subjugated to them rather than empowered by them, then you can hardly deny that as a cultural artefact this piece of artwork is reinstantiating a certain normative gender image.

SHORTT: Are you referring to Rublev's 'Old Testament Trinity' icon, in which the three angels visiting Abraham in Genesis are seen as a proleptic reference to the three divine persons?

COAKLEY: No, actually. Because one of the many remarkable features of the Rublev 'Trinity' is that even the figures themselves are of indeterminate sex, and they are visually welcoming the viewer into their circle, not excluding or subjugating us. The eye is led round and round rather than up and down, and the focus is on the eucharistic dish on the table at which the angels sit. So there are many ways of representing them as an anticipatory reference to the Trinity. But in Rublev's case, because of the masterful way in which he executes the icon, the obvious patriarchal readings are avoided.

By contrast, there are Western medieval examples of Genesis 18 done as a kind of grotesque three-headed monster, with Sarah and Abraham recoiling in front of it. There are also examples where an attempt is made to mediate the problem of the three-in-one of the Trinity so that the God-picture has a male face but with three noses – a sort of grotesque bid to do three *hypostases* (identities) in one *ousia* (substance) in a literal way. This tries to avoid heresy, but instead collapses into such appalling idolatry in the process that you see all the dangers of this attempt writ large in visual form.

But you also have wondrous examples of visual representations of the Trinity which I'm going to use at the end of the art chapter, which out of sheer ingenuity and novelty escape all the dangers, and therefore regenerate our imaginative capacity for thinking of God as Trinity in ways which don't encase us back into patriarchal ways of thinking. So systematic theology, in my view, can't be complete unless it's dealing with the realm of the imagination – either through artistic or poetic or musical material. This is a vital part of what I call *théologie totale* because, as with the fieldwork, it's a collecting up of significant fragments out of realms of endeavour which aren't strictly textual. Yet these are particularly powerful in their capacity to mould and energise our theological perspectives.

5
Christoph Schwöbel

The Triune God

SHORTT: The rationale for trinitarianism – the belief that God is a necessarily differentiated unity – could be encapsulated as follows. If the ground of creation is *eternal* love, it has no need of an object outside itself; and if it is eternal *love*, it must be in some sense relational. I take this to be a rough summary of beliefs you yourself have expressed at various stages. But it's also evident that your views evolved significantly between your twenties in Germany during the late 1970s and early 1980s through your time at King's College London, in the late 1980s and early 1990s, when you collaborated closely with Colin Gunton and the Greek Orthodox theologian John Zizioulas. Could you start by recalling these periods to provide a handle on the issues at stake?

SCHWÖBEL: I started my academic career as a theologian working on liberal theology, trying to write a book about a very significant German liberal theologian, Martin Rade, at the turn from the nineteenth to the twentieth centuries. I found that there was much that was very convincing in this kind of theology. There was an admirable ethos of engaging the problems of the modern world. There was a strong conviction that the Christian message had something to say in the intellectual climate of the times, and a great deal of openness to the new discoveries both of historical criticism and of the natural sciences.

But after engaging with liberal theology, I found that its interpretation of the Christian faith and its interpretation of reality were deficient: that on the one hand liberal theology didn't develop the Christian faith as entailing a distinctive vision of the whole of reality, and on the other hand that liberals far too easily accepted the findings of secular philosophy, and of the other sciences and arts, as givens.

These theologians – Martin Rade is a notable exception – did not appear to accept that Christianity itself could be a conversation partner with something original to say independently of the other sciences.

For me, engaging with the doctrine of the Trinity started with thinking about a notion of divine action. Reading the Bible, one finds that the God depicted there is not some timeless entity, just existing in external bliss – but is very active, involved with the story of Israel, involved with the world to the point of identifying with history in Jesus Christ. So the notion of God's being an agent seems to be one of the dominant pictures that one finds in the biblical witnesses. Now the question is, If God is an agent and if we humans are also agents, is there a possibility that God's agency can be seen *both* as the ground of the existence and structure of the world, *and* for the orientation that arises from the disclosure of truth? Is it possible to see human agents acting in consonance with God, doing God's will, being obedient to God and thereby gaining their freedom? So is there a kind of co-operation possible between the divine agent and human agents? Does God's agency allow for human freedom?

In many models of theology, the more grandly you think of God's agency, the weaker becomes the image of human freedom. And on the other hand, the more significant human freedom seems to be, the less significant God's agency becomes. On this view, it somehow seems that God must back off in order to allow humans to be free, and that was one of the starting points for me – to engage with the relationship between divine agency and human agency. The discovery I made for myself then, which was not a new thing but something that good theology had known all the time, is that we must find a differentiated view of divine agency, so that, first of all, God's agency is the creative agency that brings the world into being, and that invests the world of creation with order. Secondly, God's agency is also the agency of the Logos who discloses the structure of the world, so that it's not just a given order of being, but also an order of meaning. And thirdly, God's agency provides insight into that order of being, so that on the basis of that insight, humans can act in accordance with the structure of reality. So I developed a tripartite view of divine agency, distinguishing God's creative agency, God's revealing agency and God's inspiring agency, which was already quite close to a fairly modalistic distinction between the Father, the Son and the Spirit – that is, one which denies the permanence of the divine persons. But it also enabled me at that time to see that only a trinitarian picture of divine agency allows us insight into the complexity of God's acting, which is a presupposition of seeing how human freedom can relate to God's agency.

This was basically the kind of thinking I had arrived at when I came to King's in 1986. At that time, my thinking was very much focused on the so-called economic Trinity: how does God the Father, the Son and the Spirit act in the history of salvation, act in the patterns of interaction with his creation? The challenge that came from John Zizioulas and Colin Gunton was simply the question: How must God be if God acts in this way? So that extrapolating from God's action and reflecting on God's being as the presupposition of that action then became the crucial issue for me. And that is the transition for seeing the doctrine of the Trinity not just as the framework for the theory of divine action, but as the axis to understanding the being of God.

SHORTT: **So if the God of revelation is committed to loving what is substantively other, what must be true of God for this to be possible?**

SCHWÖBEL: Yes. That's the kind of question I'm asking. I think I'd want to add to that slightly, and say, If God is in relation to us in creation, in reconciliation and in the perfection of the world, if God relates to the world by creating the world in a particular structure and order, if God relates to the world in revelation and in the work of the Holy Spirit, is it the case that God becomes relational only when he creates the world, or is it the case that God already is relational when he begins to create and then shapes his interaction with his creation?

There's an important insight here. If God is conceived, as in classical theology, as immutable, as changeless, then it is not a very good idea to suppose that God starts to relate to the world only when he creates, so that relation comes into the being of God only once there is something outside God. So there must be relation within the godhead and a particular structured relationality that can be characterised as love, for instance. The ancient Christian language of the Father, the Son and the Spirit always used relational descriptions of their interaction by saying that the Father relates to the Son in such a sense that the Father is the source of the being of the Son, and that the Son relates to the Father in such a sense that he acknowledges that the Father is his origin. The question of the Holy Spirit is a little more complicated, since there are pronounced differences between the Eastern and the Western traditions at this point, but they both presuppose that Father, Son and Spirit are defined in their particularity by their reciprocal relations.

Now in classical theology, these relations were mostly depicted as relations of origin, so that the question of who or what a particular being is can be answered only by reference to its origins. So if I want to give an ontological description of the Son, I must say that the Son comes from the Father. If I want to give an ontological description of the Father, I must say that the Father has no origin, and therefore is the absolute first origin, and is thereby distinguished from the Son. I think modern trinitarian theology develops this relational view of the divine being more in the sense of reciprocal relationships where there is both a giving and a receiving, where there is an initiating and responding, so that one can see the dynamic of the relational life of God. Descriptions like 'God is love' presuppose not that God is or has a loving attitude, but say something about the being of God – that in God, in the Father, the Son and the Spirit, there is an exchange that can be described as love, because it is directed towards the full appreciation of the being of the other, which is the character of love, and it is so constituted that it goes beyond a bipolar relationship simply between the Father and the Son, in which they eternally sing something like a romantic duet. It sees that the very nature of love is the capacity of the lover and the beloved to relate their love towards a third.

And this is the significance of the Holy Spirit in the Trinity. The Holy Spirit is, so to say, the third to which the love of the Father and the Son is directed, and not only the *medium* of the interrelationship between the Father and the Son. So that in a personal dialogical relationship between the Father and the Son, there is an opening towards another who is addressed, who listens and who then is enabled to respond. One of the most telling pictures of this view of God is given by Luther, who depicts the being of God as an eternal conversation, so that the sentence 'God is conversation' is true. The Father addresses the Son, the Son responds, and both the Father and the Son address the Spirit, and the Spirit listens and responds, but, at the same time, the Spirit provides the means for *us* to participate in this divine conversation – because it is the Spirit who communicates to God's created conversation partners what he overhears in the dialogue between the Father and the Son.

SHORTT: Some theologians see a link – qualified, no doubt, but a link nonetheless – between theology and anthropology, or theology and psychology. But such linkages with this-worldly phenomena are clearly fraught with problems. Eastern Orthodox theologians, in particular, sound frequent warnings about the alleged monism entailed by speaking of God's triunity in terms of an individual reflecting on his or her subjectivity. On the other side, Western theologians have countered that so-called social trinitarian models run the risk of tritheism. Some of your colleagues at King's College faced a similar charge, given their enthusiasm for the Eastern trinitarian tradition. Could you fill out this picture, and defend your position?

SCHWÖBEL: In the contemporary discussion it seems that there are basically two schools of thought on the Trinity, one going back to the Augustinian tradition, the other to the Cappadocian tradition. In the Augustinian tradition, there was for a long time the tendency to interpret language about the Trinity as language about the relationship of three mental acts within the divine intellect. So that God was understood as a divine mind, and this divine mind has a particular order of mental acts, so that memory, intellect and will, for example, are part of that triad which depicts the differentiated character of the divine mind. The Cappadocians emphasised much more that there is in God the place for true particularity, so that the Father, the Son and the Spirit each have to be understood as a relational *hypostasis*, which I think one can best translate as 'identity'. Thus in God there is place for particular identities, for the identity of the Father, the Son and the Spirit. Now the Cappadocian view has always been suspected of leaning towards tritheism; on the other hand the Augustinian view was seen as a slightly more subtle version of a kind of monotheism that makes it very difficult to account for the language of the New Testament, where the incarnate Son and the Father converse, for how can two mental acts be in conversation? That's very difficult to imagine.

What's the core of that problem? It seems to me that there are two opposing metaphysical models, two opposing ontologies: one says that unity is always prior and that therefore where there are many, the many are always a deviation from the original unity. But if God is the principle of all being, then the principle of all being must exemplify, in a supreme sense, unity. It might be a differentiated unity that is somehow more sophisticated than a simple kind of monolithic unity, but nevertheless unity is the guiding concept. For other traditions of metaphysics, plurality is fundamental, and unity is always the product of different plural elements coming together to form a unity. And so, in between these views of monism on the one hand, and pluralism, ontological pluralism, on the other hand, what sense can one make of the doctrine of the Trinity?

It seems to me that Christian theology in the Cappadocians found a very unusual answer by saying the one and the many are co-equal. They're both logically and ontologically primitive, because oneness and being many are always related in a particular pattern. So that we cannot say in a Christian metaphysics that the one always has priority or the many always have priority: rather, the doctrine of the Trinity shows that unity is always a relational unity that allows for true particularity, and plurality is always a plurality, not of unrelated individual essences, but rather of a plurality of persons that form a particular communion. So what the doctrine of the Trinity says about the being of God is that unity and plurality constitute one another. They are not opposing concepts.

This is a revolutionary development in metaphysics because it seems simply to deny that there is an alternative between monism and pluralism, and says, Look a little closer and you will find that there is a way of avoiding this opposition. And the way in which that is done in Christian metaphysics is by focusing on the category of relation, and saying, If we have true unity, this unity must always be a relational unity, where the unity is constituted in a relational network. It's not monolithic. And on the other hand, we have a view of personal particularity, of identity, where identities are not individual essences, but are constituted through their relations to one another. The Father wouldn't be the Father without the Son and the Spirit, and the Son wouldn't be the Son without the Father and the Spirit, and the Spirit wouldn't be the Spirit without the constitutive relationships to the Father and the Son. Only in and through these constitutive relationships do the Father, the Son and the Spirit each have their particular identity. So the way forward in much modern trinitarian theology is to focus on this notion of relation as a primary ontological category, by saying that relation is not what you have between substances that are already established, but rather it is *the way in which* substances are established. Relation is the prior category, but relation does not only lead to relationships: it also constitutes particular terms of the relationship.

And that's where the Cappadocian view and the Augustinian view are really in sharp contrast to one another. For the Cappadocians the relationships between the Father, the Son and the Spirit do constitute terms of the relationship, and they call these terms *hypostases*; whereas on an Augustinian view, the person is identified with the relationship, so that the Father is the relationship of being Father with regard to the Son. And that's quite an enormous difference. I personally tend towards the Cappadocian view, although I would try to develop that in a conceptuality which makes more use of the concept of relation than the Cappadocians did themselves. But it seems to me quite clear that there is a distinction between fatherhood, the relation, and the Father, which is the term of the relation that is there.

SHORTT: We're in very difficult territory here, I know, and there obviously isn't space for an exhaustive discussion. My hunch about what you're saying is that a good number of other scholars would agree with the main thrust of your argument, but take a different view of the patristic texts. In particular, this group would be likely to say that Augustine isn't so vulnerable to criticism as you suggest. Take Rowan Williams' summary of his reading of *de Trinitate* as an example. He argues that Augustine's introspective method (i.e. drawing an analogy between the divine persons and our mental processes) is 'designed to "demythologise" the solitary human ego by establishing the life of the mind firmly in relation to God – and, what is more, to God understood as self-gift, as movement into other-ness ... in self-imparting love. This is hardly monism or "abstract theism".[1] For Williams, contemporary theology is increasingly taken up with forms of trinitarian pluralism that threaten to become mythological – the divine life as interactive drama – and such trends need to be balanced by serious attention to Augustine's account. Here's how he puts it:

> Modern trinitarian pluralism is often a wholly intelligible re-action to the unhelpfully formal versions of trinitarian orthodoxy current in scholastic textbooks or to the abstract unitarianism to which liberal Protestantism tended. But it is not the only possible way of retrieving this central element in the Christian grammar of God; and if it is content with a highly anthropomorphic plurality of agencies, it will miss the central point of Augustine's analysis – the understanding of the divine nature as loving wisdom, as rela-tional, and thus the integration of the doctrine of the Trinity with discourse about God *tout court*. A trinitarian theology prepared to stick close to the fundamental Christian perception of being given a share in the unlimited gift and exchange that is the joy of God will have much to learn from the *de Trinitate*.[2]

SCHWÖBEL: I think the renaissance of trinitarian theology that we have experienced in the past thirty years also makes us aware of the riches of our respective traditions. The danger is always of working with a caricature of the other side, with Augustinians saying that the Cappadocians are tritheists, and the followers of the Cappadocian tradition saying that the Augustinians are monistic intellectualists, or that Augustine was the precursor of the self-referential subjectivity of modernity – so that Augustine is seen almost as a kind of Descartes in patristic times. One clearly has to say that both these perspectives on

Augustine have enormous limitations. For him, the psychological was not an independent dimension of his view of reality. When he wrote about mental acts and psychological attitudes, the affections of the heart and so on, these did indeed all have ontological significance. They concerned the nature of being, and not just a particular form of the inner psychological life of a person.

Secondly, it has been pointed out, I think correctly, that Augustine's view of the human self is by no means a kind of self-sufficient self-referentiality which we then find as the signature-tune of much modern philosophy. I would at this point say that the unity of the human mind in Augustine is clearly a referential unity in the sense that the mental acts of a human person have their unity in focusing on God. So it's a unity which is enabled through the relationship in which the mind turns to God, but on the basis of God's prior relating to the human mind in creation.

The other innovative element identified in Augustine is that when he defines the divine being as sapiential love, then the divine being itself, the divine essence, is seen as relational. There is indeed a marked difference with the Cappadocians, because all the Cappadocians have to say about the divine *ousia*, the divine essence, is that it's unknowable, incomprehensible, unbounded, it's all kinds of negative qualifications that they attach to it in order to make quite clear that, if we relate to God, we must do so through the *hypostases* of the divine being through the persons in personal relation. We can't relate to God in confronting the unbounded, incomprehensible, unknowable divine *ousia*.

Now I think Augustine has understood that, if the divine essence is something that the Father, the Son and the Spirit hold in common but hold in different ways, each according to his personal particularity, then the divine essence must be understood as itself relational in structure. For me, the most helpful model was developed by Richard of St Victor,[3] where he used the Augustinian example of seeing the trinitarian relationship as a relationship of love in a sense that comes much closer to the Cappadocian emphasis on the particularities of persons in the Trinity. And we can see that later: both Luther and Calvin in the theology of the Reformation found it easier to apply much of the theology of the Cappadocians in their own trinitarian thought.

For Luther, for example, the Trinity is about a threefold model of personal divine self-giving, so that God gives himself to us as the Father in creation, giving us all the gifts of creation; and then the Son gives himself to us in redemption, so that the very being of the Son becomes the gift by means of which we enter into communion with God; and the self-giving of the Spirit is the way in which God illumines the mind of believers to see that they themselves can, in believing in the Son and the Father, participate in the communion with the trinitarian God by grace, and not by nature. So within the Western tradition there are many ways of trying to do justice to the complexities of the trinitarian life of God.

But there are distinctive emphases. In the Augustinian tradition, and especially in the tradition going back to Thomas Aquinas, the intellectual life of God is very much emphasised, whereas in the tradition of Richard of St Victor it's not the intellect, but the personal relationship of love, that is the primary illustration of the truth of the Trinity. And in Reformation theology, especially in Luther's theology, it is the communicative relationship between the three persons of Father, Son and Spirit, the divine conversation, which is the clearest image.

All these are conceptual ways of trying to do justice to the biblical accounts, trying to make sense of the fact that in the biblical stories God acts and speaks, and wherever God acts his act is a communicative act that tells people something, and wherever God speaks this is an effective word that creates effects, like an action: so that we have a communicative agency, and at the same time an effective communication. And that, I think, has to be taken seriously ontologically: so that divine speaking and divine action are not two separate worlds, but belong together. God speaks, and this speaking has the effect of action. God speaks the world into being. And God's action is the action in which he communicates, so that action and speech are not to be separated in any way.

From this it follows that we mustn't look at the intellectual life of the mind as the primary example of the Trinity, but rather at metaphors of communication, like the metaphor of conversation, and, as I say, take them seriously ontologically. For me as a Lutheran theologian, it's absolutely significant that being and speaking are not to be distinguished. Being itself, the divine being, is an eternal act of communication, and the particular freedom of God in creating the world and communicating with the world he creates consists in going beyond the confines of the divine essence and relating to something that is really other, and which has its distinctiveness in being another conversation partner for God.

SHORTT: Can you move on to the cluster of issues surrounding the Trinity and spirituality? I'll cite a specific example as a possible way of advancing the discussion: it's the criticism Aquinas has faced for arguing that the Lord's Prayer is addressed to the entire Trinity, not to the Father alone. He's aware of the problems this causes, given the witness of Scripture. But his justification, according to his defenders, is twofold. First, he's wanting to emphasise a point you've just made, that Christians are God's children by grace, not nature. In other words, our relation to God the Father cannot be another case of the relation between the Father and the eternal Son. And second, he's maintaining that whatever happens in the creative order in response to the act of God occurs because the whole Trinity is active. As commentators have noted, he quotes John 5:19 ('Whatever the Father does, the Son does likewise') in support of his argument.[4]

SCHWÖBEL: Yes, these are two very important points, both of which I would share, but I also have different views on how they are to be interpreted. It's quite true that Thomas Aquinas insists that we are God's children by grace and not by nature, so that we cannot understand our divinisation – that is, our participation in the communion of the Trinity – as something that is a substantive change of our nature. So the ontological order of adoption is different from generation. What that says is that we can be God's sons and daughters only because God has one Son who became incarnate and who invited us to relate to God the Father by believing in him, and so relate in the power of the Spirit to God the Father. This is the language of Romans 8. It doesn't blur the ontological distinction between our mode of filiation, being God's sons and daughters, and the Son's mode of filiation, being the only begotten Son, because the relationship of the Father to the Son and the Son to the Father in the Trinity is constitutive for our relationship to God the Father through the Son. We could never dare relate to God apart from this relationship to the Son. And that is a relationship that is given to us by God in the Holy Spirit.

The second point is that whenever we pray, we pray to the Holy Trinity, because whatever happens in the created order is in response to an act of God, and this act of God is always and in all circumstances a trinitarian act. I would agree with the principle and say, Yes, creation is a trinitarian act; justification is a trinitarian act. But it has a particular structure, and this structure does not take away the differences between the persons of the Trinity: the Father as the origin of all being, the Son as the exemplification of the communicative structure of being, and the Spirit as the energiser of the divine being: they all have a different function and only together do they form the creative act of the divine Trinity. So whenever we relate to God, we follow that pattern of divine action. It's not some kind of joint action where Father and Son and Spirit together do the same thing. They do different things, but never do them alone. Therefore our relating to God follows these differences, being enabled by the Spirit, following the pattern of the Son, being directed to God the Father. And in this sense we address the Trinity.

SHORTT: So far we've concentrated on your vision, and also said something about people who are to a large extent fellow travellers. There are others who think that the language of traditional orthodoxy is simply too confident. Many liberals, for example, argue that classical models must be recast because of the very different circumstances of modernity. But we can find other grounds for reticence about trinitarian language, especially in the negative or apophatic tradition. This stresses that whatever we can say about God is always eclipsed by what we can't say about God, and that therefore all our language needs to be relativised. Could you first say something about this – including the possible complaint that you're talking too much as though God were another item in the universe – and then a few words about some of the wider implications?

SCHWÖBEL: I don't think I'm necessarily running the risk of being simplistic. One has to say simply that the justification for all anthropomorphic language in theology is the incarnation of the Son. God was made man, and God's becoming a human being, God's inhistorisation, is also God's coming into human language, so that God speaks himself, his very being, in the incarnation, in human language. In other words, the very being of God is expressed in human words and human modes of expression, and therefore human language has the capacity to express what goes utterly beyond it. Accordingly, I would have a very positive image of human language, and would justify this by saying that, in God, being and speaking are one and the same. The silence of God is a silence between the words of God; it's not a silence that utterly transcends all the words, so that the words are merely a preliminary stage towards the true being of God. With regard to the relationship between negative theology and positive or cataphatic theology, I would say that all apophatic theology presupposes cataphatic theology, and God chose to reveal himself and to speak, and in this way God opted for the priority of cataphatic theology.

So it's a way in which we follow the history of salvation. If God hadn't spoken, we would be right to reflect, as Buddhists do, on the nature of the Sunyata, but that would presuppose that there is a silent 'God' who doesn't say anything. In the end the true character of reality is a kind of void. This is not the case with Christianity. Therefore, I'm relatively sceptical about the new fashion for negative theology, which seems to have become extremely popular with schools of postmodern theology.

SHORTT: Radical Orthodoxy in particular?

SCHWÖBEL: Yes. I think there is a tendency in Radical Orthodoxy to see the history of salvation as not quite as significant as a starting point for theology, and to see the build-up of a metaphysics in which everything relates to the one as far more important. Many of the writings of the Radical Orthodoxy group remind me of particular Neoplatonic versions of Christianity as they have been discussed in the past: a kind of theological Fall is postulated, which for Radical Orthodoxy is said to have happened round the time of Duns Scotus, and this is seen as the beginning of a wholly negative set of developments in modern theology. I cannot agree with that. It seems to me that much of the reading of the history of theology and the history of philosophy behind that would have to be corrected from a close reading of the sources. I cannot see that from Scotus onwards, everything developed negatively.

SHORTT: You're opening up further important areas of discussion that are covered in the next chapter, and I'm sorry we can't pursue them further here as well, although it's useful to know your view in outline. I'd like to ask now about the *filioque* ('and from the Son') clause in the creed, which encapsulates differences in trinitarian teaching between Eastern and Western Christianity.

SCHWÖBEL: The *filioque* is one of the more difficult questions because you have a conundrum involving legal questions and mutual misunderstandings between the Western and Eastern traditions which are very hard to disentangle. The insertion of the *filioque* clause was one of the consequences of an Augustinian theology of the Trinity, where the Spirit is breathed by the Father and the Son. This follows a Johannine description of the coming of the Spirit or Paraclete, where the Son gives the Spirit when the Son leaves this earth, so that the Paraclete is, so to say, the presence of the truth of the Son in relation to the Father in the absence of the Son. Now the Eastern side had a problem with that characterisation because, if the Father and the Son are joint originators of the Spirit, then we have two principles of being in the divine being, and that's polytheism. For the Eastern side the Westerners were succumbing to polytheism by saying that the Spirit proceeds from both the Father and the Son.

That, of course, was never what the West wanted to express. The

West wanted to say that the very fact that the Spirit comes to us in particular circumstances of the history of salvation is significant for the being of the Spirit. So that the significance of the Christ story is maintained by saying that the Spirit is breathed by the Father and the Son. So the Spirit's identity would be deficient if the Spirit were simply given by the Father like the Son, without any relation to the Son. And I think one can maintain both points. One can say, Yes, it's right that there's only one principle of origin in the Trinity, and that's the Father. There's not a second principle of origin: therefore Christians do not have to become polytheists in that respect. But at the same time, it must be emphasised that all this is not a matter of abstract metaphysics. It's always a metaphysics that engages with history, because it believes that the character of being has been disclosed in history. This is what led to a complete revolution in the understanding of the knowledge of being. For the whole Greek tradition, our experiential knowledge and historical knowledge cannot be conduits of metaphysical truths. Metaphysical truths have to be abstracted from the contingent factors of history and experience. They transcend history and experience. The Christian message says, No. Because of the incarnation, our experience, our historical experience, our bodily experience, our being in the world, are able to communicate the highest truths.

This leads to many consequences in the history of ideas – and especially in the history of philosophy – because the Greek idea that true knowledge is pure, abstract, theoretical, the pure vision, not really encumbered by the particularities of human speech led Kant, for example, to argue in *The Critique of Pure Reason* that reason could function properly only if it were pure, if it could extract itself from its historical, linguistic, culturally conditioned character, and so on. And Johann Georg Hamann, Kant's friend and opponent, who wrote a metacritique of *The Critique of Pure Reason*, said that reason is always impure: it's always embedded reason, it's embedded in history, it's always bodily reason. It's always bound up with the particularities of existence, and always connected to a scriptural source and its communicative modes of tradition, and this is because the Logos became incarnate.

So in many ways Hamann, I think, anticipated much of the criticism of a purely analytical view of reason – reason as not having a context – and rediscovered the epistemological implication of the incarnation, which I would not hesitate to call the sanctification of the bodily character of our knowledge. People knew Jesus by touching him, by experiencing his physical presence, and for the New Testament this is so important that even the risen Christ has a physical shape, although that shape is different from the way we experience our bodies now. Nevertheless, it is something that is a permanent feature of our way of knowing God: so that, even in heaven, even in the Kingdom of God, we may hope, there will be some form of embodied existence, because embodiment, corporeality, the linguistic character of communication – all these are, for God, permanent features of his interaction with the created order.

SHORTT: You're a noted ecumenist as well as a theologian. Would you favour a change in the wording of the creed in the West?

SCHWÖBEL: I think not. Most of the proposals for change so far advanced sound rather artificial, in my view. I also believe it's useful to maintain this difference, to remain attentive to the fact that the framers of the *filioque* clause were trying to say something very important at the time. They wanted to say that the way the Spirit comes to us is not apart from the Son, but through the history of salvation. To some, though, their argument was tantamount to saying that there might be two principles of being in the divine being. And therefore I would rather retain the phrase, inform people of what they're saying, and what they shouldn't be saying – but to continue being attentive to the problem, because it is highly significant. Once we forget about it and say, Well, it's quite clear we must take the *filioque* clause out, then people would forget there is something very important that it retains.

SHORTT: I believe you have a lot to add about broader ecumenical matters, especially Protestant–Catholic dialogue today. But let's stick with our main theme for a bit longer. We've discussed the renewal of trinitarian theology over the past few decades. What about some of the blind alleys?

SCHWÖBEL: At the moment, it seems to me that there are two ways in which a doctrine of the Trinity should not be developed. One is by focusing exclusively on the so-called economic Trinity, by saying that all we can say about trinitarian theology is restricted to God's engagement with the world. And the other is to say that all reflections on the Trinity must start from our view of the divine being and the way in which statements about the divine being are made in the great Councils of the Church. John Zizioulas would be a representative of this second particular approach, while many liberationist trinitarian theologies focus exclusively on the economic Trinity. The interesting insights in trinitarian theology can all be gained by focusing on a confluence between these two approaches. The inhistorisation of the Son in Jesus Christ is ontologically significant: the divine economy is not just an illustration of a pre-defined metaphysical doctrine of the Trinity. Rather, the metaphysics of the doctrine of the Trinity is worked out in creation, in God's story with Israel, in the incarnation, in the crucifixion and resurrection, and in the sending of the Spirit. So all these stages and stories and events associated with the economic Trinity are ontologically significant as well. What the Bible tells us has ontological weight. It's not just an illustration of an ontology that could be gained from other reflections. And there I think one comes to quite revolutionary ideas of the Trinity, which can perhaps be seen most clearly in the systematic theology of Robert Jenson, the American Lutheran theologian.[5]

What is more significant than simply the different theoretical ways of doing trinitarian theology is a sense of what the function and task of the subject are. If we acknowledge that we live in a world of religious and ideological pluralism, the primary question for Christians is, Who is our God? Who is the God Christians believe in? And the Christian answer to that is, The Father, the Son and the Spirit. So the doctrine of the Trinity is primarily about the identity of God, and the situation of religious pluralism really involves a battle of the gods, because one can see quite clearly that images of the divine define images of what it means to be human. So when we encounter different views of what it means to be human, there is always a theology in the background. I think one has to turn Feuerbach upside down. It's not the case that anthropology produces theology, so that a particular view of what it means to be human creates particular images of the divine. It's the other way around. Tell me who your God is, and I will tell you what your view of the human is.

And herein lies a second source of the significance of the doctrine of the Trinity. If it's true that the one and the many are both ontologically primitive and logically primitive, so that one doesn't have to argue for the priority of unity or the priority of plurality, this offers a view of pluralism which is not some kind of arbitrary 'manyness', but shows how the emphasis on the particularity of the plural elements does not exclude communion, which I think is the most important social insight that modern societies could learn from. There is a third way between individualism and collectivism, and this is rooted in the way the trinitarian God creates communion with his creatures.

A further area concerns the ecumenical significance of trinitarian doctrine. If one reviews the different Christian traditions, I think it would be quite easy to find that there are three main groups of believers who cut across the denominational and confessional divisions. The first group, one could call it the liberal group, is the one that believes in God the Father, or even God the Mother, and its beliefs focus almost exclusively on creation and providence. Behind everything there is a benevolent will that steers everything towards the good. And this group has no special significance to ascribe to the Son or the Spirit. Rather, it is a comprehensive theistic philosophy associated with what is traditionally ascribed to the first person of the Trinity.

And then there's the second group, the Evangelicals, who focus almost entirely on the redemptive work of Christ. Their emphasis is the salvation wrought by Christ on the cross. And their view of Christian faith is rather more dramatic than that of the first group, because of their insistence that we must be saved by the blood of Christ. It's a real transformation that must occur. This group one can also find in all kinds of denominations and all kinds of confessional groups within the different Churches. They tend to have a very simple creed that could be summed up in a phrase like 'Jesus is God full-stop'. There's no real reference to God the Father or to the Spirit.

And the third group consists of Charismatics of all denominations. Charismatics coming from the Pentecostal tradition, for example, get on enormously well with Charismatics within the Roman Catholic tradition. They have the same style of piety. They have the same forms in which they worship God in the power of the Spirit. And that seems to me to be the main point for them: the Spirit is a power defined by energy who grasps people and makes them transcend the boundaries of their existence. So it's a very experience-centred form of Christianity.

I think there's an ecumenism of liberals, and an ecumenism of the Evangelicals, and also an ecumenism of the Charismatics, but will the three groups find a common understanding of Christianity? How well are they able to relate to people of the other groups? And there I think the doctrine of the Trinity is tremendously important to show that each of these groups – and they're the dominant groups I think in our Churches at the moment – has an incomplete picture of the character of God, and therefore an incomplete picture of the nature of Christian faith.

The liberals, focusing on creation and providence, must learn that creation is not complete without the reconciliation of a fallen world by God the Son, which is then appropriated to believers and to the

believing communion today in the power of the Spirit. And the
Evangelicals must learn to see the reconciliation wrought by Jesus on
the cross as the enactment of the will of God the Father, which is
made real for us and changes our reality through the Spirit. And I
think the Charismatics of all denominations would have to learn to
develop a personal understanding of the Spirit, where the Spirit is not
so much understood as an impersonal force, who simply knocks
people down or makes them transcend their own creaturely being, but
who puts them into communion through the fact that he addresses
them as persons, because he himself is a person, and so relates them
to the Son in a filial relationship to God the Father.

SHORTT: And from the evidence of your writings and lectures, it
appears that you also think that the trinitarian models you've com-
mended form an effective response or antidote to the perceived
authoritarianism of the Roman Catholic Church these days.

SCHWÖBEL: That's right. The reconciliation of the three groups I've
spoken about is the main task facing the Churches in the twenty-first
century. Then, of course, the doctrine of the Trinity is also important
for envisaging what kind of understanding of unity one has. Is it a
kind of monolithic unity where everybody has to conform to a certain
pattern which is presented by a centralist organisation, which is certainly one of the temptations of Roman Catholicism? Or is it a kind
of unrelational plurality, just a pluralism of different Churches, which
is what Protestantism tends to produce, because Protestantism grows
by schisms and unions? The whole history of the spread of Protestant
missions in Asia, for example, is a history of splits between different
Churches and the establishment of unions between them.

I think both these models are insufficient on their own, because we
can also find a way of operating whereby the acknowledgement that
another Church which is differently organised from my own is nevertheless a Church in the full sense of the word becomes the primary act
of ecumenical relations. One isn't thereby saying that the content of
another Church's dogma is identical with that of my own tradition,
but one is acknowledging that it refers to the same act and being of
God. And therefore, I think an ecumenical pluralism can have a referential unity where the unity of the Church is in what it witnesses to,
not automatically in any kind of unity in church organisation.

To sum up: my hope is that ecumenism will prosper by taking
trinitarian doctrine seriously: unity and plurality are both fundamental: they're complementary concepts, and they extend to the
being of the godhead.

6
John Milbank and Simon Oliver

Radical Orthodoxy

SHORTT: No survey of contemporary anglophone theology can leave Radical Orthodoxy out of the picture. Though it has divided the critics, at times sharply, there's ready agreement about the momentousness of the movement inaugurated by you, John, in association with Catherine Pickstock, Graham Ward and others, in the early 1990s. We'll naturally need to consider the cavils in some detail, but I'd like to set the scene with a stripped-down account of your work.

Close to the heart of Radical Orthodoxy lies the immodest, but in your view vital, belief that Christian thought has to give a plausible and self-confident account of the whole world. You are saying that unless theology can evoke a coherent universe in which other things fit, then it becomes a dreary kind of ecclesiastical housekeeping or settles down into what Donald MacKinnon used to call ecclesiological fundamentalism. One just talks about the Church. And although Radical Orthodoxy is sometimes thought of as a very church-dominated or in-house discourse, it could be argued that the opposite is true.

But how can this be done in a highly secular climate like ours? Your answer derives from the argument that much modern atheism is parasitic on bad theology. In particular, you maintain that somewhere in the late Middle Ages the whole doctrine of God went badly wrong, because God got sucked into the business of running the universe. The utter difference, the utter gratuity, of God's action was overlaid, and that led to what you see as two very ambiguous effects, intellectually and culturally: the Reformation, which tries to re-enshrine the difference of God, but does so at the expense of a robust idea of participation in the divine life; and then the Enlightenment, where a challenge is placed against unaccountable authority and tradition, precisely because authority and tradition are seen as inner-worldly phenomena. From this springs a strong current of unbelief conceived as rebellion against the celestial headmaster.

A prime villain in your narrative is Duns Scotus. The specific charge against him is that he divorced philosophy from theology by declaring that being could be considered independently from the question whether one is thinking about created or creating being. Eventually this gave rise to an ontology and epistemology abstracted from theology. In the late Middle Ages and early modernity philosophers became preoccupied with the pursuit of such an ontology and epistemology, and the Reformation failed to halt the trend. On this reading of history, the sundering of philosophy and theology meant that theology lost its concern with reality as a whole. It fragmented, grounding itself on certain revealed facts, and issued in the authoritarianism associated both with Protestant biblicism and ultramontane Roman Catholicism. Western culture thereby lost the patristic and early medieval sense that reason and revelation are not opposed concepts. As you put it in *Radical Orthodoxy*, your programmatic collection of essays: 'In the Church Fathers or the early scholastics both faith and reason are included in the more generic framework of participation in the mind of God. To reason truly one must be already illuminated by God, while revelation itself is but a higher measure of such illumination . . .'[1]

I hope this introduction helps clear the ground a little, especially over the question of why the movement seeks to harness the apparently opposed categories of 'radicalism' and 'orthodoxy'. John, I wonder if you could take up the story by saying something about your background and evolution.

MILBANK: I think your report touches on the heart of what we're concerned with. We're not necessarily putting forward any one specific Christian metaphysic, but we definitely believe that in the end Christianity is going to be unconvincing if it's not connected to an entire coherent intellectual vision. Not a totalised vision in which all the details are set rigidly, but a vision in which all religious belief and practice connects with, say, nature, or the way you read history, or the way you act in society. And I think there is a fundamental conviction among all the people who inaugurated the movement that there's something unreal about a lot of quite sincere religious belief and practice at the moment, that too many people are looking at nature and society in a basically secular way, with spirituality tacked on. It's therefore right to point to Donald MacKinnon's suspicion of pietism as in fact a kind of secular phenomenon: this has had a very profound effect on me. In an almost Victorian manner he wanted to link Christian doctrine with a rigorous philosophy, and was very impatient of shortcuts and pretences.

SHORTT: He didn't teach you, did he?

MILBANK: He didn't. And in fact I've probably exchanged about two words with Donald MacKinnon in my life, but I went to his lectures and I would say that in an era when the norm in many theology faculties was disbelief in the Trinity and the incarnation, he successfully sustained an older kind of High Church tradition that had a profound understanding of orthodoxy. He was also linked, albeit critically, with many of the groups in the 1930s like the Christendom movement, and he was one of the last people really to understand the logic of Anglican divinity – in so far as this has truly existed.

SHORTT: What about your earlier career? You studied for a while at Westcott House, the Cambridge theological college, in the early 1980s, but decided against ordination. While there you were taught by Rowan Williams and another patristics expert you've identified as an important influence, Mark Santer. This was followed by the publication in 1992 of your book *Theology and Social Theory*,[2] one of the foundational texts of the Radical Orthodoxy movement.

MILBANK: Yes. After Westcott I did a doctorate on Vico, and later went to Lancaster University as the Christendom Fellow. It was a very exciting period to be in the religious studies faculty there, and I also interacted with perhaps the best sociology department in the country at that time – people like Scott Lash, John Urry and Russell Keat. I wrote *Theology and Social Theory* at Lancaster. Radical Orthodoxy extends the approach taken in that book, where I was calling into question the idea that the right way forward, if you're relating theology to other disciplines, is to see them as having their particular areas of expertise, and theology as having its own discrete sphere of competence, and then to bring them together. My argument was that the social sciences, if you dig into their history, may have already taken all kinds of theological or anti-theological decisions that you need to be aware of. And conversely, I was influenced by Nicholas Lash's view that theology doesn't have its own special subject matter: it's much more a question of the way in which the epiphany of God makes a difference to everything. That's why you can't detach theology from a certain view of society.

In the 1990s I and other younger theologians shared a concern that even some people we admired – others in the MacKinnon-influenced tradition I've spoken of – were slightly too caught up in questions of linguistic usage deriving from Wittgenstein, and not sufficiently prepared for a full-blooded engagement with metaphysics. It was not that we wanted to abandon the linguistic concerns – far from it – but more that we felt that they were being dealt with in a manner that implicitly assumed that language or grammatical structures operated rather like a set of Kantian pre-given transcendental categories. This meant that a modern predominance of epistemology over ontology – of knowledge as knowledge of our mode of knowing rather than of things known – was still surreptitiously in place. To the contrary, one can argue that if one takes the linguistic character of thought yet more seriously and recognises that the linguistic mediation of reality always exceeds any determinations of a priori structures, including those which try to fix what language is capable of, then it becomes at least possible to suppose that our mode of knowing is continuously reshaped by what there is to be known. The 'question of metaphysics', in MacKinnon's phrase, then resurfaces in a way that does not take the 'critical' character of the Kantian critique for granted.

SHORTT: **This was what propelled you to take Continental thought more seriously, given its greater concern with ontology in the wake of figures such as Hegel and Heidegger?**

MILBANK: Yes. And although we didn't want to baptise some secular theory or other, as so much twentieth-century theology has done, we still found it very interesting that postmodernism was calling human-ism into question by suggesting that there's very little mileage in try-ing to explain things in terms of purely human concerns or what human beings imagine is going on – including Kantian attempts to have a stable grasp of the processes and criteria of human under-standing. Instead you have to look at wider inhuman forces at work, at that which flows through us, operates in, with and despite us. And, while these theories are obviously often nihilistic and naturalistic rather than religious, nevertheless there's a certain parallel between them and the theological desire to go beyond mere humanism.

Perhaps even more importantly, I think that many postmodern theories – perhaps in the wake of modern physics – have questioned the idea that you can get determinate meaning and clear certainty in *any* human field. So there has been a strong insistence all the time that when you think you've got definite meaning, or some clearly grasped area of value, you're deluding yourself, and in fact you're suppressing the questions, the ambiguities that always remain. And part of our case involves the claim that theology is on the side of indeterminacy, and of a certain authentic and inescapable vagueness, because if we live in a created universe which only reflects in multiple finite ways an infinite plenitude of meaning, then there is a sense in which everything is always somewhat partial and uncertain, veiled, fragmentary and never foreclosed. I think that's a theme which also arises in Rowan Williams's writings very strongly.

SHORTT: One of the corollaries you draw from this is that perhaps only theology can question whether a recognition of indeterminacy necessarily results in either scepticism or nihilism.

MILBANK: That's true. Only theology can teach us to live with uncertainty, because of our corresponding belief that we also have some remote approximation to the truth and hope for a final disclosure of mystery which will nevertheless not cancel out its unfathomable depths. And I've become increasingly aware that to some degree this isn't just a theological attitude, but that in many ways it informs some of the most sophisticated philosophical traditions. I know little about Eastern schools of thought, but certainly in the case of Platonists and Neoplatonists, we gradually became aware of the way in which notions of revelation, grace, gift, faith, myth, significant history and epiphanic ritual saturate their writings, and not just the works of the Christian theologians among their ranks. And so Radical Orthodoxy very much wants to learn from the researches of people like Jean Trouillard or Pierre Hadot and point out that philosophy was a religious practice in antiquity, and the Middle Ages were at least half aware of this. Philosophy, in other words, was not thought of as something done in a vacuum. In the Middle Ages, when you *did* stop, as it were, at philosophy, that was often linked to certain techniques of the liberal-arts faculty or certain regional areas, such as logic or astronomy. But when you look at the full range of issues dealt with by philosophy in antiquity, the borderline with theology becomes extremely blurry, because there's no real abandonment of the Augustinian sense of an integral wisdom under which all thinking and, indeed, all human life are only possible through divine illumination.

But this observation does *not* mean, as some people imagine, that Radical Orthodoxy takes Christianity to be a mere refinement of Neoplatonism. We have continuously acknowledged that the biblical legacy introduces a radical sense that God is personal and loving, that he creates, brings about developments within time, and orientates us towards an eschatological future. If, with other contemporary thinkers like J.-L. Chrétien, we tend to point out ways in which these new aspects were nonetheless remotely foreshadowed in platonic tradition, and equally ways in which the Bible balances historical concerns with interests in cosmology, epiphany, mediating hypostases and participation, then that simply shows a concern to follow the latest scholarship in qualifying certain unhelpful dualities of the 'Hellenic' and the 'Judaic'. We also would wish to stress how Christianity is revolutionary with respect to *both* these legacies – eschatology becomes something already realised as well as yet to come; the final mystery becomes something concretely present in our midst, as well as something infinitely distant.

On our view, however, a sense of integral wisdom embracing both reason and revelation, both the perennial and the historical, does come gradually adrift, and as you've said, Scotus is a pivotal figure.

SHORTT: Your critics, including other contributors to this book such as Christoph Schwöbel, say that your approach to Scotus is simplistic,[3] that he's an exceptionally complex figure. How do you answer this charge?

MILBANK: Scotus is indeed unbelievably sophisticated, and we've tried increasingly to do justice to that – those interested should read Catherine Pickstock's detailed responses to our critics.[4] We also think that there are many other strands in this sundering of reason and revelation. It certainly begins before Scotus with Avicenna, Gilbert Porreta, Roger Bacon, Henry of Ghent, Bonaventure and others. Nevertheless, there is a justified consensus amongst historians that the shift reaches its most consummate focus in Duns Scotus.

The overall upshot of this shift is threefold. First of all, there's the point outlined in your introduction: people start to think that you can talk about being before you come to talking about God. There's a marked contrast here with Aquinas, who says that only God exists of himself. Only God has the plenitude of being. When you're talking about created beings, you can never talk about them as simply existing, full stop. Only God exists without qualification; by contrast creatures, as Augustine taught, are a kind of blend of being with nothingness. And by the time you get to Duns Scotus there's been a switch to a different outlook, according to which something either simply exists or it doesn't; so finite things fully exist, and they fully exist in just the same sense in which God exists. The shorthand for this view is known as 'the univocity of being'. It means that we can speak in a univocal sense about God's being and the being of creatures because (despite many nuances in Scotus's writings at this point) at some fundamental level both God and creatures 'exist' in the same way, even though the manner of their existing in the concrete is drastically and even unmediably diverse.[5]

SHORTT: Thus from Scotus onwards, the tendency is towards the idea that creation is outside God in the way that the quadrangle through the window is outside this room.

MILBANK: That's right. And sure enough, if you look at Scotus' treatment of causality and grace and so on, there *is* a drift towards the idea that somehow creation makes a contribution that is all of its own, that it adds something to God's action, and this is definitely problematic. Admittedly, if the classical view is right and God is the source of *all* reality, and omnipotent, it's very difficult then to understand how there is a place for something else. But I think the tradition tends to leave that as a mystery. The risk on the Scotist view is that you've started to idolise God. You've started to treat God as if he's a very big thing, and it's undeniable that people do eventually start talking about God as coming under the category of an individual, which isn't the case in classical tradition.

Nevertheless, I think it's important to concede that the 'exemplarist' view to which Radical Orthodoxy is committed does, as I've just indicated, raise the question why God bothers to create if things exist in him in a more eminent (meaning eminently different as well as eminently 'similar') manner. In the face of this question it can become tempting to insist that creation fully exists outside God's existence. However, the Scotist idea that creation embodies quantitatively finite degrees of the same goodness that is infinite in God leaves one with the same problem: Why add the finite to the infinite? One needs perhaps to say that in some sense the experience of finitude, of lack, of weakness, mysteriously 'adds' something to plenitude itself. It's a bit like the way the dependency of childhood is not just a deficiency, but something positive, later lost. But I think that thinking of this notion in a participatory, analogical context rather than a univocalist one would allow one to suggest, after someone like Sergei Bulgakov, that in some fashion God himself is still 'there' in this finite weakness, in this emptying out of plenitude, and that this is the ground of possibility for incarnation. If in future Radical Orthodoxy reintroduces *kenosis*, or divine self-emptying, as an aspect of *methexis*, or participation, our overall ontology will become better balanced.

A second way in which you can see Scotus's legacy relates, as I've said, to the shifting treatment of causality. In earlier notions of causality which were very much informed by Neoplatonic tradition, causality was seen in terms of 'influence' – literally a flowing-in – so that the operation of lower causes was caused by the operation of higher causes at an entirely different level. But under the model favoured by Scotus and some of his contemporaries, you have two factors exerting a shared influence, so that the sense of the meaning of the word 'influence' becomes different. You get the idea that divine causality is not simply operating at a higher level, but that it descends to the lower level and contributes a bit alongside the secondary cause that's contributing a discrete bit of its own.

SHORTT: **Which in turn gives rise to some pretty unhelpful views about divine action?**

MILBANK: It does. And part of our case here is that much modern philosophy is built on what appears to be a very unsophisticated and unmystical account of God: you can't talk in the normal vocabulary of facts and objects when you're dealing with transcendent reality. That's part of the argument of Michael Buckley, who's done so much to explore this subject with books like *At the Origins of Modern Atheism*. At the same time though, it's important to say that Enlightenment thinkers can't be held entirely responsible for their misunderstandings, for the reason you've already given – that they were in many cases reacting against bad theology.

And the third shift I would instance is towards something like an epistemology of representation. In the traditions of thought inherited from antiquity and sustained in the early Middle Ages (in Anselm and Aquinas, for example), the idea is that when you know something, in a sense you are part of that reality, but in a different way. In your knowing the tree, the tree is as it were 'treeing' in you: thinking the tree belongs to the life of the tree, if you like. There's a famous book by Owen Barfield, a member of C. S. Lewis' circle, called *Saving the Appearances*. While the scholarly detail in it is often wrong, I think the substance of Barfield's argument is very much borne out by recent researches indicating that there was a shift in the Middle Ages from knowing by identity with the thing known (via the transmission of 'form' from the material object to our mind), to the modern notion that the knower is completely detached. This is the idea that when one knows the tree, one is in a sense taking a snapshot of it, developing it in one's brain. It's the notion that Richard Rorty calls 'the mirror of nature'. I think that when you combine that with this new idea of a univocal ontology, what you tend to land up with is a drift from ontology towards epistemology, because if all we know are the snapshots that we take, and if you can know something adequately without referring it to God, then you're on the road to Kant – to saying that what we know is merely how we know things, not a knowledge of how things are in themselves.

And I think it's very important to say at this point that none of us in Radical Orthodoxy is all that original in terms of our historical judgements. We're just trying as theologians to do our amateur best to make sense of the finest research done by philosophers and historians of medieval thought – people like Ludwig Honnefelder in Germany, Jean-François Courtine, Olivier Boulnois and Jean-Luc Marion in France – and they are increasingly saying that the whole Kantian turn is in many ways a complex and subtle footnote to the Scotist revolution, and therefore that it has deep roots in the Middle Ages. Terminology can get very complex here: Marion tends to insist, for very good reasons, that one should describe as 'ontology' and as 'metaphysics' only those approaches that were historically given those names. That means univocalist treatments of being were in general undertaken prior to theological considerations ('natural' or 'revealed'), from roughly the late sixteenth century onwards and actually no earlier (even though the ground for such comprehensive pre-theological 'systems' had long been prepared, as I have already tried to indicate).

The implication of this is then that Kant did not really understand what he was doing, for all his brilliance. He was not overturning all of Western thought up to that point: only completing a very recent mode of reflection by reversing it. This means that to call Kant into question is not conservatively to go back to the pre-critical, but to question the whole idea of pre- and post-critical pigeonholing, and I'd suggest that the real break came earlier with univocity. If that is the case, then the truth or otherwise of this break can be assessed *only* by theology as well as philosophy. Modern philosophy then has no autonomous ability to assess the conditions of its own genesis. This is the most radical and fundamental of all the claims made by Radical Orthodoxy.

SHORTT: Simon, you were taught by John as an ordinand in the mid-1990s and your first book, *Philosophy, God and Motion*, appeared in 2005 as the final instalment in the twelve-volume *Radical Orthodoxy* series from Routledge. How have you been shaped by the movement?

OLIVER: I'd like to develop what John said much earlier about theology's relationship to other discourses, and theology itself becoming much more self-contained as a discourse in modernity. When I was studying philosophy, politics and economics as an undergraduate at Oxford, we read a good deal of British empiricism and Descartes, but with very little sense of the narrative behind philosophical thought that John's just outlined. The analytic and ahistorical treatment of philosophy places a very strong emphasis on the idea that reason is transparent and untraditioned – that is, something into which philosophy can directly enquire, and that stands over and above history, culture, practices and traditions.

After going on to Cambridge to study theology, I read the moral philosophy of Alasdair MacIntyre. This has been very influential on Radical Orthodoxy and on Stanley Hauerwas, another figure whose work has inspired many of us a good deal. MacIntyre's *After Virtue* taught me that reason – in particular, for MacIntyre's concerns, moral reason – itself belongs within particular discourses; that ideas about it change over time; that therefore there isn't a reason held in pristine autonomy by philosophy or by science to which theology has to appeal, and that this insight can give theology a new kind of confidence. Studying the Fathers, Aquinas and more recent theology and Continental philosophy with John, Graham Ward and Catherine Pickstock gave me a much more exciting theological perspective on fundamental issues. Catherine Pickstock's reading of Plato and the Neoplatonic tradition was a particularly important influence while I did doctoral research under her supervision. Although we rarely conversed, another influential figure was Nicholas Lash, whose seminars on religious language influenced countless Cambridge theologians. I remember a pithy comment of his which John has already alluded to – that theology says something about everything, while other discourses often seek to say everything about something.

SHORTT: And as John has also suggested, this has implications for theology's relations to other disciplines.

OLIVER: Yes. What has proved very attractive for a number of younger contributors to Radical Orthodoxy who have often come from philosophy or other disciplines into theology is a refreshing confidence in tackling concepts that have traditionally been held solely within the purview of other subjects: for example, the concept of motion in my own work, or society in John's, or space, or time, or illumination. All these subjects were interpreted theologically up until the High Middle Ages: you find them being examined in Augustine, Aquinas, Anselm, Grosseteste and many others. Without being unduly nostalgic, I think there is something to be recovered in their vision of those concepts which is authentically theological and radical. It can't and shouldn't necessarily supplant the accounts given in other discourses, but it can certainly complement or challenge them. For example, the understanding of motion might properly belong to physics, and yet there could be other kinds of motion analogically related to the local variety which properly belong within the purview of theology, like the motion of learning or thinking.

MILBANK: Motion is a very good example. For a long time theologians, along with everybody else, would have assumed the final truth of the Newtonian laws of motion – that physical motion is all uniform, and approximates to an abstract paradigm that describes an ideal friction-less reality. Then along come physicists themselves and start to diversify the reality of motion once more, link it back to physical realities such as light, and to deny its ideal reversibility. So it seems quite legitimate for somebody like Simon then to ask, Well, doesn't that mean that we should look at some earlier attitudes to motion within philosophy and theology, and relate those to what's now happening? I think it's a good example of the way theology can be wrong-footed if it simply assents to what the secular world takes for granted, especially as Newton's ideas were very much informed by theological assumptions – and assumptions of quite a strange kind, in his case.

OLIVER: Yes. Perhaps I could add some detail. If the universe is saturated with motion, and God is beyond all qualifications of motion and change, how does one have a proper sense of divine action within such a view? Newton, and countless others before him and since, struggled to find an answer to this critical question. Motion (which theologians and philosophers before modernity understood in very broad terms as both local and qualitative change) was seen as something that should not 'infect' the Godhead, because God should not be subject to the vagaries of change. One answer to the question of divine action is to place some kind of buffer between God and the universe, thus protecting God from the fluctuations of the cosmos. This is Newton's solution (a strategy adopted by many before him). He did not believe in the doctrine of the Trinity, and he understood Christ as the created 'viceroy' of God, putting into action the dictates of the supreme divine will. Christ is pictured as the bridge which keeps the universe from God.

Meanwhile – and this is a clear instance of an overlap between Newton's substantial, although largely unpublished, theological work and his physics – the absolute space which is so integral to Newton's *Principia* begins to take on the characteristics of an orthodox under-standing of Christ. Newton speaks of absolute space as 'eternal in duration and immutable in nature, and this because it is the emanent effect of an eternal and immutable being'. He also describes space as

God's sensorium – his sensory medium, through which he might peer at the universe. One can see that God is detached from such a universe, and one of Michael Buckley's contentions is that Newtonian physics ushers in the separation of theology from questions of cosmology. After Newton, God is bracketed from our (scientific) thinking about the universe. Nature, including motion, is now within the purview of a wholly autonomous natural science. Science and theology are separated because they have their own discrete subject matters.

One might suggest that Newton's theology is simply eccentric, and peripheral to his natural philosophy. But this is simplistic. In *Philosophy, God and Motion*, as well as examining Newton's work, I attempt to outline the way in which, for Aquinas in particular, motion is not something from which God must be preserved. Rather, motion is the means of creation's perfection, and a participation in the eternal dynamic exchange of love between the persons of the Trinity. Of course, Aquinas is clear that God does not change (there is nothing that God could 'become' or which he could 'acquire'), yet this does not mean that God is a kind of static object. God *is* an exchange of love, and this exchange is reflected, albeit faintly and analogically, within the motions of the universe. So motion can be understood as a participation in the eternal dynamism of God. Meanwhile, far from postulating a detached divinity, Aquinas has a view of God's action which is utterly intimate and yet allows genuine causal power to created beings.

So the account of motion in physics and the account of motion in theology will not be univocal, but as I've argued, there may be analogical similarities *and* points of genuine tension. The same might be said of many other concepts: light, space, time, society, language and so on. It's not an interdisciplinary outlook that claims that theology must in some sense fit itself into other discourses by finding banal similarities, nor one that seeks accommodation with the rationalities, priorities and conceptualities of other discourses, as was true of much liberal theology in the 1960s and 1970s. Rather, this approach allows us to question fundamentally the very histories of the concepts that many forms of discourse so often take for granted and deploy unreflectively.

MILBANK: But nor are we locking ourselves into a kind of a laager in the way that some Protestant neo-orthodoxy has rather tended to do, simply inhabiting a universe of biblical or ecclesiastical discourse. Reintroducing an emphasis on mystery, and challenging the anthropomorphism of certain strains of theology, might represent some kind of advance, but it's not enough if it simply drives Christian thought into a fideistic ghetto. Nor does it explain how you get religious revelation and language in the first place. Take John Montag's essay on this subject in the *Radical Orthodoxy* collection. He's resisting the idea that one should think of revelation as a bolt from the blue, or as a discrete datum that you could get hold of. On the medieval view, revelation always involved a special illumination of the mind which was also connected with a remarkable external event, or series of events. In this way revelation was still in continuity with ordinary reasoning processes – even if it also took these by surprise. For at this period *all* knowledge was seen as involving the synthesis of external with internal light.

And I think that both in the Reformation and the Counter-Reformation there's sometimes a danger of losing hold of this view, although I would want to say very strongly that we're not proposing some simplistic view of the Reformation. Both Luther and Calvin attempted to restore, against the later Middle Ages, a participatory vision to Christology, if not more generally: and the treatment of grace and faith was made once again more Christ-centred, compared with later scholasticism. Calvin, in particular, can be read in different ways. Unlike Luther, who remains basically a nominalist thinker, Calvin doesn't really have much of an ontology or a philosophy. Some later Calvinists – Ralph Cudworth or Jonathan Edwards, for example – in fact took Calvin in a way that we would regard as very sympathetic. So we wouldn't want to be read as saying that Calvin was simply part of a wrong turn.

SHORTT: I think you've now either anticipated or directly answered some of the criticisms made of the movement, but let's nevertheless turn more specifically to the queries, because there are some fairly entrenched ideas about what you're alleged to be saying. The unease, even among some of your admirers, centres on the audacity of painting with so broad a brush: they tend to say that the painstaking engagement with difficult and uncooperative detail can be absent from your canvases, notwithstanding the qualifications you've given. Another perception is that you don't allow enough for what Rowan Williams terms 'the sinfulness, the provisionality and the muddle of the Church: all subjects on which an Anglican may be expected to have eloquent views'. He adds that both the Reformation and the Enlightenment 'are unhappy episodes in the Radical Orthodoxy world, and while I'm no uncritical supporter of either, I would say that they're both, if you like, dialectically necessary worlds'.[6] In other words, the idea that authority has to defend itself, has to argue, isn't a bad idea in itself. Rowan Williams and others are also a bit sceptical of the idea that there was just one great theological fall in the Middle Ages, and instead acknowledge a need to ask questions all along the way. You've touched on this already, but might want to say more, given that the point crops up a good deal.

MILBANK: I'm not sure that Rowan is saying anything that really goes against our basic argument. I'm not trying to say that the kind of meta-history that we're talking about captures everything that matters. Far from it. Nevertheless, as I've suggested, I do think that a shift away from a participatory attitude, and a move towards epistemology and the turn to the subject, viewed as self-sufficient and autonomous, are things that one can see as very long-term trends. I entirely agree with Rowan that it's important that authority be asked to give an account of itself – this was indeed far more the case for theology and the Church in the patristic period than in the Middle Ages. Often eighteenth-century Anglicans perceived in the circumstances of their day a return to that more rigorous and desirable state of affairs – which tended to include also more of a refusal of any sort of coercion to embrace the truth. But this immediately implies that such desirable attitudes were not the unique property of the Enlightenment. In questioning the Enlightenment, Radical Orthodoxy is not primarily insisting on the need for authority and tradition: here we advocate only a kind of counter-authority and counter-tradition, which we perceive authentic Christianity to be. In doing so we expose the concealed but actually extreme authoritarianism of 'Enlightenment' as such. There's a link between advocacy of the absolutely autonomous free individual as the ultimate norm, and the subtle growth of a totalitarian politics. How can one human will find room for itself alongside others save by the imposition of arbitrary formal rules by a central authority that requires unbounded power in the absence of tacitly shared social principles? Here one has the individual autonomous subject writ large as state sovereignty. The apparent advocacy of pure reason without the intrusion of emotional prejudice is always secretly the promotion of a cold will to power. Moreover, despite the eighteenth-century critique of 'the Middle Ages' (a fiction of course, just as much as the Enlightenment break is itself a fiction invented in a later era), it actually sustained and extended the voluntarism of late scholasticism.

SHORTT: I think that a possible difference between Rowan Williams and you, John, is that he is more favourably disposed towards Hegelianism.

MILBANK: Yes. I'm afraid that Hegel, for all his sophistication, is too much of a rationalist for me, and I don't really accept his kind of historicism, with all its unfolding, dialectically necessary moments. I continue to think that Vico offers a more subtle and more Augustinian – as well as more interestingly bizarre – historicist alternative. It's always a temptation to think that events are, from a human perspective, more than a complex set of contingencies, and I'm strongly opposed to the Whig view of history. So I don't think of the Reformation as something that was always likely to happen. There had consistently been drives within parts of the Church towards reform, simplicity, personal religion and so forth, but these cropped up among the Lollards, the friars, the humanists and elsewhere. Something quite other and more genuinely Catholic and mystical *might* have emerged, and indeed for a time, especially in Spain, certainly did. If Europe had seen the triumph of a kind of pan-Erasmianism, then it is not just likely, but probable, that a quite different sort of modernity might have emerged – one perhaps where the formalities of liberty, equality and fraternity were balanced by the constant attempt socially to incarnate the virtues of faith, hope and charity, rather in the spirit of Thomas More.

Again, if the Enlightenment is essentially rejecting bad theology, and yet also sustaining some of the assumptions of that theology (one can see both things going on, for example, in its treatment of 'natural theology'), talk of its being 'dialectically necessary' doesn't seem to mean very much. Yet Rowan is absolutely right if he wishes to insist that the Enlightenment properly took further demands that personal freedom, social equality and the fraternity of the human race be legally recognised and protected. But one can say this and also see Enlightenment social norms as a thinned-out version of Christian social principles. These principles entail, in addition, a vision of our inherent relationality, of the social realm as the constant exchange of gifts within one socially material body (as for St Paul), of creation as a gift that cannot be possessed, and of a possibly realisable peace of consensus and harmony linked with the belief that all reality participates in the infinite harmony of God. Without such a faith, how can we ever trust that the Enlightenment-rooted demand that 'the freedom of each presupposes the freedom of all' is capable of fulfilment? Or perceive that it has already been anticipated for us by the incarnation?

Having said all this, I take Rowan's point to this degree. Late medieval philosophy produced a tide of extremely sophisticated, rigorously logical rationalism, and I don't think that when that's happened you can simply go back to what went before. But I don't think that critics of such rationalism – Pico della Mirandola, Nicholas of Cusa, or later figures such as Pierre Bérulle, Ralph Cudworth or Vico or Hamann or Coleridge – are simply harking back to a pre-lapsarian era. What they are commending are philosophical visions that diagnose the limits of rationalism. Although they can be read as in essential continuity with, say Aquinas, they can also be read as tacitly saying that without a better grasp of the role of metaphor, the imagination, narrative, language, history and human creativity, the slide into univocity, nominalism and epistemology is inevitable because an *uninflected* reason will be bound to favour these trends. In order to defend someone like Aquinas within modernity, one has to bring to the fore elements that were at best latent within his reflections. At the same time, the thinkers I have mentioned also showed how the notion of an 'uninflected' reason, taken apart from emotion, sign and symbol and historical conditioning, was in itself a rationally unjustifiable fiction.

SHORTT: They see, more emphatically than in the Middle Ages, that it's not rational simply to think that only reason discloses the world?

MILBANK: Yes. Reason combined with ethical, aesthetic and poetic impulses may be what discloses the world. And once you become more conscious of that possibility, you have to allow that the imagination may be playing an enormous role. This is why I think that the counter-Enlightenment thinkers, in that they're stressing far more the role of the imagination, of art and narrative and poetry and so on, are quite different from medieval thinkers whom I admire, like Aquinas, or even Augustine (although in many ways he already inaugurated such 'humanism' with his reflections on music and language).

SHORTT: Again, you've partly anticipated another criticism that's sometimes made of Radical Orthodoxy, namely that the movement represents a failure of nerve masquerading as a recovery. This is the view of people who distinguish more sharply between philosophy and theology, both in their readings of figures such as Aquinas, and in their view of the methodology appropriate to Christian thought today. Could you comment further on your approach to theological reasoning?

MILBANK: I think Newman gets it right in *A Grammar of Assent*.[7] Argument will take you only so far. As soon as we get on to the issues that really matter to anybody existentially, we're into an area where argument serves an incredibly important purpose in trying to get everything consistent and in persuading people by saying, If you think this, then that would mean you thought that, and you don't really think that. This is what Socrates does all the time. But it goes only so far. For Newman, it's the mind that thinks, and we can trust the mind because it's a function of the soul, and the soul is linked to reality. This is what you have to believe if you believe in God, or in a transcendent ground. For if the ultimate reality is self-establishing spirit, then a share in this spirit must be his initial gift to creation, which is received by humans, among other spiritual entities. This may be shocking in the contemporary world, but if we're serious about our theological vision, we will be committed to strong accounts of the soul.

OLIVER: Another way of thinking about it would be to say that syllogism and argument are put to work very differently in someone like Aquinas, because he doesn't assume that syllogism is going to get him from nowhere to somewhere, which is essentially Descartes' move. In Aquinas, by contrast, there is *already* a vision or a memory. Indeed, memory is particularly important. A central theme in the work of John and Catherine Pickstock has been to address 'the aporia of learning' which one finds in Plato's *Meno*: how do we know what we don't know about? Plato's answer to this difficulty is that, when we come to know, we are recovering a memory, something that is primordially present in us. The issue is complex, but one might think of it as analogous to a sculptor drawing the sculpture from the marble in which it is latently present. Similarly, when we come to know, our knowledge is not written onto a blank canvas by reason. Rather, it is drawn from us by persuasion. Then we realise that in some dim sense we knew all along.

MILBANK: And even Aristotle has his own version of this when he says that the order of discovery is the reverse of the order of being. He also assumes that you've got some dim inkling of what the result's going to be.

OLIVER: This is why the notion of knowledge as illumination is increasingly important for Radical Orthodoxy. Our knowledge is corrigible, not because it's simply either right or wrong in a black and white sense, but because it's illuminated, but only to a certain degree. So our knowledge is always partial: it's dimmer or brighter, and in the end it's always illuminated from a single source. Crucially, there's only *one* guarantee of truth – only one source of light – which is God's own knowledge.

MILBANK: And in a sense, truth is self-authenticating. Otherwise it would just be a trivial truth like, you know, following the rule of one plus one all the time.

SHORTT: I hope that readers who aren't that familiar with Radical Orthodoxy will have got a clearer sense not only of what the movement is saying, but why it matters. It might be helpful now to turn the soil to explore some of the implications of your arguments a bit further. As we've seen, one of your core claims is that the separation of philosophy and theology held to have been triggered by Duns Scotus led to an impoverishment of both subjects. It eventually issued in a philosophy neglectful of the big questions about human destiny, and a theology locked in the prison of revealed facts, as I reported earlier.

One of the escape routes you commend most enthusiastically comes from the French *nouvelle théologie* of the mid twentieth century: its pioneers, such as von Balthasar and de Lubac, also question the modern separation of faith and reason by recovering the patristic sense that to reason truly one must be illuminated by God. In other words, there is no human nature not already graced. Now it's this that's so dangerous in the eyes of some Protestants, given the Reformers' distinction between grace and nature, and their insistence that a corresponding gulf lies between 'Athens' (namely, Platonism and other forms of pagan reasoning) and 'Jerusalem' (that is, the purportedly very different outlook grounded in scriptural revelation). As we've seen, you both want to question this distinction. But in the eyes of those who wish to preserve it, de Lubac was downplaying the process of salvation; and contemporary Protestants have not been shy about bringing a similar charge against Radical Orthodoxy.

This debate might still seem abstruse to some, but in fact it has a crucial bearing on ways of understanding the relation between form and content in Christian proclamation, and thus for debate about the relation between the Church and the world. I'd like to quote Fergus Kerr at this point, who sums up very eloquently the multiple identity problems faced by Roman Catholics – and by extension, other Christians too:

> [I]s the way to be a Catholic these days to do your best to rethink Catholicism, to recreate Catholic sensibility, devotion, liturgy and so forth, absorbing positively ... everything that is right and good and true and beautiful in Protestantism, the Enlightenment, and modern thought? Surely what happened at Vatican II was that at last the Roman Catholic Church accepted the truth of the Reformation? ... Or, to continue this rough sketch, do you say

that enough is enough, that we have taken on board more than enough ... Karl Barth pointed out in *Ad Limina Apostolorum* that with these Catholic attempts to be modern ... we have only bought into liberal Protestantism, with its concomitant individualism. On this reading, modernity is just too dangerous to assimilate ... Look at what has happened to the liturgy, now entirely constructed around rationalist ideals of intelligibility, and, paradoxically, favouring rampant emotionalism. On this version of events, the only solution is for the Church to go post-modern – meaning by that, of course, a return to the pre-modern.[8]

At this point the picture becomes further complicated, because Radical Orthodoxy seems to lend itself to conflicting interpretations. Bridging the gap between Athens and Jerusalem is a strategy associated not only with yourselves, but also with liberalism – hardly a natural ally of your movement. Conversely, however, going 'pre-modern' in Kerr's sense places you alongside Barth, another unlikely bedfellow. Would you clear a path through the thicket here?

MILBANK: Continuing to try to make these issues less arcane, let's think of the situation of the Church, especially the Roman Catholic Church today, when it tries to speak in the public realm about moral and political issues. The dilemma is: do you speak on the basis of a natural law that should be available to everybody, whether or not they're recognising God, in which case it's very doubtful whether you're talking about any kind of natural law that the Middle Ages could have recognised; or do you, on the other hand, say that our positions are grounded in our entire Catholic vision, and here the obvious risk is that people will ask why they should listen. But you might also say that that's the only possible alternative course because, in fact, what we say only makes sense in terms of our entire vision.

I think that, by contrast, the route de Lubac's legacy points to would actually fall between those two stools, because for him it really does cut both ways: that throughout human history there is some remote glimmering of grace, there is some calling of God going on, and on the other hand the revelation we're headed towards is the consummation of an ontology of the human person, of the human spirit. So that kind of perspective would say that, speaking in the public realm, we should latch onto things that aren't completely unchristian, or that to some extent remain residually Christian. People still talk about forgiveness, reconciliation and mercy, and the idea that each person matters as much as everyone else, in a way that pagans, on the whole, didn't. And therefore we don't need to speak within a completely natural law-based kind of discourse: we can get people to try to see more deeply the implications of what they already think. This includes getting them to recognise that their vision isn't completely cut off from something that in the end resembles a religious vision; but it also doesn't mean that one has to start by over-whelming them with one's entire Christian metanarrative and ontology.

This implies that our discourse is always situated in a kind of in-between realm, which was where de Lubac and von Balthasar often sought to operate. Their approach is very easily summed up. I think they're saying that without God there really can't be any humanism, or humanism will always turn sinister, because if you try to take stan-dards simply from what's given to our humanity, in the end that will come down to something like an extension of human power and pride. But on the other hand, all theological discourse has to entail a form of humanism. It has to be an increased vision of what we are capable of as human beings under grace, and what is within our scope and capacity to see as human beings through divinisation.

So I return to the idea of a Christian humanism as an alternative Reformation and an alternative modernity. And here one can pick up again the relation to postmodernism: with it, Radical Orthodoxy refuses mere humanism; beyond it, it shares in the project of theologically saving humanism.

SHORTT: Let's look more at the future. Simon, what further ground would you like Radical Orthodoxy to cover?

OLIVER: It's certainly true that the *Radical Orthodoxy* collection of essays and the books we've referred to have been only a beginning. And as John has said, while critics have thought that the movement has put together a totalising vision, that was never the intention. I think we've laid down a distinctive view of the relationship between theology and philosophy, and theology and other discourses. I'd like to see this area developed a little more carefully.

SHORTT: John has already mentioned the soul. Is this another area that calls for more work?

OLIVER: Yes, and I think that a much more sophisticated view of the soul has obvious implications for the mind–body debate, but a return to the soul is a natural progression of the rejection of knowledge as representation. John said earlier that representational knowledge treats the mind as if it's just a tableau onto which things are stamped. If we can stop thinking of the soul in Cartesian terms as a human 'hard drive', then I think there could be very interesting and radical implications for theological anthropology more generally. There might also be a connection with contemporary science in this regard, because physicists claim that observation makes a difference to what is seen, at least at a quantum level. As we've suggested, many medieval theologians envisage a genuine mutual interaction between the observer (the soul) and that which is observed.

I would also like to see Radical Orthodoxy engage more particularly with scientific culture, because this tends to set the agenda of so many debates within politics, economics and ethics. My own work is currently concerned with teleological understandings of the natural, namely the idea that nature is orientated towards specific ends or goals. This ancient view has clear connections with Christian eschatology – the 'end times' towards which we move, yet which are intimated in the present. For the past two centuries teleology has been largely rejected by natural science, yet it now seems to be provoking renewed interest.

The contributors to the *Radical Orthodoxy* series have provided fresh readings of, for example, Plato or Aquinas, precisely through not reading them through the lens of modernity and rationalism. So much Anglo-American Aquinas scholarship has nullified his thoroughgoing theological, radical and inspirational edge because he has been restricted to the agenda set by modern analytic philosophy. Nevertheless, it would be beneficial for Radical Orthodoxy to reflect further on methodology and engage once again with philosophical and theological texts right through the tradition with a degree of attentiveness and care.

MILBANK: I agree. At the same time I would want to add that many people who accuse us of being simplistic tend to be rather vague. They never say *where* we're wrong.

OLIVER: That's certainly true. Underlining what John has already said, I think it's also very important to remember that, although Radical Orthodoxy has produced genealogies, we're not concerned simply with looking for devastating crux moments in the history of theology or metaphysics. Scotus's univocity of being or representational theories of knowledge are very important, but the claim that they are important moments is always qualified. Intimations of these crucial shifts can be seen much further back. But I don't think our sense of history is so bound to finding 'singular moments when the rot set in', as if everything before that moment had been pristine. Rather, one tries to identify stages when broad, long-lasting and complex trends reach some kind of clear articulation and distillation.

MILBANK: More generally, we're telling theologians to take courage. Secular thought is not something that you have to receive in a fearful and trembling fashion (reserve that attitude for divine epiphanies!). It's something that you can come to terms with and comprehend and call into question. The trouble is that if you say that you don't want theologians to have false humility, then immediately you're accused of arrogance and triumphalism. On the contrary, all we are doing is trying to work out what would make theology even minimally plausible by not accepting its ghettoisation – which is partly the result of separating off the biblical from the Greek legacy throughout our Christian culture. (This is less true, perhaps, of Jewish culture.) But, of course, we're sinful beings; so we probably do need to be more hesitant in some ways. Not probably: certainly.

OLIVER: One thing that Radical Orthodoxy has reinstated is a medieval sense of the massive intellectual demands of doing theology. The movement is often criticised for the scale of its ambition. But I think the ambition and scope of the many and various projects that might come under the banner of Radical Orthodoxy are warranted. Otherwise, theology gradually becomes consigned to a ghetto where it becomes much more straightforward, delineated in its aims and, ultimately, parochial and dull. Radical Orthodoxy has blown that apart and said that we've got to realise just how demanding and varied the subject is. A moment ago John mentioned the need for hesitancy. Maybe also a degree of humility is in order. But John says quite clearly in the opening page of *Theology and Social Theory* that this humility should not be false. In other words, we should not be humble before other discourses or the assumptions of the secular, but humble before God and our task.

MILBANK: There are a lot of difficulties about that, because you run the risk of having excessively tight parameters. I would prefer it if people could express partial allegiance to the movement or rather to the ideas it seeks to promote. Inevitably it has been seen in party terms to some degree, but I think we're trying to move away from this. There are obviously several cognate movements that have a lot of sympathy with Radical Orthodoxy. There's the Yale School and other groups in the United States, or the people in Britain who are influenced by Lash and MacKinnon and Williams, besides many influenced by currents in phenomenology or in Thomism. In relation to the latter two, Radical Orthodoxy has maybe been exercising something of a mediating role.

Recently I heard David Tracy of Chicago giving a paper in which he pretty much accepted the Radical Orthodoxy genealogy, and disavowed his earlier liberalism. So you get to the point where you've had your 'influence' and you've done one stage of your work and the hope is that it flows into a broader river. I think it was appropriate that the *Radical Orthodoxy* series stopped with twelve fairly polemical books, and that we're now going on to our new 'Illuminations' series,[9] which will feature a wider range of authors. The series includes people very sympathetic, partly sympathetic, and even hostile to us. It's trying to take this debate forward, and I hope to extend it also to cover the history of religions more than we've done hitherto.

7
David Burrell

The New Aquinas

SHORTT: Our conversation is the only one in this book devoted to a single historical figure, and some readers might feel entitled to an explanation. One could base an answer on Thomas Aquinas' importance alone: many people regard him as the greatest of all Christian theologians alongside Augustine. Besides that, there is the recent renaissance in Aquinas studies. The past few decades have seen some large shifts away from early-twentieth-century neo-Thomist interpretations, with knock-on effects for discussion of epistemology, the philosophy of mind, and interfaith dialogue, among other areas.

I'll leave you to review these and other developments in more detail, and confine myself to a few comments about what have been called the anti-Cartesian and proto-Wittgensteinian strands in Thomas' thought. The immensely influential model of the self in-augurated in the seventeenth century by Descartes sees us as isolated individuals prioritising our subjectivity above all else. This gave rise to the traditions of radical scepticism about the integrity and even the existence of the public world, and, it is regularly claimed, to the fundamental illusion of modernity: belief in the solitary self as sole arbiter of meaning and value. For his devotees, it was Wittgenstein who eventually came to the rescue by reinstating a common-sense or 'third-person' view of reality with his argument about the impossi-bility of a private language. A representative summary of this comes from the philosopher Roger Scruton.

> Surely we can ask the questions 'Why?' and 'How?' only if we have a language in which to phrase them. And no language can refer to a sphere of merely private things. Every language, even one that I

invent for myself, must be such that others can learn from it. If you can think about your thinking, then you must do so in a publicly intelligible discourse. In which case, you must be part of some 'public realm', accessible to others. This public realm is also an objective realm.[1]

Wittgenstein has also been credited with narrowing an apparent chasm between philosophy and theology. But this move is now seen more clearly to have been prefigured in medieval thought as well. Thomas would also have been suspicious of suspicion, as it were, given the emphasis he lays on how subjective experience depends on our engagement with objects around us. As Fergus Kerr suggests, Thomas 'takes for granted [a] non-subject-centred way of being in the world. We are inclined to begin with the mind, asking how our mental acts relate to the world; he begins on the contrary with the external objects which evoke intellectual activity on our part, and thus bring to fulfilment the capacities with which we are endowed.'[2]

This argument in turn has further major implications, perhaps the most important being that epistemology cannot be separated from theology, since we exercise our intellectual capacities by participating (to a very limited degree) in God's own knowledge.[3] It also prompts discussion of allied questions about the relative influence of Plato and Aristotle in Aquinas' work, and the clash between what might broadly be called Continental and Anglo-Saxon readings of the *Summa Theologiae*. That's a large menu. Perhaps I could start by asking you to recall some of the key moments in your own evolution as an Aquinas scholar.

BURRELL: It's fascinating, I think, to see within the forty-year period since Vatican II, how the manner of appropriating Aquinas has shifted so dramatically. This is a sign of what Alasdair MacIntyre would call the fertility of a tradition. Broadly speaking, the neo-Thomism of the early twentieth century saw a strong emphasis on Thomas' role as a philosopher – an emphasis deriving to a large extent from Leo XIII's 1879 encyclical *Aeterni Patris*, which spoke specifically of the philosophical potential of Thomas Aquinas as a corrective to the contemporary fascination with Descartes. As you've implied, one of the unanticipated but real results of that division between philosophy and theology was that people who'd styled themselves followers of Aquinas tried to find in him the same certitude that Descartes had promised. Bernard Lonergan, the Canadian Jesuit who taught me in Rome from 1956 to 1960, played a leading part in discrediting compartmentalisation of this kind. He tended to divide the world between those who search for truth and those who need certitude, and it's important to focus on the difference between those two verbs: 'search' is an intellectual verb; 'need' is a psychological verb. And a re-reading of Descartes' *Discourse on Method* in this regard helps us to see how profoundly this man needed certitude: he wanted to have done with a tradition which he thought was no longer useful, and set out in a new direction. That, of course, was to define the Enlightenment.

The divide between philosophy and theology can be very simply stated: it's that philosophy uses premises from reason; theology uses premises from revelation. So if there is a premise from revelation that appears in philosophy, you're in the wrong place: you have to call that theology. This was reflected in Roman Catholic higher institutions by the fact that there were always faculties of philosophy on the one hand, and faculties of theology on the other hand. Whereas in the United States, at least in non-Roman Catholic institutions, there would often be departments of philosophy and religion. One of the people who helped to narrow this gap between philosophy and theo-logy was a German layman, Josef Pieper [1904–97], who wrote in beautiful, lucid prose, unlike most Germans, and he remarked at one point that the hidden element in the philosophy of Aquinas is the presence of a free Creator.[4] Now that's a startling thing to say, because free creation cannot be proven from reason: it is a premise of faith, and, if that's the hidden premise in the philosophy of Aquinas, then, of course, we see that there can't be this division between philosophy and theology that neo-Thomism was built on.

Secondly, Aquinas' philosophy had been touted as a tool of apolo-getics: a mediating discipline for engaging with unbelievers. But in fact Thomism never was able to play that role philosophically because – as Pieper showed, I think – what were purportedly simply principles of reason in Thomistic philosophy were in fact undergirded by belief in a free Creator, so there were premises from revelation that had been smuggled into philosophy surreptitiously in order to make it go. I say smuggled, only because, in the context in which one was divided from the other, it looked like you were somehow subverting philosophy, making it into something that it wasn't, if you introduced these premises. After Vatican II, people began to appreciate that Thomas Aquinas was a searching figure, and that the Thomism which divided philosophy neatly from theology to give Cartesian certitude offered what I caricature as the answers to all the questions you never had. If you follow Bernard Lonergan, however, you're always asking questions. It's the search for understanding that matters, not the need for certitude.

So he and other pioneers such as Marie-Dominique Chenu, Dominique Dubarle and Martin Grabmann were arguing that Aquinas' prime motivation was with understanding the revelation that has been given to us. One of the things that happened can best be illustrated with reference to a book by a Dutchman, Rudi te Velde, called *Participation and Substantiality in Aquinas*. Building on the work of others, he showed how at crucial points Aquinas, who had been identified in the earlier mode of Thomism as an Aristotelian, had had recourse to Neoplatonic works in order to search for the best way of understanding the revelation of faith. Among these texts were the *Liber de Causis*, an Islamic adaptation of parts of Proclus, the fifth-century Neoplatonist, which had been translated into Latin from Arabic. So it was the Islamic thinkers who were showing Aquinas the way in which he might use Greek philosophy, whether it be Aristotelian or Platonic, in order to develop his understanding of matters of faith.

In that spirit, then, I was led in the 1980s and 1990s to understand how deeply Aquinas' achievement in the *Summa Theologiae* had been in dialogue with Jewish and Muslim thinkers such as Maimonides and Avicenna. I discovered that the classical synthesis of Christian theology that everyone recognises the *Summa Theologiae* to be was already an interfaith, intercultural achievement. And the reason why that hadn't been seen by Western Thomists had to do with the euro-centrism of their enquiry into the medieval period. The irony was that if they'd counted the citations he has to Maimonides, to Avicenna, and to other Muslims such as Averroës, they would have seen how influential these people were to his formation. This is especially true of Maimonides, who lived in the Islamicate, so he could also be called an Islamic philosopher, even though he was Jewish, if we think of the word 'Islamic' as more a cultural adjective and 'Muslim' as a religious adjective.

Maimonides' goal was to show his student Joseph that one could still be a Torah believer and engage in philosophy, which was exactly the goal of Aquinas. And Thomas read Maimonides' famous *Guide for the Perplexed* as soon as it was translated from the original Arabic into Hebrew, and then into Latin. He read it and responded – taking issue with Maimonides at several points, but that's how philosophers demonstrate their respect for one another – and showed how he himself had adopted the very strategies that Maimonides had worked out to reconcile faith and reason. This amounts to an amazing cross-fertilisation between religious traditions in an age that could not by any stretch of the imagination be called ecumenical. So at the same time as they were pouring boiling oil on each other's heads in Akko, sometime capital of the Crusader Kingdom, back in Naples they were reading texts from other traditions, because of this medieval sense that humankind can reach the truth. And as I've said, we've come to a richer awareness of this over the past twenty years, thanks to the work of te Velde and others such as Michel Corbin, a French Jesuit. For these scholars and myself, the relationship between reason and revelation in Aquinas is like lacing shoelaces.

To sum up, then: the earlier premise of the Thomism that sought to divide philosophy from theology and let philosophy be a mediating instrument for people who didn't have the faith – that premise has been shattered. And the tide began to turn with that almost offhand comment of Josef Pieper.

SHORTT: Before we go further, it should therefore be emphasised that the 'new' Aquinas, as we've termed him, is in your view the old one; and this is of much more than historical interest alone, of course.

BURRELL: In our own context the issue is postmodernism, which I think can be seen in a benign perspective, despite the fact that it's often derided. One such perspective can be traced back to the section of Newman's *Grammar of Assent*,[5] in which he reminds us that every enquiry has a fiduciary basis, a basis in trust, which of course is something Descartes couldn't possibly have countenanced. In our own day, Newman's insight has been strongly echoed in the work of philosophers such as Hans-Georg Gadamer.

Here's where things get interesting. If you are a firm believer in Descartes, and hold that reason has defined foundational premises that are self-evident, and then you discover that there are no such things, the rug is pulled from under you. You might duly conclude that anything goes. On the other hand, if you are someone who has already subscribed, I would say wisely, to both Newman's and Gadamer's point that all enquiry is fiduciary, then the issue isn't whether you have faith at the beginning or not: it's what kind of faith you have. So the business of letting faith and reason mutually fructify each other is the contribution of postmodernism to the understanding of Aquinas.

SHORTT: I mentioned earlier the argument that Aquinas thinks of epistemology as inseparable from theology, and you've outlined some of the ramifications of this. Another concerns Aquinas' so-called Five Ways for demonstrating the existence of God. According to the school of thought you've criticised, it's a mistake to think of these as exercises in neutral or pre-theological reasoning, still less as an arrogant bid to sideline the data of revelation – as some critics, especially those with Barthian backgrounds, have suggested. The reason for this, in a nutshell, is that it can only be on the basis of what owes its existence to God that God's existence can be brought to light for us. Moreover, since Aquinas quotes Scripture itself – 'The fool says in his heart, "There is no God"' (Ps. 14:1) – to maintain that the existence of God is not self-evident, one could also say that the Five Ways are designed in part to safeguard God's mysteriousness and transcendence.

Fergus Kerr sees the matter as follows. 'Thomas is steering his way between the claim that argument for God's existence is unnecessary because God's existence is so manifest in the natural world, and the claim that argument is impossible because God's existence is solely a matter of supernatural revelation. He wants to deny both that God's presence is transparently obvious to "natural reason" and that God's presence is totally hidden except to "supernatural faith". Characteristically Thomas is searching for a middle way.'[6]

As I've said in the preface to this book, my main object is to give my interviewees a chance to air their own views, but I think we should mention other commentators who take a different view from you. I have in mind someone like Timothy McDermott, who translated the *Summa* into English in the 1960s,[7] and who is happier than you and Fergus Kerr to distinguish between philosophy and theology in Aquinas. McDermott isn't in any doubt that Aquinas is fundamentally writing as a committed believer – but a believer who wants to argue that some things are capable of being demonstrated by muscular reason, and some things aren't, and who wants to distinguish between the two. So to start with, McDermott and other philosophers schooled in the Anglo-Saxon tradition such as Herbert McCabe and Anthony Kenny would probably want to go back and challenge Pieper's comment that free creation is the premise of faith, as you've put it. I think they'd say, No, it's a conclusion of reasoning: for Aquinas, our apprehension of truth rests on a metaphysical realism, which in turn implies belief in God. They would add that the opening sections of a work like the *Summa Contra Gentiles* has a strong apologetic element: it's saying to Jews, Muslims and other non-Christians, What beliefs do we have in common, and what

132   *David Burrell*

belongs specifically to the Christian dispensation? Moreover, McDermott would see this as a symptom of a wider problem about some of the things you've said, on the grounds that postmodernism is a slippery slope.

It's evident that you regard this as a flawed criticism. Faith and reason are not mutually exclusive. Is there anything more you can say to win over the sceptics?

BURRELL: Yes. Of course you're going to ask yourself whether or not there are things you can discuss with non-believers on the neutral grounds of reason. But at the same time the people who pretend that the *Summa Contra Gentiles* is a purely philosophical work in the sense of Descartes are displaying their hermeneutical innocence. They're insufficiently aware of the environment in which that work was produced. As I've said, the irony is that the postmodern environment in which people move today is one which is much more accepting of fiduciary or faith-type premises than the Enlightenment tried to be, and therefore much closer in spirit to the medieval period. So don't be surprised when Josef Pieper comes along and says that the hidden premise of your philosophical labours is your faith in a free creation of the universe. And if it is free, then it cannot be demonstrated; though Aquinas certainly thought we could prove the need for a contingent universe to be originated by One whose existence is necessary, following Avicenna. But *origination* of that sort falls short of *creation*, as Jews, Muslims and Christians confess it.

SHORTT: Let's pursue a subject you've already touched on: the Islamic connection in Aquinas studies. After you'd been teaching philosophy for some time you also became an Arabist, and you now spend about half your year at Tantur, in the Palestinian territories between Bethlehem and Jerusalem. Can you say some more about how your work has been nourished by contacts with Muslims and Jews?

BURRELL: A little autobiography might be helpful. When I was chairing the theology department at the University of Notre Dame in the 1970s, a Jewish Studies post was created. So I sat down with colleagues such as John Howard Yoder, Stanley Hauerwas, Robert Wilken and Joseph Blenkinsopp. We didn't want to have a rabbi off in the corner doing rabbinics: we wanted this person to become part of our wider theological enterprise. So we revamped our Hebrew Scriptures, New Testament and Early Church programme, and put them together in a creative mix called 'Judaism and Christianity in Antiquity'. That showed me the theological potential for Christians to understand their roots in the Hebrew Scriptures, in the covenant that God makes with Israel.

Our initiative followed the Vatican II declaration *Nostra Aetate*, in which the Church belatedly acknowledged that Jews will always be God's people, and God will always be their God. This is not conditional, like the promise of the land, but unconditional. I began to see in a new way that we can only really understand the Christian efflorescence after the death and resurrection of Jesus as preaching to the entire universe the God of Abraham, Isaac and Jacob, or as Paul puts it in Romans 11–13, where he struggles with his relationship to his own people: this new faith is grafted onto the trunk of Israel. So it was the Jewish–Christian understanding that really opened my mind and heart. Then in 1980 I moved to be Rector at Tantur for a year, and realised the importance of drawing the Muslim element into the equation. So when I arrived in Jerusalem I immediately learned enough Hebrew to get around the street, and in the second year I took my Arabic course in Hebrew, because the two languages have a very similar structure. I always use the expression Jewish–Christian–Muslim, not because I think there always have to be three people at the table, but because I recognise, as every married couple recognises, that bipolar relationships often need a third – so if you're trying to understand the relationship of Judaism to Christianity, triangulating with Islam helps a lot. If you're trying to understand the Christian–Muslim dimension, triangulating with Judaism helps a lot too.

To me, as I've said, the primary example of such encounters has been Aquinas, who, although he taught in Paris, came from the Mediterranean world. And when we study the map it looks as though the Mediterranean separated Europe from North Africa and from the Islamic world. But in an age when land travel was very difficult, and people didn't have to reach their destinations immediately, sea travel was the easiest way to get about. The Crusades were taking place at this time, of course, and we should never forget that the fall-out of war often includes cultural exchange. I came to discover that Thomas Aquinas' discussion in the early questions of the *Summa* on the nature of God, and about how we can talk about God, was dominated by one single concern: how to reconcile the unity of God expressed to us in the *Shema* in Deuteronomy 6:4, with the trinitarian revelation distinctive to Christianity. How is this done? Well, as people say about porcupines having sex: very carefully. And the startling thing to remember is that it took us Christians four centuries, namely from the death and resurrection of Jesus until the Council of Chalcedon, to get straight about the heart of this trinitarian revelation of God, or as I prefer to say, God's triunity.

It took so long because we were concerned that whatever we said about God as Father, Son and Spirit should never contradict the *Shema*, the foundation of Jewish and Muslim faith: that God is one. And the scholar who is best on this balancing act is the American Franciscan, Thomas Weinandy. His original work, *Does God Change?*, almost reads like a detective story as to the unfolding of Christian doctrine up to Chalcedon. It is not, as the title might suggest, a tract in process theology; rather, it's a response to the simple question about whether the incarnation entailed change in God. And he argues that you need sensitive philosophical tools to answer this. He's written a second book, *Can God Suffer?*, which also shows how Christianity uses the available philosophical tools, often transforming them, which is what Aquinas is always doing, in a bid to articulate the distinctiveness of the trinitarian revelation.

SHORTT: So to coin a familiar idea, Christians can learn much from seeing themselves as others see them.

BURRELL: Yes. It's only by trying to understand how others see us from their faith tradition that we grow in our own faith tradition. Faith traditions have always been assimilative. I've spoken here about the importance of the assimilation of philosophical tools in order to come to greater understanding, but I've also pointed out that the Christian tradition was deeply embedded in the Jewish tradition, because God, our God, is one. Similarly, to be aware of the way other people hear us and see us is going to bring us to a richer appreciation of the revelation that we've received.

Jean Daniélou, a French Jesuit writing in the 1950s on the theology of mission, put it beautifully. It's not that our missionary efforts have always gone awry, he suggested: many of them did, but many were fruitful. Yet the fruitful ones stopped thinking of bringing Christ to India – because we inevitably brought Portugal right along too – but rather started thinking about finding Christ already there. How so? In a very simple fact which we associate with reader–response criticism: that if I start talking about Jesus to someone who's been brought up a Buddhist, he or she is going to ask me questions, and in my attempt to respond to them, I'm going to discover a new face of Jesus.

This came home to me dramatically in 1975, when I was going to teach for the first time at a seminary in Bangladesh, where 92 per cent of the surrounding culture is Muslim. And on the way there I was in Uganda, to celebrate seventy-five years of Catholic Christianity in the southern diocese of Mbarara. I met some Missionaries of Africa, and asked one of them how he thought the pioneers at the turn of the twentieth century had been so effective. 'From what we can tell,' he replied, 'they started by listening to the people's stories. And then the missionaries would say, "Well, you know, we have some stories like that. There was this man Abraham whom God called out", etc.' And all of a sudden I saw that this situation recalled that of Paul in Romans 11–13.

So the sense that we can better understand ourselves by thinking about how we're seen through the eyes of others, helped me to appreciate how crucially important the presence of Islam had been for medieval Christianity in the estimation of those scholars who were open to it. Of course, many people saw Islam purely as a menace, and it was indeed a threat militarily. Furthermore, Judaism and Christianity can be seen to relate to one another in the sense that they share a large chunk of Scripture, whereas Islam arrives on the scene in about 620, after what the Church had determined was the end of revelation, and announcing a new revelation. This was a kick in the groin to Christianity. And then within a century after the Prophet's death, Muslims had fairly well dominated the civilised parts of the then known world, at a time when there were cow paths in Paris.

So Christianity was faced with trying to understand itself in relation to Islam. Admittedly, we did a very poor job for many centuries. And partly this was geo-political, because until Columbus' voyage Europe had received its luxury commodities from Asia across the Silk Road. But the Silk Road went through one Muslim domain after another which taxed the goods: Columbus secured financial backing for his adventure because the elite in Europe wanted a tax-free route to the goods of the Orient. In fact, of course, Columbus found something hugely more significant, namely two continents that Europeans could exploit. So once the Ottoman forces had been defeated at Vienna in the mid-sixteenth century, the West could afford to turn its back on Islam and begin to exploit the New World systematically, and therein lay a major source of the West's development.

When Napoleon landed at Alexandria in 1799 and began, along with the British in India, the colonisation of the once proud Muslim world, we started to get a whole new dynamic between Islam and Christianity, and one, of course, which built up the resentment within Islam that has grown exponentially in our own era. But the important thing was that during the Crusades, there were also creative thinkers who were trying to understand what the significance of this other religious faith was to Christianity.

SHORTT: And this tradition can be nurtured, even in the sombre climate we're facing now. Among the rays of hope to have emerged over the past few decades, I think you'd instance the friendship between Pope Paul VI and Louis Massignon, the renowned French Islamicist.

BURRELL: Yes. Massignon can be credited with convincing a great many people that Christian–Muslim contacts should not be about a struggle for supremacy by one side or the other, because both share the startling belief that everything around us is the free creation of God. And my own more recent scholarship of the medieval period has been to show how, linked as they were on this one point, they nonetheless follow the contours of their respective traditions, articulating the belief in different ways. And that's why in my first book, *Knowing the Unknowable God*,[8] I focused on Maimonides, Aquinas and Avicenna, because there was a matter of seeing how these different traditions talked about God and naming God; and in my subsequent work, *Freedom and Creation in the Three Traditions*,[9] I focused on Maimonides, Aquinas and Al-Ghazali, another Muslim thinker, to talk about how it was that the traditions they represented were united in trying to show that a free Creator would not just introduce a loose cannon into Hellenic philosophy. And several centuries later a pillar of Catholic spirituality like John of the Cross was producing works that display a heavy debt to Sufi and Jewish mystical thought.

SHORTT: Will you say a word about your current activities as a kind of ambassador for interfaith understanding?

BURRELL: It's best exemplified in a group called Scriptural Reasoning spearheaded by David Ford, the Regius Professor of Divinity at Cambridge, Timothy Winter, a Muslim colleague of his, and Peter Ochs, a Jewish scholar from the University of Virginia. We're trying to show, in a step beyond the Enlightenment into the postmodern world, that our Scriptures are relevant to our reasoning. It's not two hermetically sealed compartments – reason here and faith over there. Our Scriptures are relevant to our reasoning, and if we try to take on sensitive issues such as whether we should have embarked on the Iraq war, there is much that we have in common to shed light on the discussion.

SHORTT: Another subject in Thomas' thought that's received fresh attention lately is natural law, and this, too, offers scope for promoting interfaith ties.

BURRELL: Yes, and I see a further challenge to black and white distinctions between philosophy and theology in this strand of Aquinas' work. In referring to natural law, Thomas was talking about the fact that we cannot simply decide the rightness or wrongness of certain actions. Take abortion. You can argue as an ethicist as to whether abortion can be permitted, but you cannot say that abortion is simply a matter of choice, for the simple reason that certain ethical notions are built into the very grammar of our discourse. It's not for us to overthrow them – even though in practice, of course, we tend to blur the categories when it suits us.

This represents a kind of Wittgensteinian reading of Aquinas, which I elaborated in my book *Aquinas: God and Action*.[10] But grammar doesn't tell the whole story: there's also the question of how these 'grammatical' notions are employed by us. And that was Wittgenstein's whole point: it's not just language, but the *use* of language. If they are employed in a faith context, then Thomas Aquinas offers us the stellar example of how someone, in trying to use philosophy to search for the truth of our faith, will have to transform ordinary philosophical categories. And that transforming is to me the difference between the work I do – philosophical theology – and standard philosophy of religion. Because the tendency of philosophers of religion is to think that their philosophical categories will work everywhere and there's no need to transform them to talk about God. To my mind, the result of that is a procrustean picture of God – in effect an idol. If you've got to fit God into your philosophical categories, then it's no longer God you're talking about. And interestingly enough, something analogous can happen with ethical categories which have emerged in a climate without reference to a transcendent Creator – but that is a longer story for another day, yet one which I have tried to broach in my book *Faith and Freedom: An Interfaith Perspective*.[11]

SHORTT: This brings us back to your difficulties with certain philosophical approaches to Thomas, including some from the analytic tradition. Without getting submerged in technical debate, one might cite the example of Aquinas' description of God as *ipsum esse subsistens*, or self-subsistent being. For an agnostic philosopher such as Anthony Kenny, who has a very high regard for Aquinas generally, but employs categories deriving from Frege, the term 'self-subsistent being' is 'sophistry and illusion'.[12] As you've said, the case for the defence would maintain that a unique area of discussion requires that categories be stretched in a unique way. So Aquinas insists that 'being' cannot be used univocally of God and the world, because God has 'doing' or 'giving' being, while we and the rest of creation have 'done' or 'given' being. As Timothy McDermott puts it, 'What sort of being does God display? Anything Aquinas tries to say about it that would involve attributing a characteristic to God won't work, except the term self-subsistent being. For things to exist, they need "favour". But for Aquinas we don't or can't ask what favours God, because he simply is a universal favouring.'[13]

BURRELL: Precisely. As a matter of fact, Tony Kenny adopts the same approach in a number of areas, and I think that here again, what we have to do is see how Aquinas didn't just throw the formula of self-subsistent being on the table as an answer to a question you never had. It was worked out and elaborated in the context of the distinction between essence and existence which he inherited from Avicenna, who had introduced it in response to the question about a free Creator, but which Aquinas then went on to transform.

The whole philosophical enquiry was designed to articulate what could possibly be the relationship between the Creator and all of creation. That's the crucial thing. If we go back to Pieper, the hidden element in the philosophy of Aquinas is creation. One of my major gripes with most philosophers of religion today is that they haven't faced the unique causality which is required of a Creator to create the universe. They'll talk about creation, but they won't explore it philosophically. This to me is a huge lacuna.

Aquinas took it on, and it is at this point that he needed to have recourse to Neoplatonic categories to talk about a cause of being. Those are all intra-philosophical questions of great intricacy, which Kant negatively signalled in proscribing any talk of God in causal terms. But they come back fundamentally to this distinction of Creator from creation. The person who's been an ever fertile guide to me in this area is a phenomenologist at the Catholic University in America, Robert Sokolowski, who wrote a wonderful book entitled *The God of Faith and Reason*. It should be required reading for philosophers of religion, because he notes that the distinction of the Creator from creation is *sui generis*, in other words that God cannot be distinguished from the world in the same way that you and I are distinguished from one another. The things in the world are distinct from one another; they are separate indeed from one another in a way that the universe itself cannot be said to be distinct from God.

Many Christian thinkers are so frightened by the bugbear of pantheism that they will crudely and naively talk about God and the universe as two entities. The classical Christian tradition embodied in

Aquinas is then carried on by someone like Meister Eckhart, a fellow Dominican, a century later, who also struggles with trying to articulate the *sui generis* quality of this relationship. It's well expressed by Sara Grant in her book *Towards an Alternative Theology*, which draws on her study of Sankara, a variety of Hindu philosophy. She characterises the unique bond between Creator and creation as a non-reciprocal relation of dependence. All our relations of dependence are, of course, reciprocal. It's illuminated in the Arab world, where people's names change when they become parents. Let's say a couple have a child called Rasheed. The father then becomes Abu Rasheed, and the mother's name becomes Um Rasheed. So it reminds us that even though you might think the child depends solely on its parents, they, of course, experience a whole new identity through the birth of their child. So every relationship between us in the world is a reciprocal one. In Thomas' view, it's only creation which entails a non-reciprocal relation of dependence. And, of course, some modern theologians took umbrage at this idea, and invented process theology, which pictures God as changing along with the universe. We needn't discuss the inanity of that.

There's something I'd like to add in passing about style. I've been quite critical of a certain mode of Thomism, but I am now excited about the constructive approaches to Aquinas as a writer, teacher and transformer of philosophical categories into theology. And I want to mention a Dominican friend in Jerusalem, Olivier-Thomas Venard, and his book *Une saison en enfer*, which is being translated. What he has taken on in the spirit of a literary critic is the crucial relevance of Aquinas' status as a teacher to the composition of his works. And Venard makes the unlikely comparison between the poetry of Rimbaud and the prose of the *Summa Theologiae*, which has often been seen as pedestrian, but which to my mind is lapidary and incisive.

Aquinas' bringing together of faith and reason provides a great challenge to the world today. It's a place in which, after all, pure reason didn't work too well in the twentieth century, when more people were killed in the name of pseudo-scientific ideologies than the rest of human history. On the other hand, organised religion hasn't offered a very good example either, because it can also easily be hijacked by nationalist movements, as with the Israeli settlers, or al-Qaeda, or the Christian fundamentalists from Texas who give unstinting support to the State of Israel, while overlooking the fact that the promise of the land is conditional, as I've mentioned.

SHORTT: **It's based on the need for good stewardship.**

BURRELL: Yes. If you don't care for the stranger in your midst, if you don't take care of the widows and orphans, if you don't keep the Torah, then don't expect to live at peace in the land. And this emphasis is there throughout the Scriptures. In the end, neither people who believe in reason, nor people who try to follow a way of faith, can be very proud of their record. We must humbly acknowledge this in the face of the devastation in the world today.

That's why I think that the work of people who are trying to show the interaction of faith and reason is so important. The Radical Orthodoxy movement, for example, which turns around the names of John Milbank and Catherine Pickstock, may adopt a confrontational approach[14] to the kind of Thomism which divided philosophy from theology, but I think this group is teaching us to read in a whole new way, and again through postmodern eyes, the relevance of Aquinas for our time. But let's move away from Aquinas to the larger questions of how we use reason to help understand faith, and then we can yoke faith to the mode of reasoning we find in Scripture to help understand how we should proceed. That, it seems to me, is the crucial next step.

8
Jean-Luc Marion

God and the Gift: A Continental Perspective

SHORTT: Given the well-known differences between Continental and Anglo-Saxon approaches to philosophy, it's good to have a French thinker such as yourself represented in a project principally devoted to figures from North America and Britain. Much of your scholarship in areas such as metaphysics and phenomenology is exceptionally intricate, and it wouldn't be appropriate to discuss it in detail here. But I hope that our conversation can offer a few tools for looking at common conundrums in a fresh way nonetheless.

Close to the heart of your work lies a critique of ontotheology already mentioned in my preface,[1] and two corollaries you draw from this. The first is that the category of being is not a helpful or even a necessary means of helping us to talk about God – indeed that much theology and philosophy of religion has fed the naive idea that God is a being operating on the same territory as creatures. The second is that the notion of the gift or of 'givenness' provides greater purchase on ultimate reality – and, indeed, this-worldly reality too – than does being.

Before coming to this, let's start with your account of rationality itself. Generalising very broadly, one might say that in the Continental tradition philosophy has tended to be thought of as an activity of the whole person, and as consciously or unconsciously shaped by the will and emotions of the philosopher. As the Anglican theologian John Macquarrie describes it, 'reality is, so to speak, behind us in the life of the subject rather than spread before us in the objective world.'[2] I know that some people would want to take the argument a stage further, and argue that they are subverting or recasting common assumptions about what subjectivity and objectivity really consist in. At any event, I think you consider prevailing understandings of rationality should be broadened.

MARION: Yes. It's important to emphasise that I'm not moving *beyond* rationality. I disagree deeply about the opposition between faith and reason. And I don't want to bridge that gap by saying simply that faith should always try to get support in reason. Most of the time when people say there is no contradiction between reason and faith, they understand things in this way – that we have to prove by reason what we already believe by faith. On the contrary, the common understanding of reason is too narrow, because what we mean by reason is, first of all, the kind of rationality that is framed to make sense out of the most formal objects in logic, mathematics and physics – that is, to material that can be reduced to a collection of concepts, the best example being the computer. Computer science is all about reducing any information to two bits: the letter A and zero. Everything can be encoded in this binary form. This model of rationality is based on the primacy of the concept, and on the possibility of interpreting anything in terms of quantity.

What is left aside by this kind of rationality is what cannot be encoded: sensation, for example – termed subjective sensation, but better described as personal and non-abstract – and the whole field of the human sciences, where we have to interpret, and things can't be predicted. So the arts are a part of rationality: they provide a way to understand what can't be encoded. Ethics provides a way of making sense of the behaviour of human beings, which can't be understood in a reductive way: people behave as they do because they have commitments and desires: all that is also part of rationality. Politics, too, is (or aspires to be) rational. But it's a rationality based at another level – interest, desire, obligation, commitments, ideals and so on.

SHORTT: And you would want to develop this by saying that there is nothing more rational than religion.

MARION: Yes. Religion deals with real drives, real needs, real hopes, thereby giving rise to new dimensions. The question is how to understand what is at stake here, which in no way can be taken for an illusion. The only strategy some people have when they don't understand something is to be dismissive. At the moment religion forms one of the greatest challenges to the dominant, but narrow, models of rationality. It must be quite a shock to devotees of such models that religion, which was supposed to just fade away from the scene and die, is still very much alive.

SHORTT: You stress that you are a philosopher rather than a theologian, and apart from the part-time chair you've held in the Divinity School at Chicago University since the early 1990s, you've always worked in philosophy faculties in France – at Poitiers and Nanterre earlier in your career, and since 1985 at the Sorbonne in Paris. In 1992 you won the Grand Prix de Philosophie de L'Académie Française. Yet you are also known for a full-bloodied commitment to Roman Catholicism, and Catholicism of a traditionalist kind. This naturally prompts questions about how you picture the links between philosophy and Christianity.

MARION: That's too broad a question for me to answer easily. I hope that I am both a serious philosopher and a committed Catholic. I think there is no need to downsize one of the two options, and there is no contradiction between them. If by 'traditionalist' you mean someone deeply wedded to certain forms of neo-Thomism, for example, then I don't recognise myself as a traditionalist Catholic. Definitely not. I try to be a loyal Catholic. I do assume the truth of the creed without hedging and qualifications. But my Catholic tradition is that of both Chateaubriand and Bernanos, Montaigne and Pascal, so I have a very broad acceptance of Catholicism, which is after all its very definition. There are many rooms in the house of the Father. And the other point, as I've indicated, is that I don't think faith should be seen as beyond rationality, but as another way of being rational. In essence, faith and religious revelation allow us to go a bit further in the use of rationality, not only focusing on the external world and on the domains of quantity, measure and technology, but also to be more aware of, or less blind to, the world of our inner lives. And so I think simply that there is a division of labour here: science deals with a part of the world; philosophy with a broader part of the world; and theology, which is enforced by a Christian life in my case, allows us to have access to another level of reality.

To get into more detail, I began my career as a historian of philosophy, working on the role of Descartes in making possible the rise of the modern technological world, and the relation between Cartesian and Aristotelian models of science, and on the respective ontologies of Descartes and Heidegger. As you have explained, my early books in these areas are highly technical. The important thing for our purposes is that I became interested in what can and cannot be established by metaphysics. And clearly for me neither the question of being nor the question of knowing in a scientific way could ever reach the question of God. That was the main result of my enquiry. The question of God is far beyond the grasp of either science and metaphysics, and even the question of being.

And I started to study that with my two first theoretical books, which were *The Idol and Distance*[3] and *God Without Being*.[4] For *The Idol and Distance*, which appeared in 1977, the focus was on the death of God, in Nietzsche's phrase. What could be meant by this term? I studied Nietzsche, Hölderlin, Pseudo-Dionysius, and also the writings of my former teacher, Derrida, and of Heidegger and Levinas on the ontological difference. My conclusion was that if we assume God is dead, we can only be referring to a god defined in conceptual form, in other words to an idol. The 'God' we are talking about denotes a precise concept, a finite concept, one among the possible interpretations of the essence of God. And so atheism, to be rational, has to be limited to this or that precise definition: God as a first mover, God as the eye of being, God as the foundation of morals, God as the meaning of history, and so on. You can criticise those definitions of God and say, '*That* definition of God is dead'; but you can never thereby close the question of God *tout court*. Because each time you have criticised one definition of God, in front of you there are all the remaining possible definitions of God, and, by definition, God being infinite, the possibilities of getting new definitions of God are infinite too. So therefore 'the death of God' means either nothing, from a rational point of view, or it means the *possibility* of God, and this has always been exactly the meaning of apophatic or negative theology: namely, any name, any definition, that can be applied to God, can also be denied of God, because God is beyond not only definition but the denial of any definition.

And if you stick to a concept of God and insist that there is nothing beyond it, you are simply reinforcing idolatry. Idolatry is to say that we have in our possession a comprehensive definition of God, and this, by definition, is wrong. *God Without Being* dealt with this subject. My argument was that until Thomas Aquinas, all Christian theologians assumed that a better possible name of God (which was not the real name of God, because God is beyond any name) was the Good. God was the final object of desire. God was love because he was the Good, and no one could refrain from desiring God because God was the source of the Good. This was in fact a point shared by Greek philosophy and Christian thought. And there was a moment in the history of thought – I think this was with Albert the Great and Thomas Aquinas, and perhaps Maimonides – when as a result of a certain understanding of Aristotle, it came to be assumed that God should be defined first by being.

On the basis of this, the Thomist and other schools of philosophy – early modern, modern and postmodern – have shared this conception of God against the background of being. The first question about God was not, Should we desire God? or Is God good? but *Does God exist?* It's as if God were being asked to give us his credentials by producing a passport to give him access to territory marked out by us. If he couldn't do so, he was ruled out by our canons of reason. And I decided to deconstruct that, for many reasons. First of all, does the category of being tell us something about God at all? Is the transcendence of God a question of being or not? And if we stick to what being means for classical philosophy and modern metaphysics, we are talking about a univocal usage: this pen *is* in the same way as God *is*.

SHORTT: Although Thomas denies that, doesn't he?[5]

MARION: Thomas, he's a saint, that makes a difference! Thomas indeed was not at that level – he was far beyond it – but I'm not referring only to Thomas: I'm referring to modern philosophy and modern Christian philosophy as well, in which everything about God is supposed to be intelligible from the point of view of being, and I disagreed with that, arguing that in fact being does not allow us to understand God and to have access to God. After all, the Christian revelation is not about the being of God. It is the fact that, God being granted, we have to have access to him or her, we have to love him. That is the point.

SHORTT: Would you defend your intellectual genealogy a bit more here? As you know, there are plenty of people, both inside and outside the tent of Radical Orthodoxy, who deny that the tradition put 'the Good' above 'being' before Aquinas – the Cappadocians didn't, Augustine didn't: the classical Christian tradition in general thought that God was equally good, existent, true, unified – that all these transcendentals were one thing in God, simple in God, and that the really crucial shift is not in terms of where you put the stress on one transcendental or other: it's towards univocity, it's when you say that God exists or is good in the same sense that a finite being has these qualities, but to an infinite degree. And that has the consequence of meaning that you can't any more maintain the divine simplicity.

MARION: Generally speaking, it is true that before Aquinas, God was both seen as good, one, existent, true, beautiful and so on. And this continued after him. But before him, I do think that the primacy of charity and the Good was quite obvious. It is clear in Bonaventure, it is clear in Anselm, where the question of being ends up in the question of the *bonum*. Nothing better than God can be sought. This is obviously true with Pseudo-Dionysius. In the case of Augustine, what is very striking is that the way to aim for God is by saying that God is *idipsum*, the self-same.[6] The *idipsum* does not refer to the *esse* of God. This does not mean that God is not, but that the transcendence of God cannot be aimed at only with the transcendental of being. And you are completely right to say that a large part of this debate is about the univocity, or equivocity, of what we predicate both to the world and to God. My point is just that it is much easier to envision the transcendence of God according to love than according to being, because we know that charity and the Good are far above us, far transcendent to us. If we want to achieve non-univocity, it's more reasonable and more rational in relation to the Good than in relation to being. It is simply that. And when philosophy and theology decided to give up the primacy of the Good, the result was indeed not a complete collapse, but the transcendence of God was much more difficult to understand, and the consequence was ontotheology, that is, God's being part and parcel of the general being of the world.

God Without Being was well received by postmodernist reviewers, and criticised by Thomists. But over a decade on, the stance I adopted has become pretty standard, even among Thomists. They all agree – at least the best of them agree – that, for Thomas, 'being' does not carry the same meaning as elsewhere in the tradition. If the book has a polemical edge, it is aimed at Heidegger, who thought that his own attack on ontotheology was the first there had been. Heideggerians were put out when I argued that this was untrue. At any rate, I do feel that my position is in fact the only one to face the actual situation of philosophy after deconstruction and postmodernism. Because there may be an idolatry of being as well. And as I've indicated, the Christian revelation is not about being: it's about charity.

SHORTT: So we're clear that Aquinas' teaching on the being of God, though not questionable in itself, nevertheless fed a tradition which you regard as highly damaging. But if Heidegger was too hasty in dismissing all earlier eras of Christian thought, for reasons also cited in my preface, what's wrong with saying that the ontological difference *can* be read theologically, provided the right philosophical safeguards are in place? David Burrell, for example, is happy to avow that God has the being that it's appropriate for God to have – giving being as against given being.[7]

MARION: I don't disagree. You can indeed reinterpret being and meta-physics from a more Christian point of view. It's just that we don't really need to do so. In any event, even if we feel ourselves impelled to do this we don't do so from the point of view of being: in fact to do that we have to step back from pure ontology and the pure question of being and to invest on being transcendence, infinity, charity, creation, participation, and so forth, all notions which are not in-cluded in being. You can indeed say that there is no contradiction between a certain assumption about being and Christian faith. But this does not mean that you understand Christian faith from the point of view of being. It means that you understand being from the point of view of Christian faith.

SHORTT: Let's use what you've said to explore a core element of your thought, namely the call or the gift. Would you describe how this idea evolved?

MARION: I was pushed in this direction through my studies of phenom-enology, and especially of Husserl. I was very struck by the discovery that Husserl, though he draws strong distinctions between what he calls immanent knowledge and transcendent knowledge, the world and the mind, the concept on one side and intuition on the other, nev-ertheless uses the same word to describe the phenomena at stake: not 'being', because it's not precise enough, but the German *Gegebenheit*: in French, *donation*, or the less satisfactory *donnété*; in English, 'given-ness'. For Husserl, givenness is the best term we have for saying that something has happened. Take an intuition, for example. We don't know what the content of intuition is, because it's very subjective. We don't know exactly what is experienced in intuition, but we know that intuition occurs. There is a givenness about it. Even something absurd, for instance, has to be given, because to see that it is absurd and to make the distinction between an absurd statement and a formally cor-rect statement we have to allow that the absurd statement should be given to us. And we cannot say the absurd statement 'is', precisely because its very absurdity suggests that it cannot be. So for Husserl, givenness is the most profound feature of any phenomenon.

I tried to follow all this up, and my point was that, if you read care-fully both Heidegger and Husserl, you discover that although they claim to discuss the issue of being, of reality and so on, the most pro-found level of their analysis refers to givenness, and in Heidegger, for instance, it is an analysis employing the term '*es gibt*', which is often translated in English as 'there is' – unsatisfactorily, to my mind, because the German does not employ the verb to be. '*Es gibt*' is more accurately rendered as 'it gives'. And in French we have the expression *ce que cela donne*, something that can be compared to German, but in Heidegger it's very clear when he says *es gibt* that it's to avoid saying 'it is', to say something more radical. So my point, in my first book on phenomenology, *Reduction and Givenness*,[8] was that the final goal of phenomenology is to reach the given, the givenness. I suggested that perhaps there is a new definition of subjectivity, whatever you may call that, which is not, I think, or I am, but *I receive, I get*. What do I get? I don't know; but the point is, something has happened.

SHORTT: So the gift, givenness, is the primordial category, and it's not ontological – rather, it's *more* than ontological.

MARION: More than ontological, yes, since being is only a case of the gift. So I referred to a position which is both in Heidegger, in Husserl, in Levinas, in many others: the idea of the call as forming the fundamental structure of consciousness. Consciousness is the result of the call. Human beings are traditionally described as the creatures endowed with *logos*, and this has usually been glossed as a capacity to reason and speak. But in fact our first experience of speech is not because *we* speak: it's because we hear other people speak. It always starts that way. And it is not even that we are conscious before we speak; we are conscious of ourselves because first we listen to other people speaking to each other and to us. To talk of a call does not imply that I understand it, or that it's what I think it is. When you speak to a baby, you don't say anything. What is very striking is that the baby knows you are saying something to him or to her, and this is the beginning of their self-consciousness. What is important is not the content of the call, it is that it comes before me.

So my central move was to draw a correlation between the call and the given. And from that everything else followed. Crucially, it is a *pre*-ontological determination; it is also very important to see that it is not a theological determination either, because although all religious experience appears to be based on the call and vocation and election, these and related notions are not *sui generis*, but instances of what I regard as a universal phenomenon.

SHORTT: But it can yield fruit in a religious context. As you speak I'm reminded of Paul Ricoeur's insistence that theology should be grounded in an awareness that we're having to do with a world we didn't make, and with an initiative that is not ours.[9]

MARION: Indeed, but I would still stress the universality of the call. If you start with the call, you discover that theology is deeply rational from the beginning – not the rationality of arithmetic, logic, mathematics, but another rationality, and a very compelling one. And it is why I cannot agree that the first question in religion is a question of being, because I can perfectly well describe this without referring to being. People would say that your call has to *be*. Something has to be indeed, but the very fact that the call *is* does not give us anything to understand.

SHORTT: **It doesn't shed further light on a given situation.**

MARION: No. A large part of the experience of the call is that perhaps there is no call. The first experience of the call may perfectly well be a mistake. So the call comes before the decision on being, and you take the decision on being for the sake of the call. Consider a trivial example like a man in the front room of a house saying that he's heard a noise out in the back yard, and his wife replying that she hasn't heard anything. Or claims about alleged mystical experiences. Some who claim to have heard the voice of God might be crazy; others not. We discuss the reality of the thing afterwards. And in general people talk of having a vocation to do such-and-such a thing. It's individuals who decide they have a vocation to do something, and to declare that it is not their own, which is very striking. If you say that you have decided to be a philosopher, that's quite different from saying that you have a vocation to be a philosopher.

So that's the question of givenness. You might dismiss all this as too subjective, but I'd reject that charge. From the start of our lives, we are caught up in myriad responses. What is fascinating about the call and givenness is that they have no presupposition, that is, even what is not, gives itself, and that's why I ended up with the question of love. Why is love identified with transcendence? The answer is that love is not subject to the limitation of being. You can love something which is not yet; you can love something which is no more. And you can even say that you are loved by those who are no more. It is not absurd.

SHORTT: **Will you explain how?**

MARION: You can love an unborn child.

SHORTT: **But can you be loved by someone who is no more?**

MARION: Yes. Our relationship with the beloved dead is based on that principle. We do think that in some way they take care of us.

SHORTT: **Is that because their legacy lives on in the world through their effect on people who survive them?**

MARION: That's certainly one way of interpreting it, but I believe most religious traditions hold that we owe something to the dead. It's partly the fact that they are an influence on us. There's a deeper experience. You can downsize that by saying it's a legacy, a memory, something like that, but I think it's deeper, and I would say you can even assume in certain cases that you are loved by someone whom you don't know yet, and you will perhaps never meet. It's not absurd. So this means to me that love by an unknown one – to some extent a non-existent one, at least in my personal life – is not absurd. It's very strange, this property of love, not to be bound to the limitation of being. It's why love is beyond being.

SHORTT: Do you identify love with God?

MARION: No. I've recently written a book called *Le phenomène érotique*,[10] where I describe the dialectic of love from all points of view without referring to God. At the end you understand that God is deeply implied there. But I think there's a family resemblance with all the various expressions of love – the love of God, sexual love, all sorts of love. I don't believe in a univocity of being – I'm a good Thomist – but I do think there is a univocity of love. And in the Bible it's very striking that when sexual terms are employed, the usage is not metaphorical. God says to his people, 'You *were* a prostitute,' not, 'You were *like* a prostitute,' and the Wisdom of God says, 'I shall seduce you', not, 'I shall act in a way that resembles a seduction.' So I think that you can have a complete experience of love without first experiencing God.

SHORTT: Would you nevertheless say something more about the theological application of your ideas?

MARION: Although I do recognise a connection between my work and theology, including Christology. I don't understand myself as a theologian. I'm not theologically trained. This being said, I think theology is much richer, broader, more rational and fascinating than most theologians realise. For instance, I'm very surprised that many theologians haven't grasped that if they want to take a subject like Christology seriously, and even the text of the New Testament, not to speak of the Old Testament, they ought to exploit the resources offered by phenomenology. It provides another useful tool for the task of describing the life and teaching of Christ. There are all the questions about what a manifestation is, which can be completely evident and deceptive at the same time. The Christian revelation is very often about the fact that the more God opens himself, manifests himself, the more the people addressed are misled or confused or hostile. Why should this be? It's not necessarily a moral issue, it's not because people are evil. First of all, it's because it can be due to an excess of manifestation – manifestation can become unbearable. Just as certain works of art seem unbearable at first glance.

SHORTT: Picasso's *Guernica*, for example?

MARION: *Guernica*, Bacon, and others. This can even work in a positive way. You can say that the Last Judgement depicted in the Sistine Chapel is too much to bear. It's a part of the aesthetic experience, and I think there is something like that in the manifestation of God in Christ. It's not because we don't see something that we deny it: it's because we see too much. This can be explained very well by theology through the notion of the saturated phenomenon. The saturated phenomenon contrasts with common phenomena, where what we experience through intuition can always be set within the frame of a concept. So, we recognise, as we say, a car engine, for instance. We don't see it, but it conforms to one of the concepts we have already got.

SHORTT: We know it's a car out in the street rather than a tractor, for example.

MARION: Yes, even though we haven't seen it. In that case we foresee the phenomenon, because we already have a stock of concepts matching the intuition. And when we speak of evidence it is because the concept is filled with evidence, I would say. But there are cases where we have too much intuition and no concept to foresee anything.

SHORTT: And as you've indicated, we're talking here about experiences on either side of the religious boundary.

MARION: Yes. When you have a shattering historical event – September 11 or Pearl Harbor, say – the tragedy is unforeseen not only because of possible intelligence failures, but because people have no concept to match the experience. The concept wasn't available to us beforehand. The same applies for Auschwitz and the Gulag. They were beyond imagination. That's a saturated phenomenon.

You have the same thing in painting, for example, where suddenly someone creates something which is completely unexpected. And you have the same thing, according to Levinas, with the face of the other. We have no concept of that. Levinas says that in his own language, it is *noema* without *noesis*, that is, understood without understanding. So a saturated phenomenon arises when what we experience is beyond our understanding. And it is not only true for the exceptional experiences. It is true for many experiences in daily life.

SHORTT: And for Christians, this probably applies supremely to Jesus. His impact was so momentous that it took the Church several centuries to make its mind up about incarnational and trinitarian doctrine.

MARION: Yes, the career of Christ can be seen as a quite exceptional saturated phenomenon. But as I said in answer to your first question, this isn't a move beyond reason: it's an expansion of it.

SHORTT: You've been a practising Catholic since childhood, which will interest and maybe surprise a good number of people. Was it a lonely experience as a believer in French philosophy faculties, especially in the 1960s and 1970s?

MARION: Yes. I went through a lot of discussion and argument with colleagues. I'm used to that. It made my life difficult from time to time, without interfering with my career in a substantive way. On the other hand, one should never base adherence to a religious creed on whether or not it is popular. So the possibility that Catholicism may become a minority faith in France would not be a good reason for giving it up, in my eyes.

The other thing is that I've never been in real doubt about God or the incarnation, because the only argument against these beliefs is that they are impossible. And I agree that they are 'impossible' by some canons of reason. But the impossible is precisely the definition of God. If you say that revelation, creation, redemption and the existence of God are impossible, I say, Yes, and so what? Because you *start* to get into the field where the question of God may be raised when you cross the border between the possible and the impossible. So I have no difficulty in admitting that everything related to God is 'impossible'. But I feel that I have experienced in my own life the efficacy of the impossible. I've listened to the lessons of my experience. You can disagree with the Church or its representatives, but faith, Christian faith, is not about the Church, it is about redemption in Christ. And my final point is this: if you are a believer, the world is much more beautiful, much more interesting, much more rational, much more delightful than if you are not. So perhaps all my faith is based on a kind of hedonism. I am a hedonist.

9
David Martin

Christianity and Society

SHORTT: We're going to touch on some of the subjects you are best known for, particularly in your more recent books, such as *Christian Language in the Secular City*,[1] *Christian Language and Its Mutations*[2] and *Pentecostalism – The World Their Parish*.[3] But let's begin by talking more personally about your attitude to pacifism and armed conflict, which underlies your book *Does Christianity Cause War?*[4] I know you feel that provides a major clue to your evolution as a Christian and as a sociologist, as well as a key to Christianity itself.

MARTIN: That's true. The autobiographical approach is clearly a clue to the academic work, and such a close relationship is quite normal in the more 'subjective' sciences – those dealing with human beings (or 'subjects') and with subjective meanings. After all, we are studying horizons, perspectives and standpoints, and we are not ourselves entirely above the clash of standpoints, even though we try to neuter our language in the interests of objectivity.

In my case the autobiographical clues lie in two losses of faith, the first being a loss of faith in the biblical literalism of my parents, and the second a loss of faith in political idealism. My mother was a 'between maid' who read voraciously. My father was a chauffeur and taxi driver in London, and he preached in Hyde Park in between times. Our home was loving, ordered and aspiring, though our outlook might be seen as Sabbatarian and narrow. All of that broke up in adolescence, particularly after I read Schweitzer's *The Quest of the Historical Jesus*. I made a quite typical shift from religious to political nonconformity, maintaining a link between home and grammar school by adopting liberal–socialist and pacifist–anarchist views. I saw these as consonant with the gospel teaching on non-violence. I read

Shaw, Wilde, Tolstoy, Herbert Read, Aldous Huxley, the Powys brothers, and so on, and I was perhaps attracted above all else to the Jesus of William Blake who swept away the law in favour of 'life, more life'. The most important single book was Berdyaev's *Freedom and the Spirit*, which I read raw at eighteen, dictionary in hand.

I had (and still have) a visceral horror of violence so I did my National Service from 1948 to 1950 in the Non-Combatant Corps, attached to the Military Police and the Pioneers. During that time I found out too much about the brutal side of male existence and also became acquainted with the Brethren, who were virtually a majority in the NCC. It wasn't a bad preparation for a future sociologist of religion.

As I look back to my early twenties as a primary school teacher, I realise that I became a theological autodidact, taking the local preachers' exams of the Methodist Church and reading what I now realise were some of the theological classics of the period. The result was that I made my own way undirected by teachers and their pre-dilections, just as I was later to do in sociology. On the one hand I devoured biblical criticism (Branscomb, Goguel, Loisy Jeremias, Bultmann, Streeter) and theology proper (Temple, Quick, Gore, the Niebuhrs, Brunner, D'Arcy, Mascall, Baillie, Von Hügel, Tillich, Otto, Jaspers, Barth on the creed). On the other hand I wandered in the by-path meadows of medieval and Eastern Christian devotion (Helen Waddell, for example) and browsed in mystical poetry, above all the poets of the seventeenth century. I discovered writing about the Gothic and the Romanesque, especially the latter (Gilson, Markham, Mâle) and works like Knox's *Enthusiasm* and Mauriac's *Life of Jesus*. I thought, and still think, Chesterton a fine theologian. Apart from Blake, Pascal was central, and has remained so, at least in rejecting system in favour of a mosaic of fragments.

I saturated myself in Hopkins, partly because my English teacher, W. H. Gardner, was his first modern editor, and I came to know Eliot by heart. Hopkins, Eliot, Vaughan – and later Charles Sisson – were visionaries of place and natural feature, and it is out of place that the visionary world of faith emerges, all the way from the waste land and the time-kept city to the luminous pool and the rose garden. As with the visual and the visionary – visible light and invisible light – so, also, with music and its evocation of loss and exaltation, especially in Bach and Handel. Worship is made up of the iconic, the evocatory and the tangible, and all three have been profoundly focused for me in what Peter Ackroyd has called 'English Music'. I later wrote pieces on

Britten and Sisson which were about the visionary as embodied in the sound and sight of England. Contemporary theology is reclaiming our sense of place, our sense of 'approach' to luminous place in numinous landscape. We do not live in a world of abstract universals but one where the eternal is realised in a moment, where the perfect is incarnate in a fragment, and the presence is made real in the here and now. If you ask me for an argument for God I can only say 'Listen', 'Look', 'Handle', 'Receive'.

My loss of faith in political idealism began when I took a correspondence course in sociology in the years 1956–9 while still a teacher. I probably hoped to validate by social science what I already believed by inclination. At any rate, when a postgraduate scholarship took me to the LSE, I gravitated to the issue of pacifism, particularly in the 1930s. I think my faith cracked about half-way through a history of that time by Lewis Namier. Soon after that Karl Popper released me from my 'soft' Marxism, which was a huge relief, while Reinhold Niebuhr finally converted me to a Christian realism. I accepted Niebuhr's distinction between the morality of face-to-face relations and the degree of amorality embedded in collective behaviour, especially between states. I read 'international relations' and that provided me with a major model of social interaction.

SHORTT: Can you unpack what you mean by Christian realism?

MARTIN: I mean focusing on what can be done now within the limited available options, rather than exercising a roving commission of free-ranging moral judgement, ignoring real constraints and alternative costs, and big on hindsight. A Christian realist imagines being both a Christian and a Foreign Secretary, which automatically excludes the pacifist option because the national interest depends on the power and weight available for sustained negotiation. Abandon power and you lose your voice, because the power game is the 'only game in town'. You recognise policy is contingent on circumstance and to that extent incoherent, as well as economical with the truth. As alliances dissolve and re-form, the only thing worse than secret diplomacy (the great complaint of the 1920s) is megaphone diplomacy.

I think that in between the moral heroism possible in fulfilling the role of politician, and the moral heroism possible in the role of 'witness' to another order, however unlikely, there is a role based on 'critical solidarity' with those bearing political responsibility. In saying that I'm presenting the case for a morality not based on the universal space of reason, as in Kant, or the universal space of love, as in Tolstoy, but on the characteristics and virtues inherent in specific roles. If you adopt (or are placed) in a role that allows critical solidarity, then you act under certain characteristic constraints. These are less exigent than those inherent in the political role, and more exigent than those bearing on the free commentary available to bystanders or witnesses.

In fulfilling the role of 'critical solidarity' you do not attempt constantly to second-guess politicians, or keep up a running political commentary, in part because that would reduce your own credibility to the level of credibility enjoyed by partisan politicians. You choose your moment to make a broad comment, suggesting an agenda with different priorities, offering reminders about the moral costs of current policies compared with the moral costs of alternatives. But you will know that your words, however carefully chosen, will cease to be your own once spoken. They will be misused in partisan debate and be taken down for use in evidence against you by a mischief-making media.

SHORTT: This sounds like a pretty 'sombre Augustinianism', to use a term I've several times heard you employ to describe yourself. Presumably your sociology and your political theology concur. Could you say how?

MARTIN: The sociological grounds underpinning my political theology are shared with many secular writers: T. E. Hulme in his *Speculations*, Georges Sorel in his *Reflections on Violence* and John Gray in *Straw Dogs*. You do not need theology to reveal the fracture in human affairs when mere observation is entirely adequate. At the same time, mere observation in its sociological guise doesn't fully grapple with the abyss of evil opened up by certain kinds of social and human breakdown. What sociology does show, however, is the way relationships are sustained not only by reciprocal exchange and shared affections, but also by solidarity against 'the other', by scapegoating, by the threat of sanctions and violence, and by spirals of mutual repulsion. The scripts for mutual repulsion in politics as in sexuality are utterly predictable, and very difficult to interrupt.

The crux is the necessity of authority, which is a 'functional prerequisite' of social organisation, let alone civility, and includes a settled claim to power and the legitimate use of violence. Whatever the contemporary decline in deference and respect, and the proper fear of authoritarian*ism*, authority is a key to everything worthwhile, indeed the key to any reform. Just think of all the Christian experiments throughout history and it is clear that fraternity depends on discipline, on fathers-in-God as well as brothers, otherwise the wolf of chaos destroys the fold. Or think of William Morris, 'father' with Keir

Hardie of British socialism, who when his brotherhood fractured was obliged to take on charismatic leadership.

Putting this back into Niebuhrian terms, collective behaviour and political mobilisation evidence 'amoral' characteristics to a more marked degree than face-to-face relations. John Paul II acted in the spirit of 'total gratuity' when he met and forgave his would-be assassin, but he could not recommend 'release to the captive' because of the implication that would carry for third parties, in particular all future targets of assassins. When the Pope acts collectively with regard to the discipline of the Church itself, he cannot engage in particular acts of forgiveness without being arbitrary, as well as imperilling the organisation which teaches forgiveness. Instead he has to execute impartial judgement. Of course, he may be wrong or 'authoritarian', but there is no escaping the social logic of authority. Compassion has to include judgement and all the catch-phrases about 'non-judgemental compassion' are a sentimental gloss on the Gospels. Vast harm is done by the refusal to exercise judgement, just because it makes *you* feel good. Moreover, social relations have to be negotiated in terms of congruence of interests and values, as well as ideals of peace and unity, and peace itself comes as part of a bargain, in the course of which you have to demand more than you can hope to get.

All this contrasts with Christianity. Christianity confronts the love of power with the power of love, it sets out an ideal of peace based on shared humanity, not common material interests, and recommends turning the other cheek rather than maintaining face and honour through the blood feud. In the Passion narrative compassion paid the cost of this ideal in full. Yet still the world of politics stayed the same, and has done so ever since. The atonement wasn't a way through the impasse of political action, but an exposure or exhibition of what happens when the divine humanity falls into the God-forsaken abyss opened up by the impulsions and collusions of political power, and of human cruelty let off the leash.

If everything stays the same, apart from seeds of the Kingdom scattered abroad in human culture, then the implications for Christian political commentary are clear. Except for those crisis situations where the peaceable procession through the gates of the city speaks truth and humanity to power, Christian commentary faces the same dilemmas as everyone else, with no benefit of clergy or resources of extra-terrestrial wisdom. As I suggested earlier (when speaking of 'critical solidarity') you can make occasional and strategic use of the distinctive sacred space you occupy, whether literally or in terms of your sacred role, but interventions rapidly diminish that space once it is seen as a haven for the kind of fallible judgements we might all make. We *all* have the same access to moral reason, and theories of 'just war' and 'just price' are purely rational constructions. We know from everyday experience that the ends do to some extent justify the means, though within the constraints provided by proportionality.

SHORTT: But aren't there circumstances when the Church could have done more? I'm thinking of John Cornwell's arguments[5] about how Pius XII pulled the plug on the (Catholic) Centre Party in Germany as part of the price of a Concordat with Hitler. Isn't there a fine line between realism and a kind of despairing quietism?

MARTIN: You're right. It is indeed a fine line. And it is true that the Churches in Germany could have done more, but at least they did better than the universities and the arts, normally thought of as nurseries of moral heroism. Think only of Heidegger, Richard Strauss and Elisabeth Schwarzkopf. The difficulty arises because the full implications of a situation take time to unfold, and people wait, making interim compromises while all the time eroding the remaining base for resistance. One might also remember the disastrous wrecking tactics of the Communist Party. In any case, the universal Church, like the university, has had a strong instinct for survival and for conserving its material interests, as well as for protecting the understandings and values that undergird its *raison d'être*. Fear of communism played a part as well. After all, fear of communism was a consideration in both the promotion and the demotion of liberation theology, as Anthony Gill's book on Latin American politics, *Rendering Unto Caesar*, makes clear.

Churches are interest groups, with internal politics not markedly different from politics in general. The recent interventions of the Catholic Church in Chile, Brazil, the Philippines, Hong Kong, China and parts of Africa have to be seen both as courageous, and as exhibiting their own institutional and political logic. It helps that the Catholic Church disposes of personnel moving from country to country who may not be too closely implicated in local cultures and élites. Inculturation is not necessarily a good thing when the culture is corrupt, as it mostly is. I expect I'm very Protestant about all this, because I think that in a secular democracy like ours it is less a matter of what 'the' Church says by way of clerical pronouncement than of paying some attention to faithfully informed Christian voices.

I come back to what I said earlier about the role open to the Church in crisis situations, whether we are talking about apartheid, the 'National Security State' in Latin America, or a communist tyranny in Eastern Europe, Africa or Asia. In times of transition the sign language of Christianity, held in reserve in sacred space, can walk out into the public forum in peaceful procession. That happened most dramatically in East Germany, where the Church had been reduced to a depleted minority, infiltrated (like everything else) by the STASI. When other conditions were ripe, the processions emerging from the churches spelt the end of the regime. Revolution began with prayer in the Nikolaikirche, Leipzig, and in churches all over the former GDR, though you would hardly have guessed that from the secular Western media.

SHORTT: I notice that in what you have just said you defend the autonomy of reason without conspicuous benefit of theology. That was a position you also took in a review[6] of Oliver O'Donovan and Joan Lockwood O'Donovan's book *Bonds of Imperfection: Christian Politics Past and Present*. Yet elsewhere[7] you've suggested that people are more likely to find relevant discussion of serious questions in theology than in philosophy. Isn't that paradoxical?

MARTIN: Yes, it is paradoxical, and so is every serious position, Christianity included. As to philosophy I was thinking in particular of the kind of analytic philosophy offering mental hygiene to intellectual health addicts. As I understand it, Christianity is not moral philosophy or ethics misleadingly encased in archaic myth and dogma. Blake and Kierkegaard were surely right about that in their different ways, and Kant wrong. Christianity is not some excessively roundabout way to arrive at high-mindedness, duty, public decency, welfare and philanthropy.

I have always been impressed by what Kierkegaard said about Christian baptism *not* being circumcision, that is, a rite of entry into the body of the people and the community. Of course that is the *social* function of baptism, for obvious reasons to do with generational continuity, but in terms of meaning, baptism is a rite of entry into the People of God. It is a ferrying through death by water to new life and resurrection. The same tension between social function and meaning occurs where death in war is equated with the sacrifice of Christ, and where Christianity is assimilated to public decency. That is all sociologically inevitable, and such potent disjunctions are part of the irony of Christian history.

Of course, Christians are called to virtue, duty, commitment, moral prescience, neighbourliness, and what Schweitzer called 'reverence for life'. But it is not a set of ethical rules scrutinised analytically in terms of their mutual adjustment in varied situations. In St Paul's language that would once more install 'condemnation under the law' in the place of grace, acceptance and forgiveness. Rather, Christianity is about faith and hope as a journey from exile through a wilderness to springs of living water. In Bunyan's language it is the wicket-gate we *think* we see that discloses a path to delectable mountains. To have faith is a way of seeing divinity in a grain of sand and eternity in an hour. It's 'good' is not the good of G. E. Moore, but the good of creation and of Good Friday.

In one way the Sermon on the Mount can be seen as a second Sinai, affirming perfection under the law and passing a judgement on love-lessness and hardness of heart, but the sermon is preached against a horizon of beatitude and promise. It asks how you stand, how you are placed when it comes to receiving, giving and making gestures of reconciliation and inclusion. At the heart of faith is the blood offering of the Blood Donor, and of our loving communion with the Donor.

So faith is not a myth-infested way to the *idea* of the good but an apprehension of grace and judgement. When I say theology deals with what matters I mean it is about life, about waste places and abundance, losses and recoveries. It works by images and emblems comprising a table of affinities, not a logical progression. The emblems are realised above all in sacred landscapes, and they are embedded in and arise out of worship. The language of faith is declaratory, not descriptive or propositional, and to speak of Jesus as Son of God as well as Son of Man is to make a characterisation, not a proposal. Perhaps that is why I find my theology in icons, poems and music, in writers like Ruskin and Rilke, in theologians like Austin Farrer, all of whom represent this mode of understanding, and com-municate by gesture, sign and incarnate word. When it comes to music, the only art in which I have had serious training, I am deeply affected by the way composers create a sonic world answering and responsive to the sacred text, as if they have access to the 'charge' it carries, whether or not they believe. Browning wrote: 'The rest may reason and welcome/Tis we musicians know.' Perhaps the question is not so much a matter of how many things you can subscribe to, but rather, Have you heard? Do you see?

SHORTT: **In what sense are Christians right and atheists wrong?**

MARTIN: I can't think in those terms, because some atheism is rejection of a God not worthy of 'worth-ship' and, in any case, it is actually a *part* of faith to be overwhelmed as the waves pass over you. All is not for the best, or arranged by what Milton called 'the dispose of highest wisdom'. Atheism doesn't shock me, though many of the arguments people advance for atheism strike me as seriously inadequate, especially those forms of scientism adopting a reductionist approach.

There are innumerable forms of reductionism, most of them mutually contradictory, and they regard religion (or art or consciousness) as 'nothing but' epiphenomena, froth on the surface of the real. For example, the latest reduction claims that 'science' has 'explained' inspiration through observation of 'events' lighting up in particular parts of the brain. I can't see any *significance* attaching to such a claim: did the same kind of brain event accompany the composition of Beethoven's Minuet in G as accompanied the Benedictus of the Mass in D? These kinds of explanation ignore or do not even begin to understand all the different levels of scientific intentionality, with their appropriate and distinctive methodologies, up to the level of the phenomenological enquiry into the structures of meaning and being, and the sciences of meaning and being. I have been deeply influenced here by Wilhelm Dilthey's distinction between the natural and cultural sciences, that is between the nomothetic and generalising, and the particularising and ideographic.

Richard Dawkins and Philip Pullman are interesting, indeed brilliant, examples of the evasion of scientific complexity by a simple-minded identification of evil in religion itself. Dawkins clearly thinks that 'evidence' about what religion does in terms of violence is a simple matter of pointing to 'facts' rather than attempting to elucidate the social structures of violence in which religion is implicated. The propaganda could not be more crude. For example, to say that 'religion causes war' is as vacuous as saying 'politics causes war'. (Interestingly, Raymond Aron's classic sociological study of war barely mentions religion.)

Pullman, like Dawkins, is a great imaginative writer, who makes the same crude identification of evil with religion or rather with what he calls 'The Authority'. Only eliminate the Authority, and we can troop into the freedom of the republic of heaven. There is a whole class of such identifications, claiming and proclaiming innocence and locating evil in a particular social structure which is collapsing or must be destroyed: patriarchy, capitalism and so forth. Utopia is constantly being predicated on such exemplary surgeries and the exemplary final violence they legitimate.

Blame can usually be heaped on Christianity because it is a continuing identifiable institution. Its critics can fire from hidden positions because they only represent their own views and cannot be nailed down collectively and institutionally as caught up in the general dynamic of social processes. Richard Dawkins can dissociate science as an activity from the murky reality of science as responsible for weapons of mass destruction, and roundly condemn Darwinism in all its monstrous social realisations. He wipes his hands in asserting the innocence of 'knowledge'. Christianity can be blamed for Torquemada while science cannot be blamed for the misuses of biology, or the Enlightenment blamed for Joseph Stalin. Yet the governing metaphors of Darwinism are far more apt for misuse than the key images of Christianity. Any commitment to science requires us to abjure superficial indignation in the interests of understanding how social processes give rise to such deleterious outcomes.

If we think of faith as a response to manifestations of grace, then it really is not open to the kinds of argument deployed either in the natural or the social sciences. Christianity would be verifiable or falsifiable following standard criteria, and would have been consigned to the vast corpus of misconceived science. This is where I think the advance of science actually clarifies the nature of Christian language by cleansing it of false science. You have to be very careful in devising premature reconciliations of science and faith.

Scientific criteria are central to my professional activity, but they have no intrinsic purchase on the unique, the gratuitous, the iconic, the emblematic, the embodied and manifested, the declarative, the trustful, the hopeful or the faithful. Sir Thomas Browne wrote of 'an O altitudo', and faith begins in that 'O'. Faith is exclamatory, not explanatory. To say 'Give, sympathise, control' has nothing to do with the givens of science. The gift is not the datum. Any god located at the end of a telescope or infallibly deduced by reason would not be God, because his inevitability would destroy our free response. A demonstrable God would be only an idol. God is 'known' in showings and what Donald Davie called 'sightings'.

SHORTT: It's naturally true that God can't be located at the end of a telescope, but a very large number of believers would say that religion is exclamatory *and* explanatory – that it entails the fullest application of reason, based on the impulse to seek a fundamental and inclusive context of meaning. Such an interpretation is defended at length elsewhere in this book; so I shan't say more about it now. But can you at any rate say how you understand the definitiveness of Christianity?

MARTIN: I can certainly say something about how I understand the distinctiveness of Christianity, and perhaps I should begin by saying that indiscriminate 'respect' for each and every religion and for all the elements in them is the negation of intellectual integrity. We are obliged to discriminate because we have to judge from a coherent standpoint. I'm also against any attempt to abstract some common elements of the world's religions as true, because that denatures each and every religion and falsely assumes that the languages of faith can be translated into a super-language. The universe of meaning is too rich for that kind of dehydrated Esperanto, and Hinduism is at least wrong in imagining we can all be right.

In this I follow Max Weber in seeing Christianity as placed at a critical point on a spectrum of possibilities based on how we say 'Yes' or 'No' to the world, and how we understand 'the world'. The world religions of what Karl Jaspers called the 'Axial period', roughly from 1000 BC to AD 600, are ranged along this spectrum, overlapping but distinct, and the contemporary 'spiritual' variant of faith seems to me to weaken the tension of 'Yes' and 'No' with a confused and indiscriminate 'Yes', for example its indiscriminate embrace of the Erotic and the Natural. The point is that this spectrum is multidimensional and each position along it implies a *range* of possibilities with respect to the Erotic, the Aesthetic, the Economic and the Political. For example, the Christian 'Yes' and 'No' to the world (the *saeculum*) actually generates the notion of 'the secular' central to contemporary consciousness, as well as our sense of movement in history.

The meanings lodged in the different world religions are simultaneously shared and opposed. For example, Christianity and Islam share the notions of victory (and martyrdom), but in the one there is a victory *over* the world and in the other a victory *in* the world. We are back again, then, with the Christian fruitful ambivalence towards the dynamic of secular power as compared with the Islamic realistic acceptance of it. These differences are clear in the foundation stories of the two faiths. In the Christian story an unmarried prophet enters the city unarmed, and in the end converts the city and its Temple into his own spiritual body; whereas Muhammad is a prophet who is a family man and a soldier who simply takes the city and issues edicts of world conquest. No wonder Carlyle chose him for his lectures *On Heroes*. Both prophets claimed to have 'overcome' the world but the meanings of 'world' and 'overcome' differ radically.

In practice, of course, an established Christianity comes to terms with the world, and its vocabulary as used by emperors and nations more closely approximates to Islamic usages. Thus Christian meanings bifurcate under the pressure of political realities, and Christian civilisation is internally riven by a double entendre or whispering gallery of alternative and primitive meanings. People can overhear a different Kingdom of God still embedded in the proclamations of a Church with pretensions to plenary power on earth and to constituting a 'perfect society'.

In an article I once commissioned from a Muslim scholar for an encyclopedia he claimed that the West was a civilisation without any notion of honour. I think that is partly true, except that the dynamic of the political is *always* driven to a great extent by honour and shame. One must not lose face. However, the truth of the comment lies in the way Christianity in its primitive form actually pitches its tent in the idea of losing face to retain inner integrity. 'His face was marred more than any man's'. The world demands a 'king' be royally attended. A potentate is all-glorious and his face is aweful. But this 'king of glory' is woefully attended, girded by nothing except his inner conviction. The 'passage of arms' in the two faiths illustrates a different relation of 'Yes' and 'No', 'Now' and 'Not Yet', as well as of inwardness and externality. Christianity has an inner potential for self-destructiveness, Islam for self-protective externality. In his *The Making of the Yoruba* John Peel suggests that Islam works inward from the outward action as ritually prescribed, while Christianity works in the reverse direction. That is quite a 'clash of civilisations'.

In Christianity the 'Yes' is given to a good creation, and the 'No' to the infestation of evil in the resistant 'world'. Faith claims to have 'overcome' the world, but the victory is pursued in steadily hostile territory by colonies of divinity and secret agents of heaven. Monastic and Utopian communities make up the colonies, and images of reversal and renewal comprise the secret agents. Even the Church as firmly established in the seats of power still sings 'He hath put down the mighty from their seat and exalted them of low degree.' Faith cannot help but throw possibilities of a different order onto the screen – above all the basic oxymoron of Christianity: When we die, we live, when we fall, we rise. The creed itself embodies the pattern of descent and ascent.

SHORTT: **This, then, is the Trojan Horse notion of the way Christianity infiltrates civilisation even when having been taken in by it.**

MARTIN: Yes, exactly. I would only say that what slips out of the Trojan Horse does not overturn the city and the powers-that-be. It spreads unsettling rumours, but there is no way it can abolish the 'powers'.

There Islam is more realistic. For some three centuries Christianity remained voluntary and dependent on the sword of the spirit until, as I said, classical Rome supplies the sword of state, as well as the political concepts to back it up. Christianity as a sign language of peace, love, sacrifice and brotherhood is deficient in terminology to cover the exigencies of power. That is the opportunity cost of its 'angle' on the world, and of saying 'No' as well as 'Yes'. There is a similar lack in the sphere of everyday ethics, as distinct from the perspectives of the Kingdom. That is another opportunity cost. The cost, the gap, is intrinsic to the subversive tilt of its angle on the world. I disagree with John Milbank here, because he thinks Christianity generates its own politics and sociology.[8]

However, as I said earlier, the concept of 'the world' does generate the idea of the secular, and the distinction between Caesar and God, the Church and the state. It brings into being the possibility of autonomous spiritual space which can in due time be expanded by the Christian emphasis on inwardness and conscience. Already, you can see our modern world prefigured and anticipated, though all kinds of social mutations will have to occur until it can be realised. For example, the distinction between spirit and world may be articulated as the two cities or the two realms, or as the clash of theocracy with empire, or as the Lutheran reserved area of the spirit, maintained while the secular polity runs its own affairs in its own way. You find another example in the assertion of spiritual autonomy by dissenting groups in England and Holland in the late sixteenth and early seventeenth centuries.

Here you see the interaction of theological conceptions, like inwardness and autonomous spiritual space, with social conditions, allowing them a range of realisations from a minimal realisation in the Byzantine Empire to a maximal one in the United States. This range constitutes a series of possible solutions to the Church–state problem, which is *in part* problematic precisely because the established Church has disseminated the seeds of its own unsettlement. However, even where the distinction between Church and state is maximal as in the USA, the dynamic of 'the political' remains as it always was. As a polity the USA combines Joshua and Rousseau, the claims of conquest and the claims of innocence.

State-bearing élites in Christian societies understand what a peaceful Palm Sunday entry might mean, in part because the liturgy of the Church keeps it in perpetual recollection, but they also retain the option of the old-style triumphal entry practised by the Roman

emperors. To understand the systematic ambiguities and ambiva-
lences built into Christian civilisation you have to observe the
fluctuations in meaning between the original Palm Sunday and subsequent entries into the city. The Passiontide hymn '*Vexilla regis
prodeunt*' – 'The royal banners forward go' – expresses precisely the
capture of military metaphor by the spirit, and its recapture by the
powers that be. Crosses turn to swords more easily than spears turn
into pruning-hooks. It is the way of 'the world'.

There isn't time or space to elaborate now, but one of the problems
with the Enlightenment is that it both carries forward Christian
notions in mutant form, as Charles Taylor convincingly argues,[9] *and*
begins to close up the bifurcation of sacred and secular space derived
from the distinction between God and Caesar. Like any other structure of power, religious or secular, it seeks to neutralise whatever
points beyond it. From the perspective of an Enlightened society the
Christian relativisation of the political points dangerously beyond it.
From a Christian perspective 'the political' is not at the heart of what
faith takes to be ultimately serious. Liberal theologians are too often
Christians who transfer faith to politics, and so give to the contingent
a religious loyalty and resonance. Their real credence is given to
political doctrine, with Christianity lending adventitious rhetorical
weight.

I want to make a distinction here between the ironic and the innocent. A Christianity conscious of its own whispering gallery of
contrary notions will generate irony on account of the gap between
hope and reality. But Enlightenment (as the very word suggests) seeks
a point of innocence from which to judge where lies the source of corruption. *Bien pensant* thinking, understood as the infinite resource of
the high-minded, elevates itself to the secure ground of innocence to
comment on the ubiquity of failure and identify its source, which in
the cases already cited may be in religion itself. Feminist theologians,
who after all have a serious case against patriarchy, write as if they are
the embodiment of the innocent party. In a similar way the religion of
America has become so innocently proud of American achievement
that it has lost access to irony.

There *is* no innocence, and the closest we may come to the perfect
society and Yeats' 'ceremonies of innocence' is in the special liminal
time of liturgy. Liturgical time recapitulates loss and restoration, and
anticipates perfection by fast-forwarding into the present. But just as
monasteries and utopian sects require discipline and boundaries, so
does liturgy: it requires courtesies, obeisances, placement, choreo-

graphed movements and scripted responses. Most liturgies maintain a chaste reserve with respect to personalised interventions and random initiatives. A 'spontaneous' Pentecostal liturgy can only work when its implicit semaphore is universally understood and obeyed.

Liturgy is a received poetry of the perfect and fulfilled achieved through abnegation and purgation. Light, wholeness and presence are uncovered through darkness, fracture and absence. This reconciliation is realised theologically through typology and binary contrasts: the death-dealing and the life-giving, fountains of life and bottomless pits. Theology is not so much a form of linear argument as the evocation of 'types' embodied in contrasting icons and images: the valley of the shadow and the mountain of transfiguration, Babylon and the New Jerusalem, the Law delivered on Sinai and the Spirit given at Pentecost. The code-language of faith works by potent contrasts: 'He gave up all but love; He is crowned with glory and honour'.

SHORTT: Does all this give us more of a handle on your sociological work on secularisation and its paradoxes?

MARTIN: It does, precisely because the Christian faith creates the space of the secular, and the sacralisation of the Empire under Constantine is, therefore, the first full-scale secularisation of the Church. Religious motifs are constantly being secularised, as when inward faith becomes sincerity, or Madonna and Child the bond of maternal affection. The question is not secularisation as such, but whether Christian images have been earthed without remainder.

It is a question that becomes very urgent when you are suffering under an Enlightened tyranny, which in its own practice falsifies its own promises and its claims to innocence. Those promises and those claims motivate and justify the suppression of faith as an alternative source of 'light' based on spiritual autonomy. At that point liturgy, by including both fracture and promise, becomes a point of resistance. As the Romanian dissident Petre Tutea pointed out from his experience of re-education in prison, the liturgy, reduced to a pure gift passed from open hand to open hand, witnesses to a different presence in a waste land. Under *those* circumstances the gesture conveys a plenitude of spiritual power. Even empty sacred space witnesses to some other power than brute force. Spires puncture horizons with another dimension.

SHORTT: I recall a tart comment at the end of one of your reviews[10] where you said we are constantly told to be attentive to what happens in other parts of the world with the signal exception of religion. There we still treat Europe as 'the lead society'. How does that relate to your emphasis on the way 'general tendencies' delineated by sociology are inflected or even negated by particular histories?

MARTIN: Very closely, of course. Evidence from France or Sweden definitely counts as more significant than anything in Brazil or South Africa. The European 'exception' understood as the one place where secularisation is most clearly evident, still provides the model, with France or Sweden or Holland promoted as likely futures for us all. This is where the 'proclamation' of the future derived from the Enlightenment (and most persuasively illustrated by intellectual history) shows up most obviously. 'Secular theology' since the 'Death of God' movement in the 1960s is only a variant on this, except that sheer proclamation without evidence comes to some secular theologians just as naturally, as it does to Richard Dawkins.

The point of my *General Theory of Secularization*[11] was to bring all the observations together, both empirical in the form of trends in the figures, and structural, for example the increasing independence of each sector of social life, such as education and welfare, from church control. I then showed how the data varied in different historical circumstances: for example, the different relationships, some negative, some positive, between religion and Enlightenment, and between religion and nationalism. In France, the relationship was negative between religion and both the Enlightenment and nationalism, whereas in the nascent USA it was positive on both counts. The other factor was the degree of religious pluralism or monopoly, because pluralism in the USA allowed religion to adapt under the spur of competition, whereas in France a religious monopoly reacted to change by associating itself with an older France and entered into a war of attrition, particularly after 1870. The Anglo-Scandinavian trajectory lay in between the French and the American, and there are several more intermediate cases.

There were many variants, all making for complicated cultural ensembles, with interesting questions to be raised later about why there was a 'second confessional phase' arising with the onset of modernity in the nineteenth century when religion rather successfully mobilised to meet the challenge, but which then tailed off. My whole aim has been to indicate what Eisenstadt calls the multiplicity of possible futures. Secularisation in the European style was born *in* Europe *of* Christianity in the specific form of Christendom. Those circumstances won't be repeated elsewhere. The decline of Christendom is clear enough, and that is specifically European. Even the Latin American extension of Christendom is developing quite differently, as my work on Pentecostalism there (and in the rest of the non-Western world) shows. Latin America combines some elements of the European with the North American situation, and it seems that religious pluralism has really taken hold there. Africa is, of course, something different again, and (apart from the Islamic North) provides an amazing example of exuberant religious pluralism.

Even in Europe the Eastern countries have had a quite distinctive experience because of the ethnoreligion stimulated by Muslim or Russian communist colonialism. For most of 'the East' the experience of Petre Tutea is exemplary, even in Russia itself. In Russia one asks oneself how it is possible after an Enlightenment influenced by France and seven decades of communist indoctrination for Christianity to have revived so spectacularly. I was recently in the Nevsky Monastery in St Petersburg, *the* great city of Russian autocratic Enlightenment, and realised that the only resource of this Church was the liturgy and being Russian. Western ratiocination *about* religion hardly mattered: what mattered was lighting a candle while waiting on and being attentive to the Spirit.

In a curious way that links up with my work on the spread of Pentecostalism seen as a movement of Christian revival comparable to Islamic revival. Yet when it comes to Pentecostalism, there isn't even a margin of violence. One has to ask why people in Latin America, Africa and the Far East with much more to motivate hostility to 'the West' than the Middle East are so resolutely peaceful and anxious simply to work hard to improve their own circumstances by the classic path of individual and group mobility. Pentecostalism had an autobiographical resonance for me because I saw it as the kind of religious mobilisation of the poor seeking 'respectability'. By that I mean the self-respect and the respect of others, through the respect shown them by the grace of God that had moved my own parents. It is why I revived the theory of Halévy about Methodism and the entry of England into modernity and reapplied it to the vast changes occurring in the developing world.

And here comes the connection of Pentecostalism with Orthodoxy: both are direct encounters with the Spirit, but one is a kind of *stasis* – *iconostasis*, while the other is *dunamis*, the dynamic outpouring of ecstatic speech confirming your identity as precious to God, though not to the contemptuous world. This is the noisy ecstasy of the poor, and I do not see why it receives so much less respect from the liberal intelligentsia than (say) the meditative silence of a Buddhist monastery. As David Lehmann – an agnostic Jew – has pointed out, the great offence and triumph of Pentecostalism in Brazil is to create a popular movement indifferent to the patronage of the intelligentsia – as well as to good taste.

SHORTT: So Pentecostalism in Latin America refreshes the parts Catholicism doesn't reach. I wonder if Catholicism could have the resources to achieve the same end?

MARTIN: It might if it were a minority, as in Korea, but for those on the underside of life in Latin America, Catholicism is part of the structure of status and power, even though the base communities and Charismatic movements do cross over the divide to some extent. Pentecostalism is the walk-out of those trying to create an autonomous space where they can re-create themselves. It *is* re-creation, carried out in a self-protected environment able to move on and up in a capsule of shared mobility. The virtues Pentecostals pursue are like those recommended in Leo XIII's 1891 encyclical *Rerum Novarum*, and they are often rather close to standard Catholic teaching. Indeed, they agree with episcopal pronouncements about family life more than Catholics do, but they can realise their goals only by shepherding themselves, not by being shepherded. The priest, even a priest *for* the people, doesn't speak their language. They want a tangible tongue of fire on their own lips, not a lecture on the structural and political conditions holding them back. After all, the corrupt world of politics has not done much for them so far, and those Pentecostals who venture into it find their purity all too easily sullied.

My research on Pentecostalism reminded me of my grandfathers, who preferred standing up as 'speaking men' in the street or the chapel to taking a back seat while the military and the squirearchy read the lessons. After all, that is analogous to what happened when 'ignorant and unlearned men' got up to speak at the first Pentecost, and it happened again in 1906 in Azusa Street, Los Angeles – the founding moment and founding story of Pentecostalism. Of course, a remarkable ability to cross lines of colour and ethnicity among blacks and whites also encountered the constricting social logic of 'separate development'. Social apartheid was bound to reassert itself.

SHORTT: How does your study of Pentecostalism and secularisation link up with your most recent concerns, such as the ecology of sacred space and musical reception theory?

MARTIN: Some new directions have emerged from my work on Pentecostalism. In one way I was extending the study of secularisation to the developing world in order to trace paths to modernity other than the particular experience of European Christendom and the break-up of that kind of society. However, I was also following through the Halévy thesis about Evangelical religion and the way it helped by-pass revolution in the French style and all the progeny spawned by that version of militant secularism. I wanted to show how certain kinds of Christianity, separated from the state, and coming up from below, could help initiate a *peaceful* transition to modernity by a cultural revolution which included a feminisation of the macho psychology. So my interest in peace was engaged as well as my critique of master narratives pointing to a single dénouement.

All that complemented my own family's experience in the English context from the 1880s on, and I could see my parents in these aspiring hard-working Pentecostals of Latin America and Africa. Indeed, I once addressed a service of Pentecostal rural workers in Chile in which I traced the parallels; and they were immediately enthused and moved because it was all so recognisable. I, the distant person from the remote world of the university, knew their story. The issue for us now is not the parallel between the two situations, which is obvious, but whether the movement would largely empty itself into political nonconformity, as it did with the radical Liberal and Socialist movements in England, or continuously flourish as it had in the USA. In the USA it flourishes religiously, and as a source of the moralistic and righteous tone of American politics.

The study of Pentecostalism also stirred up a return to my earlier concern with the mystery of music and of sacred place. Clearly Pentecostalism is spread by narration and by healing, by tongues and singing. The moment my wife and I went to a Two Choirs Festival in Campinas, São Paulo, we knew where we were. It *had* to end with the Hallelujah Chorus sung to a vast, mainly black, congregation who broke out into an afterbirth of 'Gloria, Gloria, Gloria'. This was the Halévy thesis in its musical version: the power of harmony to subdue and elevate. In just the same way a background of hymns and choruses had opened up for me a life-long love of Bach, Handel, Brahms and (later) Schütz.

Perhaps I can add that I've always argued that the 'secularisation story' with regard to music was significant and distinctive among the arts, and I believe that is because it 'touches' us in the same place as religion touches us. I mean the place of revelation, ecstasy and transformation: the last duet of Handel's *L'Allegro*, the middle movement of Bach's last motet, *Singet dem Herrn*, the three women in *The Magic Flute*.

Turning to the subject of sacred space: in a village in the Yucatan,

Mexico we found what was architecturally a Welsh chapel, and it occurred to us that the Evangelical peripheries of the British Isles have spread in other 'peripheries', like the American South and the Yucatan. Maybe periphery speaks to periphery, mobilising what has been neglected by 'centre'. Maybe Evangelicalism mobilises and energises neglected areas as well as neglected classes – and women. Then in a Jamaican town I saw an ecology of sacred space that told me everything I needed to know. In the centre was the Anglican church next to the police station, then in the High Street were the established Methodists and Baptists, while all around the peripheries were the encroaching Pentecostal chapels – the 'offscourings of the earth' (in biblical terms) 'finding their place', mobilising and preparing to advance. They had found their place as well as their voice – the coal of fire placed on the tongue empowering the tongue to sing.

There, then, was another map to superimpose on the other two. It struck me that the varied sacred ecology of land and city was the spatial, visual clue to be integrated with the varied musical clues and the varied historical narratives. It all lay in front of my eyes, not just in some tiny town in Jamaica but in the centres and peripheries of Europe. I could 'read' the variable historical narratives by comparing the sacred ecologies of Paris and London, along the lines of the Halévy thesis, and going on to compare Paris and Strasbourg, London and Edinburgh. This could be a mode of understanding employed from St Petersburg to Washington. The history was in the stones and the disposition of space, so that in Paris, for example, you can trace the militant opposition of Notre Dame and the Place de la Bastille, the Sacré Coeur and the Panthéon, together with the 'triumphal ways' of enlightened absolutism and absolutist enlightenment. I could compare them with the muted complementarities of London, its clusters of alternatives, such as the state–Church cluster in Westminster with the Catholic cluster in Victoria as well as the Nonconformist clusters, and I would underline the *absence* of triumphal ways. So that's what I'm doing now, constructing visual and sonic maps to accompany the varied historical narratives. The sociology of religion has to be a sociology of the arts and peace, as well as of politics.

SHORTT: Could you maybe say a little by way of a coda about the state of your subject, the sociology of religion?

MARTIN: Well, I should say that I remain committed to sociology, and do not regard it as a pseudo-science, even though I believe there has to be a greater answerability to history. Sociology needs history because it is ideographic, concerned with the contingent and particular. Otherwise, sociology denatures itself by conceding too much to the nomothetic, concerned with the law-governed and generalised. When I came into the subject it was focused on the analysis of structures and data, especially structures and data relating to inequality (social mobility, the welfare state), and the analysis was positivist and purportedly 'value free'.

That was reversed in the 1960s, and I felt the reversal went too far in its denial of some kind of control exercised by the social world 'out there'. I welcomed the interest in phenomenology, but felt that relativism destroyed our academic *raison d'être*. One genuine gain was permission to take seriously people's own accounts of their experience and situation. They were no longer dismissed as suffering from false consciousness or luckless creatures of 'anomie'. It was not even necessary to reduce religious phenomena to a residue of the pre-modern. (I speak with controlled irony.)

Rather surprisingly, the sociology of religion, once at the centre of concern for the classical sociologists, managed to be marginal to the mainstream of sociology and the mainstream of Christianity. The pioneering and distinguished work of Bryan Wilson led to a focus on new religious movements and the New Age, to the relative neglect of (for example) Catholicism, or changes in European religion and politics. Vast changes were also coming about in the developing world, and it was a pity intellectual and financial resources tended to go elsewhere. There was, of course, the ground-breaking work of Peter Berger in *The Sacred Canopy* on the structures of religious consciousness in the modern world, and both Peter Berger and I initiated a dialogue with theology. My *Reflections on Sociology and Theology*[12] was a modest contribution to that. A great deal of valuable work filtered in from anthropology, for which religion was not marginal, as well as from political sociology and history. I was always keen to relate the sociology of religion to the sociology of politics, including politics in the developing world.

One of the difficulties arises from the way some people file religion under ethnicity and can only be persuaded to consider religion if it presents a problem – for example, as a consequence of post-colonial migration to Europe – or can help solve one, for example, the decline in social capital identified by Robert Putnam.[13] A major focus at the moment is with religion outside institutions – for example, burgeoning kinds of 'spirituality'. People who deal with the big questions and the long-term mainstream include Rodney Stark, Steve Bruce, Richard Fenn and Grace Davie, all from very different perspectives.

Rodney Stark has even raised the question of what difference belief in God has made over the centuries. Nowadays I don't feel a deviant by being interested in the mainstream.

In the wider academic sphere, sociology itself has been squeezed into marginality, so you can imagine the pressures on a subject at the margin of a margin. Sociology became a diffuse influence, on historians, political sociologists, religious studies people, and (say) regional studies people, like Africanists and Latin Americanists. When I moved to the USA in 1986 and studied Pentecostalism in the developing world, my immediate peers were often regional specialists or political sociologists, or development specialists, or anthropologists. When I later returned to the secularisation debate, some of my key reference points were historians. It was they who enabled me to see that it is better to think in terms of mutations and of successive christianisations and recoils rather than the one-dimensional master-narrative of secularisation, and all the associated nouns of process, like rationalisation and privatisation.

Perhaps you need to remember that four out of five sociologists of religion are American, because they have so much more obvious religiosity close by to think about, whereas on the Continent there is either '*sociologie religieuse*', often French, Belgian or Dutch, with some concentration on the Catholic Church, or the proponents of big theory. I hope that part of my contribution has been to try and bring the different approaches together.

10
Stanley Hauerwas and Samuel Wells

Theological Ethics

SHORTT: Stanley, in the last chapter David Martin defended the so-called Christian realism of Reinhold Niebuhr, and what it implies about the answerability of theology to secular disciplines. You take the opposite view – that 'realism' is symptomatic of a monumental loss of nerve, and its exponents indistinguishable from worthy citizens. In your way of thinking, a theological ethics rooted in a vision of the revealed character of God will entail a radical corollary: that the Church 'outnarrates' the world: it establishes 'what is prior to the world, more basic, more comprehensive', as one reviewer of your Gifford Lectures, *With the Grain of the Universe,* has put it.[1]

HAUERWAS: The review you refer to puts it well. The heart of much of what I do depends on the assumption that the Christian language *works.* At the time I was educated, there was an assumption that there was something wrong with Christian language, because people didn't understand it, and it had to be translated into terms that they understood. I thought that if Christian language doesn't work, it ought to be abandoned. Quit trying to resuscitate a corpse. My big question – and it owed much to reading Wittgenstein, as well as to my theological convictions – was, What kind of people do we need to be to be able to perform this speech? What kind of communities do we need to be to perform this speech? I also take it for granted that part of what the Christian speech says is that you have to be transformed to speak it: it doesn't come naturally – whereas the question asked by people like Bultmann, Tillich and John Robinson was, How do we make Christianity fit into the world as we know it?

SHORTT: **Could you describe your personal circumstances?**

HAUERWAS: I became a theologian because I couldn't get saved. I was a member of an Evangelical Methodist church in the American South, and you could attend on Sunday morning, but everyone knew that didn't have anything to do with getting saved. You had to get saved on Sunday night, after a sermon of at least an hour. And I wanted to get saved, but I didn't think you should fake it. And so it didn't happen.

And some young people in the church were beginning to dedicate their lives to the ministry after they had been saved. So I thought, if God isn't going to save me, at least I can dedicate my life to ministry, and then he will have to do something good for me. And I started reading seriously. I read a lot of very bad books, and then I discovered the work of Nels Feree, an early Swedish Barthian, and he said that religion probably hid God as much as it revealed God, and I thought, That's true: I'm going to give it up. So I did.

At college during the late 1950s and early 1960s I started to major in history, and I ended up majoring in philosophy. I was *the* philosophy major at South Western University in Georgetown, Texas, and I had a wonderful teacher who helped me to see that I didn't know enough about Christianity to reject it. I then decided to go to seminary to try to find out more. The pastor at the liberal church I was then attending sent me to see Schubert Ogden, who urged me to go to Chicago rather than Yale. 'Don't go to Yale,' he said: 'you'll only end up a Barthian.' And he was right. I went to Yale, and I'm a Barthian.

Before that, though, I was very impressed by liberal Christianity, and especially by Tillich. But I'd also become convinced that one of the major challenges for Christianity was the destruction of the Jews. And at Yale I was absolutely stunned to discover that it wasn't the liberals who had stood against the Nazis. It had been Karl Barth and Dietrich Bonhoeffer. So I really started reading Barth seriously, and also, at the same time, discovered the work of Wittgenstein. From Wittgenstein I learnt about the importance of paying attention to the concrete and I thought that that had deep implications for how theology ought to be done. Theology after Hegel tried to make itself look like philosophy – to be systematic, with discrete compartments for metaphysics, epistemology and ethics. And I thought that was a deep mistake for how theology should understand itself, because it was making theology look like a structure that becomes more important than the practice of the Church itself.

SHORTT: Sam, you were the first person to write a doctoral thesis on Stanley's work, and it has influenced you decisively. You are also joint editors of *The Blackwell Companion to Christian Ethics*.[2] Would you start by commenting on the relationship between theology and philosophy in Stanley's thought?

WELLS: There are probably three ways to answer this kind of question. One is to start where Stanley started, and that's with Wittgenstein. As far as his role in shaping Stanley's ideas is concerned, I'd go back one beyond Hegel, and say that the liberal theology Stanley's talking about is too much in thrall to Kant. Kant said it's impossible to talk about the transcendent: you can only talk about the immanent; and so theology then parked itself in the irrelevant quarter from the start, and became engaged in special pleading to transpose somehow that irrelevance onto the edges of our ways. It parked itself a long way from the cinema, and tried to say, Actually, this parking lot *can* be quite interesting!

And Wittgenstein gives theologians a new ability to speak because he suggests it's the ordinariness of our lives that really counts. For those dominated by Kant, theology spends its time reflecting on the 'limit moments' of our lives, so-called religious experiences: and these make up the substance of what 'religion' is. I'm thinking of people like William James and his enormously influential *The Variety of Religious Experience*, which is still required reading for perhaps the majority of liberal arts undergraduates in America doing an introductory course in religion; whereas Wittgenstein is not talking about the once-in-a-lifetime transcendent encounter, but about the vast majority of things that people do: the things they take for granted. And that's where Stanley's theology sets up its tent.

You can quickly see from this distinction why Stanley begins his career pointing out that ethics is not so much about moments of decision but about the character of the person making the decision: the 'moment of decision' in ethics is clearly analogous to the 'religious experience' in religion. Stanley sees both as being the footholds theology has mistakenly assigned itself in order to avoid being thrown off the philosophical mountain altogether. You can also quickly see why Stanley began his Gifford Lectures by dismantling William James' hold on the American theological imagination.

But you could answer your question a second way, and say that much of what Stanley got from Wittgenstein led him back to Aristotle. For Plato, the real is fundamentally the transcendent – the great ideals of truth, goodness and beauty are the truly real. This runs up against Kant's unbridgeable gulf between the realm of sense experience and the unreachable realm of the transcendent. Aristotle, on the other hand, is directing attention all the time to the concrete, earthy ordinariness of human and communal life, and so, like Wittgenstein, Aristotle gives theologians a language after many have fallen silent in the face of Kant. Stanley doesn't really express his debt to Aristotle and Wittgenstein until his later career.

Perhaps the most topical way to answer your question would be to point to Alasdair MacIntyre, because it's common to describe Stanley in shorthand terms as a theological version of MacIntyre. MacIntyre draws on Aristotle and Thomas Aquinas to say that ethics lies in ordinary practices and traditions and narratives that form communities who take the right things for granted.[3] But the most significant criticism of Stanley at the moment is coming from Jeffrey Stout, the Princeton philosopher, who endorses a good deal of MacIntyre, but questions how Stanley can sit MacIntyre alongside the Mennonite theologian John Howard Yoder.[4] Yoder has influenced Stanley's theology enormously,[5] but Yoder does not share a great deal of Stanley's philosophical heritage – Aristotle, Aquinas, Wittgenstein, MacIntyre. Stout's challenge is a constructive one and it'll be interesting to see how Stanley responds in the years to come.

But whether you start with Wittgenstein, Aristotle or MacIntyre, they all mean that the ordinary practices of the Church become the substance of theology, which breaks down that divide that so often exists, and which Stanley has referred to, between the Church and the theological academy – because in Stanley's thought they're actually both talking about the same thing: they're theologically reflecting on the ordinary practices. Wittgenstein and the others enable Stanley to find a whole way of expressing theology confidently, without constantly apologising to Kant for being an academic discipline at all.

HAUERWAS: I think that's exactly right. It also has to do with the occasional character of my work. I can't do system. By system I mean the assumption that you have to discover a non-problematic starting point before you begin to think through the various loci of theology. Systematic theology wants to make theology look like philosophy, or at least like how philosophy used to look. Under the systematic gaze, theology becomes divorced from the Christian body.

Now that doesn't mean that theology can't be quite critical of Christian practice. Theologians are set aside to help the Church remember what it's about, and that means that we have to help the Church see why sometimes it has gone astray. Even what was a success in one generation can become a failure in the next generation. And once you buy into my way of doing things, you don't really want to talk about ethics. We say God is Creator, and then we say that God

requires justice. Now people think, Aha, the latter statement is ethics
and the former statement is theology. Really? Have you tried to learn
to be a creature? I mean, you don't know what justice is until you've
learned to be a creature. So part of what I've been trying to do is to
help us get over the idea that you have to get your theology straight
before you ask what the ethical implications may be. Theology is
ethics all the way down.

SHORTT: Let's move on to the notion of narrative as a potent means
of communicating human experience. It's been back in vogue in
philosophy and theology generally over the past two or three
decades, as well as playing an important part in Stanley's work.[6]

WELLS: A turning point in Stanley's thought, it would seem to me, is
the moment where he says that he actually doesn't have a particular
stake in the idea of narrative in general – the 'narrative quality of
experience', as certain philosophers described it in the late 1970s. His
interest is in forming and shaping the faithful lives of Christians in
communities, and those arise through striving to adhere to and
participate in the narrative of Jesus. And that narrative is incomprehensible without the narrative of Israel, which in many ways it
realises; and the narrative of the Church is realising the narrative of
Israel and of Jesus. It's not that Jesus is important because he's part of
a really good story, but that that story becomes important because it's
the way God reveals himself to us in Christ; and the other ways in
which God reveals himself – such as the Eucharist – all presuppose
that definitive story.

One could cite two implications that flow from this – just to give a
pair of opposites that might help in understanding what it means. The
first concerns the distinction between faithfulness and effectiveness.
Christian ethics is usually considered to be a debate between faithfulness, which is usually the ethics of obligation, versus effectiveness,
which is the ethics based around consequences – that's a classical
ethical division. What Stanley's work, especially inspired by John
Howard Yoder, enables one to see is that actually faithfulness and
effectiveness are really talking about the same issues over different
time frames. The reason why you're faithful is you believe that that's
effective over the very long term, and what Stanley's work enables
Christians to do is to see that they are actually part of an everlasting
narrative, which far transcends the story of one's own individual life.
The question isn't, Is this faithful to the narrative quality of my
experience?, which might be true (a virtue ethicist might be happy
with that kind of form of expression in a philosophical vein) but

rather, Is this true to *the* story, the unfolding story of God? That's a much bigger narrative. So they're both using the word narrative, but one's using it in a theological sense and the other in a philosophical sense.

SHORTT: This connects, I think, with a distinction you both make between the saint and the hero.[7]

WELLS: Yes. The hero is in many ways still the model we look up to in contemporary society – even though we want to be very democratic and egalitarian about heroes and say we can all be heroes spontaneously. We all feel it's our job in our generation to make the story come out right, which means stories are told with the heroes at the centre of them and the stories are told to laud the virtues of the hero – for if the hero failed, all would be lost. By contrast, a saint can fail in a way that the hero can't, because the failure of a saint reveals the forgiveness and the new possibilities made in God, and the saint is just a small character in a story that's always fundamentally about God. So the saint's story is a very different story from the hero's story, and I think the distinction between saint and hero can portray the difference between philosophical ethics and theological ethics quite sharply and effectively. They're both narratives, but the theologian is looking to choose between them, rather than simply affirm the category of narrative in general.

HAUERWAS: I got into the narrative theme from diverse sources, but primarily from working through a philosophy of action in terms of identity descriptions concerning continuity of the self. This is where I began with my doctoral work. And in a sense, I didn't believe in a strong substantive self; so I had to find some way to display an ongoingness that gives you some continuity between the past and the present, and that will give you a way forward, yet appropriately displays that what we call 'me' is always to be renegotiated.

Now I know that sounds very complex, but it comes right out of Elizabeth Anscombe's *Intention* – a great book. Once I started down that track, as Sam indicated, I suddenly discovered that some people who were talking about narratives were turning it into exactly the kind of apologetic strategy I hated, namely, You've got to have a story: why don't you try ours? It doesn't matter whether it's true or not. And so I backed away from talking about narrative *qua* narrative, even though there are some interesting philosophical issues there, and just started talking about the Christian story. But I still think narrative is helpful in preventing the language of virtue becoming too abstract. That's why I talk a lot about novelists like Trollope in my work.

SHORTT: Sam, can you shed further light on the philosophy underlying this argument?

WELLS: Pretty well everyone in philosophy is wanting to affirm there is such a thing as the 'self', because it's hard to think in terms of human interaction without it. But by the time you've looked on the one hand at determinist theories that suggest the self has no ability to withstand the forces of heredity, nurture, biological and environmental forces, and on the other hand at ideas of freedom that reject determinism altogether, it becomes difficult to give a description of the self that explains how humans maintain their identity over time. How am I still me, even though I'm different from the person I was ten years ago? So that's where narrative comes in: it's a helpful, perhaps indispensable, way of displaying how the self is contingent (i.e. could always have turned out differently) and yet continuous (i.e. I'm still me). But narrative quickly becomes a panacea to smooth out a number of other unresolved issues – rather as terms like 'journey' and 'wholeness' tend to be used in discussions of spirituality. For theology, the point about narrative is not just whether it's helpful, but whether it's true.

HAUERWAS: There is a strong metaphysical issue here, and it's this. If we are created, it's like that Indian story about the earth resting on an infinite series of turtles: it's contingency all the way down. So you will never have an adequate theory that presupposes necessitation to account for the way things are. The only way you account for the way things are is by telling a story. Now that's a very strong metaphysical claim: if you could show that we all exist by necessity, you don't need a narrative. So as I've indicated, I don't want to back away from narrative, as I think it helps to express a very strong theological claim that Christians make about the way things are – that is, that they didn't have to be this way: they were *created*. The interesting question is not whether God exists, but whether we do. Which reminds you that existence is an analogical term.

SHORTT: And we don't 'exist' in this way. You're using 'exist' in a technical sense here, not as a synonym for 'being alive'.

WELLS: Yes. In Aquinas' terms, God is pure act. He can do things without changing his very nature – certainly without impairing his perfection. This is the definition of existence: he is *being*: he is not in the process of *becoming* something else. But only God can act without loss. We, his creatures, change every time we act. Every action closes off the possibilities of alternative outcomes and thus 'reduces' the potential of the person acting. Prayer is the closest we get to perfect activity, because it aligns us most closely with the being of God. Because we can't act without loss, we don't fundamentally exist – at least not in the way God does. This is the kind of theology that becomes possible when one reverses the Enlightenment 'turn to the subject' and remembers that theology is essentially about God, and only secondarily (or analogically, as Stanley puts it) about human beings.

SHORTT: So how then can we continue to talk about human existence in this way of thinking?

HAUERWAS: The word is 'gift'. You only know what it means for us to exist in relationship to God's existence when you recognise that our existence is gift: it's not necessity. God didn't have to make us. He chose to have us as his creatures. It's all grace. One of the ways to think about it is that Christianity is ongoing training to help us accept our lives as gifts. It's a very hard thing to accept our lives as gifts, because we somehow want to have control over them, and there can never be control when your life is gift.

WELLS: I can think of one piece of work that would make a good Ph.D. It would be to take the notion of gift in Hauerwas and gift in Milbank. Milbank's discussion of gift is subtly different because it arises with the whole tradition, going back eighty years to Marcel Mauss, of gift exchange in primitive societies.[8] Mauss' anthropology leads to discussion of the kind of obligation that's created by giving a gift. That discussion of obligation emerges in a treatment of forgiveness, which is where Milbank's thinking about gift is at the moment.

In Stanley's work the category of gift is more in terms of notions such as life, creation and contingency. It comes out differently, and to contrast and then to find the points of contact between those two would be a useful piece of work. Then you would contrast it with the notion of the given in people like Reinhold Niebuhr,[9] for whom the givens of life – death and taxes – are really what ethics is all about. And then you appreciate that in the early twenty-first century, where we are now, people like Stanley and John Milbank have captured the imagination of contemporary theology so that its assumptions are becoming that theology is about gift, whereas a generation or two ago for everybody, ethics was really about locating oneself between competing givens.

SHORTT: I think you've both brought us to the heart of the matter. Sam, would you talk more about what is at stake philosophically here?

WELLS: Too often the 'givens' reflect a Stoic recognition of our human predicament. We find different strategies to overcome or contain the givens of our human existence, whether by becoming so strong-minded we don't notice them, or by collaborating with others of 'good will' so that we can somehow deal with them. By givens I mean death, I mean the limitations of the body, I mean the limitations of our imaginations, intellectual limitations, the state, politics and so forth. If you want to know what I mean by Stoicism, think of Rudyard Kipling's poem 'If' ('If you can meet with triumph and disaster/And treat those two impostors just the same...'). And so we have Reinhold Niebuhr's 'moral man and immoral society': immoral because once we become corporate and collective we lose that sense of the genuine-ness of ethics which we find in the Gospels, which then become simply written for individuals; whereas gift, on the other hand, is a much more theological notion through and through. It's recognising, as Stanley is saying, that the interesting issue is not, Does God exist, but, Do we? It's all of life experienced as a gift. And to take the example of how Stanley writes about the time-consuming and dis-tracting practice of bringing up children: God gives us time to do the things he really wants us to do.

That's the key to it: there's plenty of time. It's a theology of abun-dance. There's no shortage there, and I mean to put that on a much larger canvas: the whole of Niebuhrian ethics, the ethics that domi-nated twentieth-century thought in this area, is actually about shortage. There's not enough – not enough life, not enough resources (a classic issue in global ethics today), not enough wisdom, not enough goodness, there's not enough revelation – fundamentally there's not enough God. All of these are a problem for Niebuhr, whereas especially for John Milbank and potentially for Stanley, though Stanley doesn't talk as much about this, there's *too much* God. The problem is, either our imaginations develop resistances because we want to be our own creators – we sin – or our imaginations sim-ply aren't big enough to take in everything there is of God. The things that we need, really *need*, are things like love, joy, peace, patience, kindness, goodness ... It doesn't matter how many resources we've got, if we haven't got those things, we can't actually use those resources appropriately. Well, the Holy Spirit gives us those things abundantly, but many discussions of ethics are written as if there were no Holy Spirit and no Church. Niebuhrian ethics rules out of court the things that are abundant and then perceives the Christian life as one of scarcity. Well of course it's about scarcity and Stoic endurance if you've ignored all the gifts God has given. But whose fault is that?

Niebuhr takes out the part played by God in giving us the gift of our existence out of pure grace. He takes the gift out of ethics. He takes out the Church, which is given to us to practise and model what it would be like if we lived as if the Holy Spirit were giving us a super-abundance of these things. We have somehow to scrabble around and manage without it. So with no Church and with no Holy Spirit – and a good deal of the time without much help from Scripture, either – we really scratch around to do the best ethics we can. And that's Niebuhrian ethics.

Stanley and John Milbank, on the other hand, are in different ways challenging that and saying, Well, what if we think about ethics *with* the gift of the Holy Spirit and *with* the gift of the Church? What if we started by saying God gives his people more than everything they need – not everything they want, of course, but everything they *need* to follow him? Surely that is the meaning of the New Testament. The Christian life is not some kind of unsolvable puzzle – a dynamic jigsaw with key pieces missing – which we're supposed to carry on playing anyway, even though we surmise the joke must be on us. It's a wonderful gift with far more breadth and depth than we need, and a never-ending supply of examples (saints) and encouragement (Holy Spirit) as to how to enjoy it. If I were to say to Stanley, one thing I'd like him to write more about in the next ten years, it would be the Holy Spirit, because that's drawing out the implications of the gift of God. I'd like him to write about the Holy Spirit the way Yoder writes about Jesus.

HAUERWAS: I agree that a dissertation comparing John Milbank's work with mine, along the lines Sam has spelt out would be fascinating, and I would learn from it because I'm not sure how John Milbank and I do differ, except that he has a natural metaphysical mind and I don't. I worry about abstract accounts of gift that are not first-order theological language, though I'm not saying it can't be done.

I'd like to underline something Sam has just said. It's that Reinhold Niebuhr wasn't just recommending a certain understanding of Christianity. I think he reflected the Stoic character of Christianity in modernity. In other words, he was giving voice to what 'is'. And that 'is' became Christian because Christians assumed that it was the Church's task to run the world, to make Britain work, to make America work. As a result, Christianity became a disguised Stoicism, in which it helped people come to terms with the limits that were assumed as givens. And Stoicism was always, in my view, the most attractive alternative to Christianity other than Judaism, because

Stoicism trains us not to expect, to hope for, too much. Stoicism underwrites empires, because it will give the fragile conscience of the bureaucrats who run empires comfort when they have to do such great evil in the name of doing good. For me the disengagement of Christianity from Stoicism is one of the greatest tasks we face.

SHORTT: You're revealing some of the roots of your pacifist stance here, and we ought to look at this subject in more detail.

HAUERWAS: Yes. I don't like to be identified as a pacifist, as if that's really what all of this is about, because what it's all about is Christ, the second person of the Trinity. And one of the things I learned from John Howard Yoder was that we make a Christological mistake when we try to talk about Jesus and then say, We really think he is the Son of God, and second person of the Trinity, and therefore, these implications about pacifism follow. What Yoder helps you see is that non-violence isn't one aspect of what people might identify as the Christian way of life separate from telling one another the truth, as we are enjoined to do in Matthew 18. It's not separate from Christians' understanding of how it is that they don't have ownership of their possessions.

SHORTT: But the Church *has* interpreted the matter in a different light, hasn't it? There's the fact that the just-war tradition arose in the first place. No one in the Church has ever seriously doubted that telling the truth is always the right thing to do, but the notion of the just war was coined in response to changed circumstances.

HAUERWAS: Yes, that is what's often said. In reply, I always ask why the Church didn't develop a position on just adultery. So the assumption that just war is some kind of faithful mode of discipleship needs to be carefully examined. Some think the just war is a series of exceptions from the general Christian commitment to non-violence, but I think the stronger justification of just war involves claiming that it is what is required if you are to do justice. Accordingly, justice requires punishment; it will even require armies. I take that as a very serious position. And I just want to see if you can pull it off.

SHORTT: Are you making an important concession to some form of realism, then?

WELLS: What you've got to see is that Yoder helped Stanley see that he, not Niebuhr, was the realist. If the most powerful force in the universe is not armies and markets but cross and resurrection, then the real realists are those who follow the way of the cross. That's the argument at the heart of Stanley's Gifford Lectures, and that's why he called them *With the Grain of the Universe*. Stanley's objection to conventional Christian realism is that it isn't Christian and it isn't realism. But the proof of the pudding is always in performance – can the just-war approach be put into practice?

SHORTT: A good deal of serious work has been done on this subject, however: look no further than Oliver O'Donovan. His book *The Just War Revisited* argues that armed conflict is not only justified in self-defence, but as a means of delivering judgement when all other means of judging a dispute have failed. The proviso is that such a judgement must be a truthful pronouncement on what has been done, and an effective foundation for what is to be done, and this applies to all decisions at whichever moment in the course of the conflict they arise. And the principle behind this, of course, is that resistance is sometimes required if this world isn't to fall away from what it's meant to be; which is why those who endorse this argument feel that the pacifist is a spectator of violence, and thereby in collusion with it.

HAUERWAS: The question is, What does that have to do with Jesus? I mean, if you think that Christ has made a way of life possible that would be otherwise unimaginable, if Christ had not done what Christ *has* done through his death and resurrection, then where do you start saying that we just can't follow him in *this* context. Why not? I mean, I had a friend say to me once that Christians can't be non-violent because there are just too many of us. And I said, Let's talk about life-long monogamous fidelity. What kind of disciplined community would you need to have in order to be a community capable of life-long monogamous fidelity?

SHORTT: I can see the force of your point that the gospel makes costly demands on Christians, and that vigilance against bad faith and complacency is always necessary. But many people would still insist that the relevant New Testament passages need handling with care. After all, most textual scholars think Jesus believed in the imminent end of the world, and that he was simply mistaken about this. That's a matter of technical exegesis with important implications for what we're talking about.

WELLS: I'd say, if you're going to settle on one text where you can see the divergence between someone like Stanley and the conventional Christian ethicist, it would be, 'No one can be a follower of mine unless they deny themselves, take up their cross and follow me' (Matthew 10:38 and Mark 8:34). Because for a conventional Christian Stoic, if you like, taking up your cross means the cross you have to bear if you're the Defence Secretary, and you have to realise that something must be done about this country that's threatening to have nuclear weapons and the whole point is that only a handful of countries are supposed to have nuclear weapons, and so we must do something about it. And it could be brutal, but it'll be good for Western democracies and therefore all life as we know it, in the long run.

But for someone like Yoder, Jesus died on the cross because that's what Rome did to political threats, and he was a political threat because he didn't take the path of establishment conformity, but also because he didn't go off into the desert with the Essenes and wash his hands of the whole thing. He stood there in Jerusalem being that alternative: you know, in that market place, as a member of God's people, obviously a particularly significant member. Now for the establishment-responsibility people, the cross becomes domesticated as something we all have to bear. For people influenced by Yoder's reading of the cross, it becomes the definitive way in which we follow Jesus.

HAUERWAS: One of the crucial things that comes into focus once you start thinking along the lines that Yoder teaches, is how you understand the sense of 'we'. My way of putting it is to cite a show we had on TV in America for years, *The Lone Ranger*, about this white guy who was saved by his faithful Indian sidekick, Tonto, and he went around the West doing good. Once, the Lone Ranger and Tonto found themselves surrounded by 25,000 Sioux in the Dakotas. And the Lone Ranger looked over to Tonto and said, 'This looks pretty tough, Tonto. What do you think we ought to do?' And Tonto answered, 'What do you mean "we", white man?' Now Christians have assumed that the public we is us. What are 'we' going to do about Iraq? George Bush Sr said that we must oppose naked aggression wherever it occurs around the world. American Christians said, That 'we': that's us. Until just-warriors see that that 'we' isn't their 'we' either, they're not going to have a political stance that will give their work any bite. We badly need to recover a stronger understanding of the relationship between the Church and the world. I want to stress that we're surrounded. The question is, How do we, as a surrounded people, not circle the wagons, but keep going through in a way that enables us to be of service to God and our neighbours?

WELLS: A reference that I picked up from Stanley's book *After Christendom?*[10] and have taken on with a lot of the work I've done, is Michel de Certeau's distinction in his book *The Practice of Everyday Life* between a tactic and a strategy. A strategy is basically the art of the powerful, the establishment 'we', which operates from a citadel, whether that be of medicine, the law or the military; they all make forays into the hinterland, and if they have a good time, then they control a greater territory, and if they have a bad time, then they pull up the drawbridge and they are safe in this citadel, and they stay there until the next foray.

For a tactic, on the other hand, there is no citadel. There's no place of security for Christians to withdraw to, no place to stockpile their weapons. They're in hand-to-hand encounters in the hinterland the whole time. That's all they've got. So to me, that makes a very helpful distinction, a different way of putting the same point about the 'we'. Christians are not in a position to ask a question like, What are *we* going to do about Iraq? – because if we're being faithful we have no stockpile of weapons to bring recalcitrant world leaders to heel. In liberation theology terms, what it means to be in solidarity with the poor is that if Christians were living their gospel more faithfully, they *would* be poor in that sense, poor in the sense of powerless: powerless, that is, in terms of access to conventional routes to coercive power. So that, to me, makes more sense of where Christians will find themselves if they are more faithful to who they should be. And part of what Stanley has named so accurately is just how much conventional Christianity has bought into a kind of 'we' that hasn't got all that much to do with the New Testament, or an appropriate telling of the story of the Church.

HAUERWAS: Yes. Could I add a word about Oliver O'Donovan's critique of my position. His argument, as you've said, Rupert, is based on the idea that the Church had to develop and recast its position as it grew into an institution and took on more responsibilities – and therefore that I'm tied to a romantic view of the first four centuries of Christianity. I think that's wrong. What I'm trying to do is name a Christian faithfulness that has always been there. After all, the Constantinian Church produced the monastic movement. It's not as if my position resembles that of a bunch of people withdrawing into farm culture in Northern Indiana because they're Amish. I'm a full professor at Duke University: that's not withdrawing. I don't pre-suppose that Christians can't run for public office at all. I think whether you're going to be elected or not depends on what kind of populace there is, and whether candidates tell the truth. John Howard Yoder said he always thought that a Christian could probably be elected to public office once!

WELLS: It's the same with the establishment of the Church of England.

People often say to me that, since I agree with Stanley on a lot of things, I should be campaigning for disestablishment. But the way I see it is that the Church is called to faithful witness. I'm quite happy it does so from within the veil of the power elite. I just can't quite work out why they haven't yet asked us to leave. Is it because they've found ways of not listening, or is it because we long ago lost the art of speaking?

SHORTT: **One criticism made of you, Stanley, by Jeffrey Stout and others, concerns an alleged failure to take responsibility for the influence you've had, an influence that is out of all proportion to what might have been forecast. Part of this hinges on interpretations of the word 'exile'. Could you comment on this please, Sam?**

WELLS: 'Exile' is a word that Stanley hasn't yet fully defined. Many theologians, including people like Walter Brueggemann and Tom Wright, use this term. It's obviously in the Bible, but it's also rooted in a sense of lament in contemporary society. For me, the heart of the matter is whether exile is looking back to, say, the 1950s, when everybody went to church, and we all obeyed our parents, and we didn't need to lock our front doors; or whether we are mourning an exile from a kind of Christian enclave, a kind of pseudo-state of Israel, where everybody was Christian and therefore we all obeyed the laws and we were all nice to each other and everything worked – the Pat Robertson vision; or is it that we are exiled simply through not being in the Kingdom of God, heavenly or earthly? Have we not fully embraced the gift?

I think Stanley would be more interested in talking about this last kind, but actually he's become very attractive in a casual way to the people who are really talking about the first two. And he doesn't know really what to do with those kinds of people, because it doesn't occur to him to think of the United States as the Promised Land. But there are a lot of people in America who think that it is.

HAUERWAS: I don't want to say that all forms of nostalgia are without possible interest. Nostalgia is often a very interesting form of social critique. I think Marx was quite a nostalgic thinker as a matter of fact – and I have a lot of Marxism in me. But it's curious how people identify me with the conservatives harking back to happier times. None of these conservative critics claims me. If you want to know where I think questions about exile are leading today, I would point to the question of Christianity's relation to Judaism. If the Jews are a diasporate people, and if our lives are unintelligible without the Jews, that ought to lead us into thinking of ourselves as a diaspora as well.

Christians should be 'exilic', and the temptation will always be to find a home. I just hate the boredom of home. And Christianity's just so damned interesting!

SHORTT: **Let's turn to medical ethics, another area where Stanley has made his mark.**[11] **Both of you have some sharp things to say about the unwarranted expectations behind some of our demands of medicine these days.**

HAUERWAS: My argument is that physicians and nurses have to be present to suffering in such a way as to absorb it without passing it on. And they have to know that finally they're not going to relieve it.

SHORTT: **Because we're all going to die in the end?**

HAUERWAS: Yes. There are all sorts of conditions we may have that are not cured by physicians. I don't mean to suggest there aren't some cures, but what doctors often do is help us go on in the face of the illness by teaching us what *they've* learned from other people who have learned how to go on in the face of illness. One of the demonic things that has happened to medicine is to change its purpose from care to cure, and that puts an unbelievable burden on doctors. It gives them a lot of power, but they break apart under the strain.

My argument is that all suffering creates loneliness, because it is not clear we ever know how to say to another what we're undergoing. Physicians and nurses enter into a world of suffering that means that loneliness becomes part of their lives, though they themselves often can't acknowledge this. The way they deal with it is often through the cultivation of professional distance. This is absolutely necessary: I don't criticise it at all. But that loneliness can become an occasion for power and manipulation, precisely because it can't be shared. What the Church does is say, We're in this business. We understand that you physicians and nurses can't be heroes. Share with the whole Church the life you share with the sick.

Now I believe we're coming to the point where we are going to recognise that there really is something called the Christian practice of medicine. Right now, we just think medicine is the scientific application of knowledge to illness, which is just rubbish. But the moral incoherence of our society makes it very hard to practise medicine as a coherent activity. And so I think we're going to discover that Christians may well have to train physicians in accordance with our fundamental practices – which will put them out of step with the wider society.

SHORTT: **How strong a similarity do you see between the American and British medical cultures?**

HAUERWAS: I don't think there's that much difference. I think in Britain, too, patients think that doctors offer them an opportunity to beat death, whereas no doctor works for long without realising every patient they have is going to die on them. And the Church can only produce a Christian practice of medicine by having Christian patients who refrain from forcing unwarranted expectations on medicine. I know that the health service has faced, and still faces, a lot of criticism in Britain, but it's a great thing that you've got to queue up. It's a great, good thing. No one in America with money has to queue up. Which means that, if you're rich, you're going to be subjected to an extra-ordinary torture called medical care, because you're going to get everything you want.

People are caught in these terrible binds that are created by their expectations about what health means, with the result that America is going to go broke on medicine. We're now spending 16 per cent of the Gross National Product on crisis-care medicine. And if you ask what the most important developments for the health of the population over the last century have been, they don't have anything to do with crisis-care medicine. They have to do, of course, with sewerage, windows and better diets.

But people believe we should put all this money into crisis-care medicine – and 60 per cent of the figure I just mentioned is going to people in their last year of life. You don't know it's their last year of life until you've spent all the money. And we can't afford it. This has everything to do with the control that modern states have over people's lives, because what creates the legitimacy of modern states is that they promise to make sure you get the best medical care possible. Michel Foucault saw the irony and the circularity of this with great clarity: we now police our bodies to make sure we're going to get the medical care we need to live as long as possible in order to underwrite the state legitimations that are necessary in the kind of world in which we find ourselves. And we call that freedom.

WELLS: A couple of things, just to epitomise what I've learnt from Stanley on this subject. One is that there is one key decision that's at the centre of medical ethics, and it's not whether to have an abortion or not, or whether to say goodbye to a loved one when they're in desperate, desperate pain. It's the fact that we – and I think it is appro-priate to use the word 'we' in this context – agree not to give up on people when they can't offer anything to society in any tangible form, certainly economic. We don't. We agree to sit with them, just as Job's comforters sat with him for seven days saying nothing because his suffering was so great, and actually that's why I think it's wonderful that whenever Stanley does talk about this he always begins with a paean of praise for those who are committed to doing that: people in the nursing and medical professions who make that fundamental choice not to give up on people because they're sick.

But the second key moral term in medicine is the word 'patient', and we should just keep remembering its moral significance. Everything that Stanley has just described in the last few minutes shows the absurdity of continuing to use that word when 'dissatisfied customer' is the actual definition of that term now, especially in America.

SHORTT: Stanley, I'd like to see how you think out loud; so let's end on an uncommon note. What's your line on transsexuals?

HAUERWAS: I don't know that I have one. I don't know what to make of transsexuals. I don't like the general notion that we get to make up our lives, but I do know that people are born with ambiguous characteristics that make it very hard to know how to negotiate their lives. And I guess I want to say that what bothers me always about this kind of area is the assumption that the question whether I'm a male or female is more important than whether I'm a Christian. That seems to me to be the issue. I'd hope that the Christian community would be a kind of place that wouldn't make an overriding issue of people's gender.

WELLS: I think that's a good question to have asked Stanley, because in listening to him reason out loud theologically, one sees quickly where his core, his gut, goes. I think what we've also just seen in his response is the absurdity of thinking of him as a sectarian, because the arguments that he's taking on are the prevailing liberal democratic arguments we find in mainstream society. What he's not doing is going straight to other Christian arguments, if you like, which is what you'd assume a sectarian would do. A sectarian would be interested only in discussing issues like 'Male and female he made them': does this apply to Christians today?' Also Stanley asks, Wouldn't it be great to be part of a community which actually transcended your ambivalent feelings about who you are as a person? This directs us to practices, community and worship.

So it actually ends as a kind of apologetics, although Stanley would never use that term. 'Wouldn't you want to be part of a community that placed your discomfort over your identity within the context of a far more enthralling narrative and practice?' That's the question he's putting to the transsexual – and to the world. It begins and ends in a mission-oriented context and in dialogue with those outside the Church. That shows how absurd most of the criticisms of his work are. And that all came from a spontaneous question; so I think it's very telling.

II
Tina Beattie

Feminist Theology

SHORTT: I'd like to start by quoting Natalie K. Watson's account of a core question posed by feminist theology:

> [D]oes the fact that women have been marginalised, silenced and oppressed by the Christian Churches throughout most of their history mean that Christianity as such is bad for women, or is it possible to write theology in a way that advocates the full humanity of women in the image of God? Is it possible to write a theology in which women are seen as those without whom the body of Christ is incomplete? Could the message of Christianity in fact be interpreted in a way that advocates women's experience and equality?[1]

In other words, feminist theology highlights a large injustice, but there's disagreement about what's implied by this recognition. Has the sidelining of women been an accident of history – a mark of the Church's collusion with what are at root secular mores and prejudices – or is Christian doctrine inherently patriarchal? As might be expected, mainstream scholars and pastors tend to favour the first of these alternatives, while the second is endorsed by a combination of post-Christian feminists such as Mary Daly and Daphne Hampson, on the one hand, and, on the other, by some very conservative voices who seek to defend Christian patriarchy.

Another response to Watson's definition might involve questioning the questioners. Has the male sex as a whole been as powerful and culpable as she implies, or are we talking for the most part only about an élite coterie of largely celibate men? And in connection with this, what are the dangers of portraying women almost exclusively as victims? I'm reminded of a warning by Angela West, another feminist theologian, about the problems of confining one's definition of sin to patriarchal structures alone. Christianity teaches that everyone stands in need of redemption.

Behind West's point lies the sense that tradition can sometimes subvert the assumptions of conservatives and liberals alike. What might be called the symbolic ordering of Christianity is very rich – perhaps the right word is kaleidoscopic – and it can give Christian feminists the means to talk in a confident theological voice, rather than making everything they say answerable to secular theory. Many instances of this fresher thinking could be quoted. Elizabeth Johnson, for example, observes that Sofia, the female symbol of Wisdom, is the most developed personification of God's presence and activity in the Hebrew Scriptures.[2] Preparing for this conversation, I was especially interested by Janet Martin Soskice's argument, which we'll look at later, that supposedly masculine-based narratives can be mapped on a feminine grid.

That's by way of a curtain raiser, one merit of which, I hope, will be to reassure readers that this discussion involves more than just qualifying the work of earlier feminist theologians, necessary though that may be. I'll ask you to describe the scene – and the distinctive contribution being made by a newer generation of thinkers – after beginning with your life. You became a Roman Catholic having started out as a Presbyterian. Surprisingly, perhaps, you evolved as a feminist and Catholic at much the same time. How did this happen?

BEATTIE: I was brought up in a Presbyterian family in Zambia during the late 1950s and 1960s. Even as a child I always had a fascination for Catholicism, partly because I was educated at a convent school. Like many people I drifted away from religion during my teens and twenties, and it was when I had the first of my four children and the question of baptism arose that I began to think again about what Christianity meant to me. At that time my husband and I were moving around, working in different countries, and then we settled in Zimbabwe in the early 1980s, just after the end of UDI. I returned to my Presbyterian roots there, but the church I joined was quite Evangelical, and I never really fitted in. I was also becoming more politically aware, and I wasn't too impressed by the track record of the Protestant Churches during UDI. I was attracted by what I read of the Catholic Church's role during those years, particularly since the then head of the Catholic Justice and Peace Commission had been imprisoned by both Ian Smith and Robert Mugabe. So there was now a political basis – a liberationist motive, perhaps – to the renewed attraction I felt towards Catholicism.

I went to see a Catholic priest and he was keen to talk about transubstantiation, assuming that was a stumbling block for me, but I said that my problems centred on the Pope and the Virgin Mary. He replied that if I could say the Mass and the creed with my heart in it, I'd have the rest of eternity to sort out these lesser problems. I went on to do my doctorate on the Virgin Mary, and I sometimes say that just leaves me with one problem to sort out as a Catholic.

We moved to England in 1988, and three years later I went to study theology at Bristol University, where I discovered feminist religious thought under the aegis of Ursula King, who is one of the great pioneers of feminist theology and is still a great source of inspiration to me in her enthusiasm and commitment. Apart from reading Germaine Greer's *The Female Eunuch* when I was eighteen, that was my first real exposure to feminism, but a great many questions began to slot into place. I started to realise why I had felt so ill at ease during my Evangelical days when, as a member of an organisation called Homemakers, I'd tried very earnestly to be a devoted mother and a good submissive wife (much to my husband's bewilderment. He feels much less threatened by my Catholic feminism).

Inevitably, I felt to some extent tugged in different directions by Catholicism and feminism – I still do. On the one hand, I was beginning to discover that the Marian tradition I'd been so nervous about was spiritually very nourishing. Suddenly I was in churches full of statues, symbols and devotions that allowed me to explore my relationship with God for the first time in language that wasn't exclusively masculine, as it had been in the Presbyterian tradition I'd known. The relationship between motherhood and God began to seem interesting and full of rich possibilities, based on that encounter between my own experience and this new form of Christianity. At the same time, my reading of feminist theology was highlighting the problems with some of these symbols and ideas. I've been living with this tension ever since, but most of the time it feels like a creative challenge.

SHORTT: I believe the matter is focused by your mixed feelings about **Rosemary Radford Ruether, Elisabeth Schüssler Fiorenza, and other pioneers in feminist theology. You've been influenced by them, and readily acknowledge their large achievements. But your own thought, like that of other second-generation feminist theologians such as Sarah Coakley, Susan Parsons and Mary McClintock-**

Fulkerson, has to some extent been prompted by the urge to move in a new direction.

BEATTIE: Yes. I learnt much from the standard bearers and their work, particularly Ruether's *Sexism and God-Talk*,[3] which was one of the first books I read on the subject. I still think it's a book that repays careful reading, even though some of her arguments are questionable – for example the claim that whatever contributes to the full humanity of women is redemptive, and whatever denies the full humanity of women is not. In recent years feminist theology has been influenced by what's sometimes called the 'linguistic turn'. Feminist thinkers have become more aware of the extent to which experience is shaped by language, so that a feminist critique of theology cannot appeal to women's experience *per se*, but must look at the ways in which experience is linguistically constructed and communicated. There's been some criticism of this approach by those who see the first task of feminist theology as political – it's about the transformation of women's lives, not about keeping up with the latest fashionable theories in academia. I think this is an important point, particularly for many women theologians in Africa and Asia and Latin America who are living much more on the frontline of these political struggles than their Western academic counterparts; but one approach does not necessarily preclude the other.

I think it was Augustine who said that any theology that can't be communicated to the people in the churches is not Christian theology. So those of us who find it fruitful to engage with postmodern theoretical perspectives must bear in mind that our first responsibility is to the Christian community, and this means constantly striving to balance the demands of good scholarship with the demands of prayerful and ethically engaged practice. As it happens, few Western feminist theologians ever refer to the significance of prayer – and some are quite resistant to the whole idea. An exception would be the theologians you've just referred to – particularly Sarah Coakley, who has written some fine reflections on the significance of spirituality.[4]

There's a connected point here. It's important to bear in mind that women have always been doing theology in the Christian tradition, as opposed to the academy. One of the shortcomings of Natalie Watson's definition you quoted earlier is that she confuses theology and Christianity. If you define history in terms of what theologians have been doing, then women are excluded and silenced for much of the time, particularly since the rise of the universities in the twelfth century; and theological rhetoric is often highly misogynist. But if you define the history of Christianity as a story of faith and a way of life for millions and millions of people, then I'd have my doubts about such a clear-cut characterisation. Women have always been as much part of the Christian story as men have, and their influence has been considerable. I think we have to guard against a risk of arrogance in the ways we criticise the past. It's anachronistic to judge history by the standards of contemporary feminism.

Nevertheless, you said something very important at the outset. On the whole, the people who have defined the Christian tradition in doctrinal and theological terms have been a fairly small élite of white, celibate, European men, and that has excluded vast numbers of the world's people, male as well as female. Today, it's not just women but non-Western cultures and religions that are changing the shape of Christian doctrine. It's an exciting time to be a theologian.

This distinction between history and theology is also important if we want to ask what the vast majority of people might actually have been doing, rather than what a religious hierarchy was saying they ought to be doing. I tell my students that one should probably assume that religious populations are often doing pretty much the opposite of what their moral authorities are telling them. For example, if you thought no Catholics were resorting to contraception or abortion at the beginning of the twenty-first century because recent popes have said so much against these practices, you would be reading those teachings in the wrong way. We have to appreciate that many of the Church's writings on women may have been provoked by the fact that women were never so docile as the texts suggest.

SHORTT: **In brief, then, you're saying that your subject needs to be approached with more humility.**

BEATTIE: Yes, even though that's not the most popular word in the feminist lexicon. It's an important quality, not only in terms of the past and what we can know about it, but even more importantly in terms of what theology is. If theology is not a prayerful, self-questioning activity that allows itself to be continuously broken open and unravelled by the mystery of God, then it becomes the most hubristic of all forms of thought. I mean, if you can invoke God as being on your side, what could be more powerful than that?

Fulkerson has written very interestingly on the relationship between feminist theology and power, drawing on the theoretical perspectives of Michel Foucault.[5] She argues that feminists like Ruether risk being blind to the power of their own rhetoric – and incidentally, I include myself in this. We are in academic jobs; we decide who counts in terms of experience; we decide who gets invited into the conversation. An interesting insight into this comes from Jean Bethke Elshtain.[6] Her argument is that historically men have had institutional power – what she calls *potestas* – conferred on them in all sorts of structures, from the family up. But that doesn't mean that women have been powerless victims. Elshtain uses the term *potentia* to refer to the kind of charismatic power of women that can be used for good or for ill, just as *potestas* can. That kind of informal, non-institutional power can be manipulative, it can be very cunning; but it can also be a power that subverts the oppression of institutionalised power through relationships of care, through the loving it does beyond the control of those structures. When we look at great literature down the ages, we see women as well as men exercising this kind of power.

SHORTT: **Chaucer's Wife of Bath saw off five husbands pretty comprehensively, didn't she?**

BEATTIE: Yes, and think of some of Shakespeare's women. I suppose Lady Macbeth is the classic negative example, but what about Rosalind? Or Mozart's women. Donna Elvira, perhaps. I'm not saying these are feminist icons, but they're characters who challenge some feminist stereotypes. And look at some of the women in the Hebrew Scriptures. Think about Sarah in her dealings with Abraham, or about Abigail, who goes off to make peace with King David and tells him to ignore her husband, Nahum, because he's such a buffoon. God conveniently strikes Nahum dead, leaving Abigail free to marry David. Or there's the story of Ruth and Naomi, and how they plotted together for Ruth to seduce Boaz. In the Gospels, too, women are highly significant, and they always seem to come off well, even when they challenge Jesus, as the Syrophoenician woman did. It's the male disciples who are held up as lacking faith or as misunderstanding what Jesus is about, never his women disciples. Feminist biblical scholars are reclaiming these women of the Bible, and bringing new perspectives into view. The same is true of women in the early Church. These are constantly evolving areas of feminist scholarship.

What I'm saying is that we need to be aware of the way power operates. It's rarely simply a case of men's power over women, and only in the most exploitative or violent situations is it the case that one person or group has absolute power over another. Normally, we're caught up in complex negotiations of power all the time, and that's an important point if we're talking about the ways in which women might use and abuse power, particularly today, when women are acquiring institutionalised power for the first time.

SHORTT: Does that take us back to the question I raised earlier, about feminist theology's handling of sin?

BEATTIE: Yes, absolutely. One gets the impression from reading some feminist theologians that sin is either an anachronistic concept, or it's mainly to do with patriarchy and androcentrism; but it's a perspective that's often lacking from feminist discussions of women's agency and ways of being in the world. To say this is not to imply that the Christian understanding of sin is adequate from a feminist perspective – it's not. For men as well as women, we need to draw on the psychological and sociological insights of the twentieth century to rethink the question of sin and what it involves. For example, Valerie Saiving wrote an influential article in the early 1960s in which she suggested that the Christian understanding of sin might be informed by masculine concepts such as lust and pride, whereas women's sins might be more to do with excessive self-humiliation (which of course is not the same as humility), and a failure to take the self seriously enough.[7] Since then, theorists such as Carol Gilligan have brought a psychological perspective to bear on some of these issues.[8] In her study of women's moral development, Gilligan identified a tendency for girls to lose confidence in their own moral insights as they approach adolescence. She argues that women tend to form moral decisions based on the imperative to maintain relationships of care, while men tend to be guided more by principles based on appeals to autonomy and individual rights. Gilligan argues that we need to integrate these two perspectives, to develop a more holistic approach to moral issues. Work such as hers has something important to contribute to Christian moral theology.

SHORTT: And I imagine you also think it's vital for feminists to challenge traditional Christian ideas about the relationship between sex and sin – particularly since these have so often been bound up with portrayals of Eve, and an allied association of female sexuality with sin and death.

BEATTIE: Yes. Christian ideas of sin are heavily invested with an unexamined fear of female sexuality that runs through the tradition, which hasn't been helped by centuries of compulsory celibacy. We must also recognise that our concepts of sin are culturally conditioned, which means asking far-reaching questions, not only about sexuality, but about war and violence, racism and nationalism, economics, the environment, politics – in a democracy, we can sin in the polling booth just as easily as in the bedroom. Liberation and feminist theologies have made an important contribution to Christian thinking in these areas.

On the other hand, feminists need to take seriously the question of sin as a mysterious but profoundly personal experience of alienation and distorted desire which does seem to be part of the human condition, and this can't simply be attributed to the effects of patriarchy. Freud pretty firmly introduced into the twentieth century the idea that all of us are fundamentally alienated by some kind of primal experience of desire gone wrong, and although thinkers such as Luce Irigaray have challenged Freud's androcentric bias, there is still something there that we can't ignore. Whether you call it original sin or the Oedipus complex, there's wisdom about human nature in these terms, and it needs a deeper theological response than criticising unjust social structures, important though that is. Sin might affect women differently from men – it would be surprising if it didn't, given the different forms of cultural conditioning we're exposed to – but as you've indicated, women need God's grace, healing and redemption just as much as men do.

As soon as we ask what we mean by sin, we also have to question some of the ways in which we understand God. I've referred to sexuality and Freud, but it's also interesting to note how influential René Girard has been in recent years, in raising questions about Christian attitudes to sacrifice and violence. Girard hasn't made much of an impact on feminist theology, and he tends to be quite dismissive of feminism, which is a shame, because he shares the concerns of many feminist theologians, not least in challenging the idea of God as a sacrificial father figure who demands the death of his Son. Some feminists have questioned the doctrine of the atonement along those lines. Others ask if the idea of God demanding the crucifixion of his Son is a terrible image of child abuse. Again, these are important questions, and it's premature to expect feminist theology to come up with adequate solutions to these vast issues that it opens up. After all, it took the early Church over three centuries and much political wrangling to get round to the Council of Nicaea. We might have to wait a few centuries yet before we have a Council of Lesbos that gives doctrinal recognition to women's theological insights.

SHORTT: So feminist theology has asked many of the right questions, but hasn't always offered the right solutions. This isn't surprising, though, given that it's still early days for the subject.

BEATTIE: Yes. A fruitful approach is to keep going back to the roots – to be really radical, in that sense – in order to ask why these doctrines first entered Christian language and what the earliest thinkers were trying to get at. Christianity didn't begin as an enterprise whose whole purpose was to oppress women, although you wouldn't know it to read some feminist theologians. In fact, the earliest Christians believed that the core message of the Christian faith was freedom from all structures, practices and beliefs that enslaved the human spirit, for women as well as men. Sarah Coakley and Janet Soskice both recognise the value in asking what theological ideas meant to the early Christians, and often we can discover material in these early sources which challenges some of the later developments that have been detrimental to women. For example, the understanding of sin, certainly in the early Church, had much to do with the idea of our being vulnerable, in a terrible predicament, and in need of Christ's rescue. Having fallen into the clutches of death, we were powerless to escape the suffering that ensued. This offers an understanding of sin that can allow us to criticise some later concepts that have been particularly negative for women, without going so far from the tradition that we begin to use a rhetoric that doesn't hook into it.

SHORTT: I know you feel that patristic theology is also a valuable resource for both upholding and rethinking traditional teaching about Mary. Would you say a bit more about that, including your belief in the virgin birth?

BEATTIE: The idea of Mary's virginal conception of Jesus wasn't about sexual morality, but about the human and divine natures of Christ – about the vertical and horizontal dimensions of the incarnation, to put it another way. Christ is fully human because he has a human mother. He is one of us, born into the human story that begins with Adam and Eve. Like us, he's born, eats, suffers, dies. But Mary's virginity says that Christ is God incarnate, because this is something miraculous that interrupts history, something entirely new that comes about through God's power and Mary's assent. I think that's very important for feminism. If Mary had conceived Christ sexually, then ultimately it would have been a man's consent, not a woman's, that was needed for the incarnation. But the fact that no male mediation or intervention was needed has profound implications, not least for a theology of priesthood that says a man always has to mediate between humankind and God. If Mary's 'yes' was enough to incarnate Christ in her body, a woman's prayers of consecration ought to be enough to incarnate him in bread and wine. And incidentally, in the Catholic tradition it's of the utmost importance that Mary did consent, which is why Catholics and Protestants disagree about whether or not she co-operates in Christ's saving work. Catholicism says she must have co-operated, because she freely consented to what God asked of her. God doesn't violate human freedom in the incarnation.

The idea of Mary's virginity got bound up with ideas about women and sexual morality from about the late fourth century, when the Church was becoming more hierarchical and more institutionally organised along gendered lines. I think there's much truth in feminist claims that the virgin–mother dichotomy has not served women well. But the way beyond that is not to invent a sex life for the Virgin Mary, but rather to look at why the early Church thought her virginity was important.

Perhaps it's easier for Catholics (I'm including the Orthodox and Anglican traditions, as well as the Roman Catholic) than for Protestants to trace these ideas back through history. But feminist theology is impoverished when it's not sufficiently rooted in doctrinal history.

SHORTT: **I think you've already given a hint of how you might answer the charge of sectarian bias here. Since you've faced this accusation explicitly, from a Protestant feminist reviewer of your book *Woman*,[9] I wonder if you could reply to it in more detail.**

BEATTIE: I referred earlier to the importance of balancing academic scholarship with the needs of the faith community, and I think this is one area where feminist theology often falls down, because it pursues a kind of well-intentioned but woolly-minded ecumenism in its theological arguments. Certainly, I see ecumenism as vital in prayer and Christian social action, and ecumenical debate and discussion are important, but these are nurtured by good theology, and that entails not sectarianism, but particularity. Christianity might be one story about the world, but enfolded within that are many different narratives, and what is theology if it's not the telling of a particular narrative and an exploration of its possible interpretations, meanings and contradictions? Of course that process entails dialogue with other narratives, but for that dialogue to happen, we have to know where our differences are.

Nowhere are the differences between Catholicism and Protestantism so conspicuous as in the significance accorded to maternal feminine symbolism – Mary, the saints, the maternal Church. These are not peripheral to feminist theology: they concern its pivotal symbols and concerns. There's some fine work being done by Protestant feminists in some of these areas, including on Mary, but by definition that must be a different theological enterprise from the kind of work Catholic theologians would undertake, even if we

discover large areas of common ground. I'm also interested in
sacramental language and symbolism, and again, that's an area of historical and doctrinal difference between Catholics and Protestants, as
is the whole theology of creation and grace. So I do make clear that
my theology is written from a Catholic perspective, not because it's
intended to be exclusive or sectarian, but because my own experience
makes me deeply conscious of the differences between Protestantism
and Catholicism in the areas that I work in, and it would be
intellectually dishonest to say that this doesn't matter.

SHORTT: Turning more to the wider world, one of the positive mes-
sages of your work is that despite appearances, Christian theology,
and Catholic theology in particular, have huge amounts to contribute towards the theory and practice of being a woman in the
twenty-first century. Jane Williams has given the following précis of
your book *Woman*:

> Beattie argues that modern post-feminist non-religious women
> are in a pitiable state. She quotes the front cover of *Cosmopolitan*
> magazine from March 2002 and concludes from the topics listed
> that this is what a modern woman might well be like: 'somebody
> who worries about her weight and appearance, is fascinated by
> Hollywood stars, has improbable sexual fantasies while fretting
> about her sexual performance and is quite possibly being beaten
> and abused by the man she shares her home with'. Her main func-
> tion in society is as a consumer whose self-doubts and anxieties
> can only be fed by buying things.
>
>   What *Cosmo* girl has given up to live in this world of un-
> certainty is a secure domain of 'benign patriarchy' whose moor-
> ings in religion gave women a strong sense of self-worth and
> belonging and a satisfaction in knowing the value of marriage,
> motherhood and married life. But Beattie is no naive conservative
> ... [she] is simply raising the question of whether secular femi-
> nism has actually made life more fun for women (answer: in some
> ways, yes, in some ways, no), and whether we are now any nearer
> to a definition of 'woman' than we were when men did all the
> defining (answer: no).[10]

One of the corollaries of this is that if women and men alike could
appreciate the richness of Christian symbolism, then traditional
Christianity would become a much more wearable garment than it
appears.

BEATTIE: There were lots of big ideas in *Woman* that I didn't do justice to, and I'm not sure I was entirely fair to modern secular women. But yes, something in me does want to say, Look beyond the façade, and see what you're missing. Secular culture in Britain is hostile to religion, as a result of which lots of women dismiss what the Church has to offer without ever trying it for themselves. Women have gained enormously in some areas of modern culture, but there have been great losses in other areas, including religion and spirituality. No matter how patriarchal Christianity has been, it has also been an empowering faith for women, not only medieval mystics, but women like Mary Wollstonecraft, Florence Nightingale, Josephine Butler, Dorothy Day, not to mention the many women founders of religious orders in the nineteenth century. Daily Christian life is often focused on communities of women, particularly mothers, but also on the activities of religious sisters in the Catholic Church. And is modern culture really any more women-friendly, with its *Brave New World*-style science, its war and violence, its brutal economics, and its vacuous consumerism? What I see today in secular culture – and I don't think you have to be a theologian or religious believer to sense this – is a sort of disintegration verging on despair. I think there's a hunger for meaning and an insatiable consumption that masks some terrible unmet need at the heart of human experience in the most affluent societies.

SHORTT: But there's a challenge here. On the one hand, Christianity does have a great deal to offer women, but on the other hand that's not always apparent, particularly in the Catholic Church, which still presents a very male-dominated image to the world.

BEATTIE: It's true that you have to be quite determined to sit through a Mass where a priest never once attempts to use inclusive language, and where the homily is a vague mumble through a few platitudes that have absolutely no relationship to anything real going on in your own world or anybody else's. So I'm not saying that what the Church offers can simply be taken at face value by women, but, rather, that it offers something more substantial and more challenging than anything you'll find in the 'Mind, Body, Spirit' section of your local bookshop.

Nor am I implying that the Church should bend over backwards to reflect all the latest political and cultural trends, feminist or otherwise. One of the great weaknesses of modern Catholic liturgy is its bland impoverishment as a result of trying to be too 'consumer-friendly', so that much of the mystical or transcendent quality of worship is sacrificed in the interests of participatory sing-alongs. This isn't an appeal

for a return to a form of pre-Vatican II Catholicism – although to some
extent I agree with those who say that too much was sacrificed in the
democratisation of the liturgy. It's not just reactionaries who are saying that, either. Charlene Spretnak – a radical feminist – has written a
book in which she appeals for the recovery of a more mystical, potent
form of Mariology, instead of the rather diminished figure of modern
Catholic devotion.[11] Sarah Jane Boss's recent book on Mary argues
along similar lines.[12] This suggests a need to rediscover the sacramentality of Catholicism, but in a way that makes it appropriate for the
questions people are asking of faith and life today. That means recognising that liturgy needs to tap into those levels of awe and desire that
so often get covered over in our everyday lives.

The symbolism and sacramentality of Catholicism is a remarkable
heritage, as is its mingling of Scripture and tradition. In my
Evangelical days, Scripture was the ceiling I banged my head on.
Whenever a question was too hard, you just had to believe such and
such a tenet because the Bible said so. As I read more Catholic
writings, I began to see that Scripture could be the trampoline
beneath your feet. It could be where you started from to go to some
very exciting places rather than what stopped you asking.

Good theology is like great literature and poetry – it makes its
point by its lyrical capacity to evoke other possible worlds.
Postmodern feminism has yielded an appreciation of the ways in
which our bodies are part of a linguistic performance of faith, that it's
the symbols we use and the narratives we tell that position our bodies
in the world. That's not just a theological point, of course. Judith
Butler is the feminist theorist *par excellence* on this. Sarah Coakley has
written a very interesting essay comparing Butler and Gregory of
Nyssa, arguing that he offers an eschatological perspective that Butler
lacks, but that in other respects they're on a similar wavelength as
regards the significance of gender.[13] This is feminist theology at its
best – that creative inter-reading of the ancient and the contemporary.
As I've indicated, this is of much more than academic interest alone.
The question of justice for women can't be separated from the question of sacramentality and gender, in a Church whose sacraments are
still so skewed by a one-sided understanding of the significance of
gender. How can we expect the Church to be serious about women's
rights in the secular sphere, if it's still so reluctant to acknowledge our
significance in the liturgical and sacramental sphere?

SHORTT: Could you spell out in more detail your ideas about
sacramentality and how it relates to gender?

BEATTIE: If one emphasises the significance of symbolism and sacramentality, then one has to recognise the extent to which gender is the
   kaleidoscope through which the Catholic imagination views the
   human and divine worlds and the relationships between and among
   them. The association between divinity, masculinity and transcendence, and nature, femininity and bodiliness, is a hugely significant
   construct that continues to shape theological language. But I use the
   term 'kaleidoscope' deliberately, because when one starts to look at
   how gender functions in the Catholic tradition, it's very dynamic,
   with constantly changing patterns and relationships. I don't deny that
   women have always been positioned in terms of their bodies in ways
   that men haven't; but both sexes have also had access to gendered
   language as a form of expression that goes beyond sexual dualisms.

   The problem today is that Catholic feminists and conservatives
   alike have lost this fluidity, so that there's a much more literalistic
   understanding of sex and gender, whether it's liberal feminists talking
   about women's experience, or conservative Catholics adhering to the
   essentialist theology inspired particularly by Hans Urs von Balthasar.
   On the one hand, von Balthasar insists on an absolute difference
   between the sexes, which is a very modern way of putting it; traditionally, that hasn't been the Catholic understanding of sexual difference.
   He's had a huge influence on a recent movement that calls itself 'new
   Catholic feminism' and declares itself the rightful heir to the so-called
   old feminism, which is said to have failed. This is inspired by John
   Paul II's call for 'a new feminism' that doesn't simply model itself on
   masculine values, but recognises women's fundamental qualities as
   nurturers. I'm not unsympathetic to some aspects of John Paul's
   feminism, and in fact I've suggested that he has quite a lot in common
   with a feminist figure such as Irigaray.[14] But the new Catholic feminism is utterly anachronistic nevertheless. It's based on the old sexual
   stereotypes, and it's heavily dependent on von Balthasar. Yet his
   theology is shot through with contradictions and denials in its understanding of sexuality.

   Despite insisting on an absolute difference between the sexes, he
   also says we're all women in relation to God, because to be human is
   to be open and receptive to God's initiative, just as Mary was: we're
   back with the old stereotypes that the divine initiative is masculine,
   and the human response is feminine. He also says that on Calvary,
   Mary's identity becomes that of the Church, so that the Church is now
   woman in relation to Christ. But then you have to ask, What's happened to the female body? The answer is that the female body has no

redemptive significance in von Balthasar's theology, although female sexuality serves as a metaphor for sin, death and hell at various points, in a way that I find quite pornographic.[15] I've been studying some of this recently, and it makes for dismal reading. It's interesting how few theologians pick up on these problems with his work. Even among those who are critical of him, I've never come across any who have questioned the violence of his sexual rhetoric. It makes me think that there's still a deep insensibility in the Christian theological imagination to questions of sexuality and violence.

Pursuing Balthasar's scheme, what we have is male bodies acting as women, and the only manly man is the priest, because he stands in the person of Christ, who must be male because he is God – and incidentally, when you read von Balthasar, the priest's role in the Mass is represented as a kind of cosmic male orgasm. It's worrying when you think of how widely he's taught in seminaries now. Yet even the priest, even Christ, is feminine in relation to God, as far as his humanity is concerned. So von Balthasar colonises the female body. Men are women and priests are men, but women are always and everywhere women and can't ever be men or priests. Queer theology has nothing on this.

SHORTT: **Balthasar is naturally extremely important, both in his own right and as an influence on the powers that be in the Catholic Church. Do you think the problem you identify sullies his theology generally, or is it restricted to certain parts of his oeuvre?**

BEATTIE: His output was vast; so I'm a bit wary of generalising; but I'd say it's a pervasive failing once you know what you're looking for. Feminists sometimes use the term 'reading as woman', which means that you adopt the woman's standpoint when you read a text, and then it becomes clear how many texts are written from the male point of view. So reading von Balthasar's *Theo-Drama*, for example, there's a section in Volume III which deals specifically with woman, and which makes all these points about a fundamental difference between the sexes which, he claims, runs through the whole created order.[16] So you think, Well, von Balthasar's *Theo-Drama* should be entirely scripted with that difference in mind, so that it should be possible to read it as a woman throughout and discover one's own distinctive role and mission, which is equal to but different from that of the man. But then the rest of *Theo-Drama* is written about human subjects and persons with only occasional reference to sexual difference; so either that contradicts von Balthasar's point about sexual difference – if you can say most things about humankind in a non-gendered way, then there's nothing so fundamental about gender – or it means that *Theo-Drama* is just another example of theology written by a man for whom the male is the normative human being, and the woman, when she gets mentioned at all, is entirely positioned in terms of his perspectives and projections. This is all complicated by von Balthasar's friendship with Adrienne von Speyr, who had a significant influence on his theology. She's a classic example of what Irigaray refers to as '*la mystèrique*', which is a play on the idea of the female mystic as hysteric.

SHORTT: **Let me try to summarise your argument at this stage. You're saying that good feminist theology faces a complex challenge: it needs to reclaim the sacramental significance of sex and gender – which is wrongly seen by liberals as the province of conservatives alone – but must do so in a way that challenges the conservatives on their own ground.**

BEATTIE: Yes. The new Catholic feminists include some highly educated women, and I don't want to sound as if I'm dismissing them out of hand. They make some valid criticisms of secular feminism, but with a few exceptions their hostility to mainstream feminism, and their unquestioning loyalty to the Vatican, make their work highly problematic, not least because it lacks the kind of critical edge that academic theology needs. An example of the kind of material I'm referring to is a recent book called *Women in Christ*, edited by Michele Schumacher.[17] Her essays in the collection are well worth reading, but some of the others are little more than anti-feminist polemic.

I suspect that some of these ideas were behind the document issued to the world's Catholic bishops by the Congregation for the Doctrine of the Faith in August 2004, 'On the Collaboration of Men and Women in the Church'. Only the Catholic Church could issue a letter written by one exclusive group of men to another exclusive group of men about collaboration between men and women; but in fact the document says nothing about collaboration. It's just a thinly veiled attack on feminism. The challenge we face today is to recognise that, for an incarnational theology, the body matters, the body signifies, and Schumacher is good on this point. A Christian theologian can't adopt the kind of radical linguistic approach of Jacques Derrida or Judith Butler, say, which denies the body any inherent significance. We need symbols and sacraments that allow us to explore the creative potential of our bodies, to express what it means to be sexual persons made in the image of God, and that's where I think aspects of the tradition challenge the sexual dualisms of the contemporary Church.

Feminists debate about the relationship between sex and gender – between our biological bodies and cultural constructs of masculinity and femininity – but pre-modern Christians knew that gender was primarily social rather than biological. It referred to characteristics, attributes and social functions before it referred to being a sexual male or a sexual female, and that gave them conceptual freedom to explore these issues.

For example, there are Julian of Norwich's well-known reflections on the motherhood of God. St Ambrose speaks of Christ as a virgin mother who bears us in his womb and nurtures us with his milk. In St Anselm's Prayer to St Paul, he refers to Paul and Christ as his mothers in faith. He calls Christ 'the Great Mother'. I sometimes read that prayer to students and ask them who they think wrote it. They usually suggest it was Rosemary Radford Ruether or Mary Daly. If you used that prayer in church today, you'd probably be branded a feminist heretic.

SHORTT: **Let's turn to the subject of women's ordination. The implication of what you're saying is that it's a sacramental necessity.**

BEATTIE: Yes. it's not a matter of equal opportunities or rights (priesthood isn't a right), or of power sharing or any of those other secular ideas that are utterly inappropriate for a theology of priesthood. It's a function of believing that the liturgy is an anticipation of heaven, an acting out of the promises of the Christian faith; and if we believe that the female body is redeemed, then we must recognise that the female body has sacramental significance. Again, this isn't to judge history. It's not to say that it's always been wrong not to have women priests. It's to say that in our own time, this question has become an urgent issue concerning the development of doctrine, and the theological arguments against women's ordination don't hold up.

A female priesthood might inevitably mean a change in some symbolic meanings – von Balthasar's kenotic male orgasms might have to go, for instance – but it would still remain coherent in the context of the Mass. For example, some anthropologists and psychologists argue that the idea of sacrifice is deeply rooted in a masculine religious imaginary, so that there's a relationship between an all-male priesthood and cultic sacrifice. Now, if you're going to say, 'This is my body, this is my blood', and you believe that Christ is essentially male, then of course you're going to think of Christ's suffering and death, because bodies bleed only when they're wounded. But if a woman says, 'This is my body, this is my blood', the symbolism might be that of fertility, menstruation, childbirth. She represents a dimension of the incarnation of Christ and the life of the Church that's about fecundity rather than sacrifice, and a number of feminist thinkers argue that it's important to move away from a sacrificial religious symbolism to one that is more holistic and life-giving, that offers a more positive sense of nature and the body. This is a central theme of Irigaray's writings, and it's supported in Grace Jantzen's recent work on feminist philosophy of religion.[18] This would put Christ's death within the wider context of his incarnation and resurrection, and that would be an enrichment of eucharistic symbolism.

SHORTT: One of Janet Martin Soskice's examples that I had in mind at the outset involves the juxtaposition in the Synoptic Gospels of the raising of Jairus' daughter with the healing of the woman with the flow of blood. Tradition links this woman to St Veronica, the histori- cally shadowy figure whose cloth, when she wiped Christ's brow on Golgotha, was imprinted with the true icon – thus vero-nica. Accordingly, Soskice can turn up a link between the blood of the flow and the Passion of Christ: '[A]s the cloth of Christ's garment stopped the flow of the woman's blood, so Veronica's cloth stopped the flow of Christ's blood. As the woman's flow of blood is stopped and her fertility restored – she is made fertile with faith – so Christ's flow of blood is turned from death to new life.' Soskice goes on to argue that the pairing of the woman with the flow of blood and Veronica sug- gests an interpretation of the Synoptic story that isn't concerned with unclean female bodies, or with the dismissal of the law. 'Rather we are drawn back to the life-giving power of female blood, a power that the Jewish purity laws reflect, and that this reading aligns with the blood shed on the cross ... [T]he blood of the cross is mapped on the symbolics of the feminine.'[19]

BEATTIE: That's a very good example. Feminist theologians are work- ing at reclaiming some of these sacramental possibilities, in order to ask how we can live our bodies through these symbols and narratives in a way that responds to the challenge of feminism, but doesn't just cut free of any kind of traditional roots. This means allowing a femi- nist critique to unmask the hidden ideologies and assumptions that exclusively male scholarship has brought to the theological tradition over the centuries, but not giving up, if you like, on the raw materials that are necessary for all theology: preserving that matrix wherein Scripture, tradition, prayer, the body and God illuminate one another.

This means, as I've said, that Christian feminism needs to position itself in the often conflictual relationship between postmodernity and traditional Christianity. Figures such as John Milbank and Stanley

Hauerwas have important things to say about this, although I'm wary of their theological style. The late Walter Ong SJ wrote about the agonistic masculinity of traditional Christian theology; he describes it as a form of combat in which men pit themselves against each other in order to prove their strength. It's hard not to see a revival of that kind of macho theology in Milbank and Hauerwas, whose style seems at odds with their pacifist claims. But if we look more widely at theologians associated with the Radical Orthodoxy movement, there are some, like Graham Ward and Gerard Loughlin, for example, who have a richer appreciation of the significance of sexuality and gender, and don't indulge in combative rhetoric. Loughlin's work epitomises what I was saying earlier about lyrical theology: a style that can create visions through the beauty of its language. It's no coincidence that much of his recent work has been on the relationship between film and theology.

But what thinkers like Milbank and Hauerwas can help us to see is the extent to which much liberal theology, including feminist theology, dances to a secular tune. It's as if feminist theologians are desperate to win the approval of the secular sisterhood, when, in fact, secular feminists tend to be completely antagonistic towards religion, at least in the English-speaking world. Feminist theologians read feminist theorists, but not the other way round. Secular feminism is very closed-minded in that respect – but then, I think that's true of much secular thought vis-à-vis theology and religion. It's different in France, where figures such as Irigaray and Julia Kristeva allow for much greater fluidity between secular and religious perspectives. I've referred to Irigaray several times, but Kristeva also has a growing influence on some forms of feminist theology.

Ultimately, if Christian theology can't provide an adequate response to feminist theory, I'd invoke Alasdair MacIntyre's argument that if you find another tradition that answers your questions more coherently, then in conscience you should convert to that tradition. If secular feminism really is so persuasive, then why persist with Christianity? I think people like Daphne Hampson and Mary Daly have a high level of intellectual integrity in acknowledging that the Christian tradition can't answer their questions, and therefore that they're post-Christian.

SHORTT: **How do you think feminist theology will evolve over the time ahead?**

BEATTIE: I've sounded a number of critical notes, but it's important not to lose sight of the fact that feminism is a very new movement,

and it embraces many, many women from different cultures and perspectives, working across religious and cultural boundaries. It's a
developing conversation, if you like, that's open to different voices.
Women in every religion and culture share some common ground.
One way or the other, we're all up against male authority structures
and the historical exclusion and subordination of women, whichever
religious tradition or society we're talking about. The world is still
threatened by an aggressive culture of masculinity – think of
terrorism and the war on terrorism. This is where feminism,
including religious feminism, can give women an alternative voice.

As to whether feminist theology has a future, I hope the answer is
no. I look forward to a time when theology speaks with an openness
to revelation which allows us to see God in everyone and in all
creation, filtered through the lens of a rich sacramental tradition.

Miroslav Volf

Faith and Reconciliation: A Personal Journey

SHORTT: All those interviewed between these covers talk to a greater or lesser extent about their thought through the lens of their lives. This seems a particularly worthwhile approach in your case, because you grew up in Communist Yugoslavia and pursued a theological education against the odds. It was hard enough to lay your hands on books that challenged Marxist orthodoxy, let alone to get on the college course of your choice. Your life has been interesting for many other reasons besides, including your shifting church allegiance – from Pentecostalism via Presbyterianism to Anglicanism – and the peripatetic pattern of your work. You studied in your native Croatia, then the United States, and finally in Germany. You now live in the United States and have won renown for promoting reconciliation among Christians, and between Christians and Muslims in the Balkans. Although the worst of that conflict was over before the turn of the millennium, your reflections, encapsulated in books such as *After Our Likeness*[1] and *Exclusion and Embrace*,[2] provide rich materials for confronting the even stiffer interfaith challenges that the world now faces, as well as the sceptics who see religion as creating more stumbling blocks than solutions to the search for peace. We'll turn to the subject of violence later. Could you take us back to 1950s Yugoslavia to start with?

VOLF: I was born in 1956 in Croatia but grew up in Novi Sad, a multi-cultural city in northern Serbia, where my father was the Pentecostal minister. Ruled as we were by Communists out to destroy religion, we lived in interesting times, especially since we were not only religious but also belonged to the small Protestant minority, and within that minority to another, namely, Pentecostals. At school, for instance, a teacher would ask in front of the whole class what my father did. 'My dad is a pastor,' I would say. 'What on earth is a pastor?' would be the reply. This caused me almost unbearable shame at the time. I remember swearing to God that I would never do to my own children what my dad did to me by being a minister. My vow was soon broken, of course – superficially, because some visiting Swedish teenagers made faith attractive to me, but more deeply, because of the genuine and life-giving faith of my parents and my saintly nanny. So the hostility of that secular environment in my childhood and young adulthood contributed a lot to my self-understanding as a Christian and a theologian. I never had the luxury of entertaining faith merely as a set of propositions that you do or don't assent to. Nor was faith part of the cultural air I was breathing. I always experienced it as a distinct way of life, because it was a contested way of life. Through its educational system, political institutions and mass media, the dominant culture was telling me that religion was nothing more than superstition and a form of false consciousness that legitimised violence and served as a bulwark against progress.

When I look back on those years, I realise that as far as my faith was concerned, I faced two fundamental challenges from early on: faith's ability to help human beings flourish, and its intellectual plausibility. To what extent can faith in the God of Jesus Christ be intellectually compelling to the larger public? To what extent can such faith be generative of human flourishing in all spheres of life? These are the two large questions engendered by understanding faith as a way of life, and I've been pursuing them, especially the subject of human flourishing, throughout my career. The centrality of these questions explains why I could never do just religious studies – that is, examining the phenomenon of religion from various angles. Such study is important, even indispensable. But it's not sufficient. The challenge is, I think, to shape religious and so-called secular realities in the light of the reality of God as revealed in Jesus Christ. That's why I'm a theologian.

SHORTT: It also explains why you're well equipped to be Director of the Yale Center for Faith and Culture. Can we return to this after hearing more about your early life?

VOLF: I devoured novels, especially by French and Russian authors. One of the first extracurricular books I remember reading as a sixteen-year-old was Bertrand Russell's *Wisdom of the West*, an accessible and masterly history of Western philosophy. The book had just been translated into Croatian, and my brother-in-law gave it to me as a present. It was through the atheist Russell, paradoxically, that I discovered Plato as well as Augustine, Aquinas, Pascal and Leibniz, and much else that was of immense theological significance in the Western philosophical tradition. By that time I was keenly aware that my faith was subversive, and before the age of twenty I had bruises on my body caused by an angry anti-Christian mob, and a brief spell in jail, to reassure myself that I wasn't making it up in an act of self-importance.

I also felt I needed to do some serious intellectual work to make its subversiveness more effective. Before I enrolled to study philosophy and classical Greek at the University of Zagreb, and theology at the Evangelical Theological Seminary in the same city, I taught myself Greek and was deeply immersed not only in writers such as C. S. Lewis, but also in theologians such as Wolfhart Pannenberg, Karl Barth and Joseph Ratzinger, whose *Introduction to Christianity* was just translated into Croatian. From Zagreb I was able to go on for further studies at Fuller Theological Seminary in Pasadena, California, in the mid-1970s. There I was exposed to a generous kind of Evangelicalism: rooted in classical Christian convictions, yet open to exploring new theological movements. It was there that I first encountered liberation and feminist theologies.

Having graduated from Fuller, I returned to Yugoslavia and taught at the seminary where I'd studied, founded a Christian monthly magazine, and then went to Tübingen in Germany to do doctoral work with Jürgen Moltmann. My research dealt with Marx's philosophy of work. Some of my friends found this very surprising. To me, it was all to do with loving one's enemies. A dissertation on Marx, I felt, would not only immerse me in the work of German Idealists (especially Hegel and Fichte) and their critics (Feuerbach and Nietzsche, as well as Marx), but also have some bearing on my original milieu. In the early 1980s, when I was writing the dissertation, Marxism was still officially alive in Yugoslavia. Soon it was to give up the ghost, at least for a while, but the lessons Marx taught me remained: first, deep analogies between religious and economic forms of alienation – between idolatry and love of money, in biblical terms – second, suspicion of attempts at whole-scale social transformations based simply on moral appeals; and, above all, the centrality and pervasiveness of work in human life. For example, you sit in your shop repairing bikes or in a corner office managing a global firm, and an interpretation of the entire world is implicated in your activity.

SHORTT: Your doctoral work was interrupted, wasn't it?

VOLF: Yes. I was about two months away from submitting my dissertation when I received a summons to do military service in Yugoslavia, and I had several unattractive options. If I said no, I'd face imprisonment if I ever returned from abroad. Saying yes, on the other hand, would not only interrupt my studies but go against my pacifist convictions, which I still hold in a modified form. Eventually, I decided that I would yield to the request but tell them from the outset that I wouldn't do anything that involved killing people. This was in late 1983, and as soon as I arrived at the base, I was spied on by virtually the whole unit: all my movements on and off base were tracked, my mail was read, my conversations with students were taped after I had been dragged into discussing potentially dangerous topics, and so on. Four months later, the interrogations began. I was completely at the mercy of my tormentors. They threatened me with years of imprisonment. I had no recourse to an independent lawyer. Even though the threats eventually proved empty, I had a vivid sense of the subversiveness of my faith.

After my demobilisation, I spent the next few years in Yugoslavia and Germany, first finishing my doctoral work, then teaching, and finally doing the postdoctoral research that formed the basis of *After Our Likeness*. The research for the book grew out of my ecumenical experiences. In 1985 I was invited to take part in and write a position paper for the dialogue that Pentecostals were conducting with the Vatican, a dream opportunity for a very young theologian. The topic was communion, and it got me immersed in Roman Catholic ecclesiology and the ecumenical movement.

SHORTT: There's a strong trinitarian element in your ecclesiology, and a corresponding insistence that false ecumenical moves are often based on defective models of God. Take a very influential figure like Pope Benedict XVI. I think you would want to see his model of church government as excessively centralist, because rooted in a sense of the priority of the one divine substance over the three persons of the Godhead.

VOLF: There are many tributaries to Benedict's excessively centralist model of church government, and an inadequate account of God's being is one of them. But my main concern was not to engage in a critique of Catholic ecclesiology, but to mend Protestant ecclesiology. Protestant tradition in general and in particular the Free Church tradition to which I belonged, have often failed to connect the nature of the Church to the nature of God as Trinity. The consequence has been religious individualism: each person connects directly with the Lord through the Word proclaimed, and each person is 'saved' by himself or by herself and only subsequently enters into communion with other believers. My sense was that Free Church ecclesiology, both for the sake of the Free Churches themselves, and for the sake of their relation with other Churches, needed to be enriched by theological reflection about the relationship between the Church and the Trinity that has been going on for centuries in the Roman Catholic and Eastern Orthodox traditions. And that's part of what I've tried to do, while at the same time arguing that the Free Churches should properly be treated as Churches, and not as second-rate assemblages of Christians. They may not be the best possible Churches, they may be even significantly deficient: but they are Churches in the full sense of the term, and therefore partners of equal dignity in ecumenical dialogues.

SHORTT: There's evidently a high level of agreement between you and Christoph Schwöbel on this point.[3] Let's turn to the categories of exclusion and embrace which are also central to your thought, and based on your experience during the bloodbath that followed the break-up of the former Yugoslavia in the early 1990s.

VOLF: After Croatia declared independence in 1990, war was almost pre-programmed. Serbia would not let Croatia go, because Serbia had territorial aspirations that extended over a good deal of Croatia, especially places that historically had had a significant Serbian minority. With most of the military might concentrated in Serbian hands, one-third of Croatia was soon occupied. Its towns and villages were emptied of their populations: some people were killed, and others were driven out. Though I had moved to Germany in 1989 and then to California at the very end of 1991, I still continued to teach for roughly a semester each year in Croatia at the Evangelical Theological Seminary. In fact, in the fall of 1991 my wife and I, together with the students and staff of the seminary, watched from exile in Slovenia the fall of Vukovar and relentless attacks on Osijek, the seminary's home town.

At that time, the big question for me, as a Croatian, was, How do I respond to this aggression as a Christian? My knee-jerk reaction was that a few B52 bombers would do the job. We wanted to respond to Serbian aggression in kind: drive out and wipe Croatia clean of Serbs who pursued the policy of ethnic cleansing. But it took only a moment's reflection on some basic Christian teaching to see that this was wrong.

SHORTT: And did you bracket the just-war tradition with a 'common-sense approach'?

VOLF: In a sense, yes. I was, of course, familiar with just-war theory. It is a dominant tradition in Christianity – though manifestly not *the* traditional Christian position – and it has been pre-eminent ever since Augustine formulated it. Modern just-war theory has become divorced from any concern with the practice of reconciliation. But reconciliation lies at the heart of the Christian response to transgression and enmity. A compelling alternative to the just-war tradition does not rest primarily on the many New Testament passages dealing with non-violence; rather, it rests on the broader pattern of God's action toward sinful humanity, which in the New Testament is universally seen as a model – with adjustments, of course – for Christians to follow, and which is echoed in New Testament passages advocating non-violence.

I argue strenuously in *Exclusion and Embrace* that the practice of reconciliation doesn't leave questions of justice behind. Rather, it reframes them by setting them in a larger context. No authentic reconciliation is possible if you disregard justice; but equally, no genuine justice is possible if you don't pursue reconciliation. Similarly, the notion of forgiveness, which is, of course, much more at home in interpersonal than in inter-communal relations, does not negate the concern for justice. On the contrary, the very act of forgiveness both affirms the rightful claims of justice and sets them partly aside by not letting them count against the transgressor.

SHORTT: So your approach to conflict resolution draws on Christian teaching about identity, among other factors.

VOLF: Yes. The wars in the former Yugoslavia were waged partly in the name of pure identity: with Muslims, especially in Kosovo, Serbs and Croatians alike insisted on the purity of their respective soil, blood and culture. So I was also looking at the Christian tradition for resources to help me think about identity. What does it mean to be a self, to be a bearer of identity? What does it mean to be a community, and as a community, a bearer of identity? What kinds of boundaries should we have? By looking at the Christian story, I came away with two conclusions. First, identities are a positive good. Therefore, boundaries must also be good and be maintained, for without boundaries there would be no identities and the world would be one large undifferentiated chaos, which is to say that nothing would exist. Second, identities are a result of interchanges between their bearers. Consequently, boundaries cannot serve simply to keep things out: they must also serve to let things in. So identities are dynamic. Selves are always being enriched by others, even as they are in the process of remaining themselves.

Let me give a simple example. I like to bring works of art home with me from foreign trips. So here's a piece of a foreign culture that now has been put in my office, in my living room or wherever, and shapes the space that's properly my own. It is a sign of porous boundaries and of an identity that's not self-enclosed. Such a notion of identity – one that doesn't exclude the other from the self – is very clearly visible in some basic Christian tenets. Take the trinitarian idea personhood. A divine person is itself by being 'inhabited' by other persons so that, for instance, the Son is never the Son without the Father, and vice versa. Or take a key idea in the account of Christian community. A church is a local church only because its ties to other local churches are part and parcel of its very identity. It seems to me especially helpful to think of identity along these lines in the context of conflicts that involve claims to purity.

SHORTT: Let's return to reconciliation. Some people might endorse much that you've just said about reconciliation and justice, but have questions about how it applies in practice. That would be the Niebuhrian view. This says that B52 bombers might be your only available means of arresting a cataclysm that is involving tens of thousands of rapes, and hundreds of thousands of deaths. And paradoxically, in view of the Iraq situation, in Britain it was the Left that tended to rattle sabres over Bosnia. It was the Right that was associated with calls for non-intervention, on the grounds that UK interests were not threatened. Many on the Left replied that force was required to satisfy the demands of justice, regardless of one's national interests. As you know, Europe then proved itself ineffectual in bringing the warring factions to heel. Many believe it was American might that eventually averted an even graver catastrophe.

VOLF: Two questions need to be asked with regard to military intervention. One has to do with a situation that has got out of hand, as clearly happened in the former Yugoslavia. Another has to do with creating the climate in which such catastrophes are far less likely to arise in the first place.

SHORTT: I'm talking about the first sort. Sometimes the Christian will have to think and act in the heart of the maelstrom. Can one infer that you now believe military action is justifiable in some circumstances?

VOLF: When American might and its role in former Yugoslavia are invoked, it's good to keep in mind that the American military needed to step in because US diplomacy had been complacent when the conflict was still brewing and there was an opportunity to prevent it. This just underscores, I think, the importance of creating good climates at an earlier stage. But to answer your question directly, I do believe that some forms of military action are justifiable in certain circumstances. That's what the very end of *Exclusion and Embrace* is all about. In all circumstances, it's wrong for a person to take the life of another, but in some circumstances one can take upon oneself the sin of taking the life of another so as to prevent graver evil from occurring. In a world where violence is committed in the name of religion, this position has the advantage of clearly showing that taking the life of another – in war or otherwise – is sinful from a Christian perspective, even when it is needed.

SHORTT: So there's a difference here between you and David Martin, who consistently draws a tighter distinction between private and public morality. An example, on his view, would be the attempt on Pope John Paul's life in 1981. John Paul could forgive his would-be assassin, but couldn't recommend release for the captive without violating a moral order.

VOLF: That distinction is valid if applied in a proper way, but it can be misused. If it's turned into a simple disjunction, it becomes deeply problematic. And it looks to me as though that's what David Martin has done with it in his contribution to this book. Certainly, atonement was not 'a way through the impasse of political action', as David says.[4] But to say that after atonement 'everything stays the same' in the world of politics seems to me either to privatise faith illicitly, or to compartmentalise faith and make its central convictions irrelevant to the world of politics. Though politics can't be based on atonement, atonement should certainly shape how Christians engage in politics. David Martin also seems to think that Christians must take rigid, overarching stances in the world, like being a 'realist' or being a 'witness', so that you have to choose between the two. I'd say that the social reality we face is so varied that I could well be a witness in one situation, a full participant in another, and a something else in yet another. The penchant for typologies one finds in writers from Max Weber through Ernst Troeltsch to David Martin obscures realities as much as sheds light on them.

SHORTT: In other words, you want to defend the integrity of being a conscientious objector in one situation or at one level, while at the same time paying your taxes and driving a car.

VOLF: That's right. I can imagine myself being an adviser to a government in a Cold War situation on the one hand, while, on the other, deploring that government's policies in other spheres if they conflicted with my convictions. Even if I felt that complete non-involvement with the government were appropriate, I might well be involved in many other spheres of life, such as business or medicine or education. Typologies are straitjackets designed with specific values and interests in mind. John Howard Yoder's critique of the kind of typology that H. Richard Niebuhr adopts in his book *Christ and Culture* is exactly on target. Some aspects of culture we can accept at face value. I don't know how to make a hatchback car as distinct from a saloon in a Christian way, for example, and therefore would not know what it would mean to make it in a non-Christian way. In other areas of culture I might participate at a critical distance. In yet other areas I might refuse participation completely. Moreover, these areas and these situations are not static; they may change and therefore necessitate a change in my stance.

SHORTT: **Nevertheless, you've owned up to a significant change of outlook by conceding that in some circumstances B52 bombers *are* the appropriate response to cases of intolerable aggression. To that extent, you yourself have become more of a 'realist'. Isn't it surprising, then, that you're commending the pacifist John Howard Yoder, but criticising the ex-pacifist David Martin?**

VOLF: I'm not sure about B52 bombers. They may be too crude an instrument. But as I've mentioned briefly, I do think that a military response may be appropriate in cases of intolerable aggression. I shifted from the pacifism of my childhood and early adulthood to the position I am taking now by extending the obligation to love my neighbour when that neighbour's life is threatened by a third party. After reading Oliver O'Donovan's book *The Just War Revisited*, in which he understands war in the context of a 'reconciling praxis of judgment'[5] and argues that it is not 'essential to warmaking that you should kill, merely that you should remove by all necessary means the forces that oppose you',[6] I find that I'm not as far from just-war theory as I thought I was.

As to the question about Yoder and David Martin: I am commending and criticising here only narrow segments of their thought. I've learned a great deal from David Martin, and I like his account of secularisation and analyses of Latin American Pentecostalism. My point is very simple. I don't have, and I don't think it is good to have, some overarching stance toward the world. It is to Yoder's credit that he rejected such stable, overarching stances. His opponents, who have a stake in painting him as a sectarian so as to dismiss him more easily, seem to me much less subtle on this point than he was. On this issue, my position is somewhat analogous to that taken years ago by another Yale theologian, Hans Frei, on theology's relation to particular philosophies. He recommended an ad hoc approach, based on the extent to which a given school of thought can help illuminate the Christian story. At the same time, he insisted that other philosophies should never control our understanding of the Christian narrative, which in reality means replacing it. In my opinion, that's what it means to think and act in a Christian way. To use Augustine's image, I don't see why I should either melt all the gold of the Egyptians, or simply use it as it is. My term for such a stance is 'soft difference': there is difference, but the difference is soft in the sense that boundaries are not impermeable. For me, our engagement across the boundaries should be governed by the demands of generosity and justice.

SHORTT: Moving on to your approach to Scripture: I know this isn't the place to ask you to develop a fully-fledged hermeneutical theory, but liberal Christians in particular might want to query the central place accorded to biblical models in your reasoning about religion and society.

VOLF: There are two principal explanations for my approach. First, the biblical texts are extraordinarily rich, richer than theologies based on them, and much richer than those theologies that have discarded them completely. Have you noticed how much more complex and interesting and close to life the Jesus of the Gospels is than the Jesus of historians' reconstructions? The one is pulsating with life; the other is a bloodless abstraction. The conversation we have just had about sectarianism is another example. Theologians often go on assigning particular biblical texts to particular categories and then interpreting them in the light of these categories. But when you enter the world of a text such as John's Gospel, you find the text is much richer and more subtle.

Second, these texts are authoritative for Christian communities, in my view. They are the Word of God, and they have been authoritative for centuries, thus shaping not only the convictions of individuals and Christian communities, but also the sensibilities of whole cultures. Theology disregards interpretation of biblical texts at its peril. Liberal Christians who advocate the position you refer to might find themselves irrelevant rather quickly, without a basis from which to speak to Christian communities, having little of interest to say to the rest of the world.

SHORTT: They, for their part, might complain that you are begging the question here, because the Bible is *not* always life-affirming. In their view it's missing the point to accuse bigots and fundamentalists of misinterpreting the texts, because the problem – the intolerance or ignorance or whatever – is in Scripture itself. Take an example like 1 Samuel 15, where Saul is commanded to destroy the Amalekites, and then censured by God for showing mercy towards some of them, rather than blind obedience to the divine will. Or Exodus 32, where an orgy of violence follows God's command that the sons of Levi slaughter 3,000 of their own kin.

VOLF: It's crucial not to read the Bible simply as a collection of texts that themselves may be collated fragments of texts from the Ancient Near East and Greco-Roman antiquity. That is, of course, what the Bible also is. But a person of faith and a constructive theologian will read the Bible as *Scripture*, which is to say that at the very least she or he reads the Bible as a unity, however loosely or subtly defined. The texts you mention, and many others even more troubling, should be read not on their own but in the context of the larger unity, and for Christians, evaluated in light of the story of Jesus Christ. I'd be first to admit that Christian faith in particular has been gravely misused, and this corruption has partly sprung from appeals to sacred texts. But the proper response to such misuse is to engage in responsible interpretation of these texts as part of the whole of Scripture, which culminates in the story of Jesus Christ. The procedure will be somewhat different for Jews and Muslims, of course.

Here's a related consideration. I don't see any signs that religion is withering away, except maybe in Western highbrow culture, or disappearing from the social scene. Given present trends, the likelihood that religion is going to cease to be an important factor in social life in the foreseeable future is close to zero. On the contrary, the social importance of religion is going to increase, because the two fastest-growing faiths in the world today – indeed, the two fastest-growing overarching interpretations of life – are Christianity and Islam. Between them, they have close to 3.5 billion adherents, more than half the world's population. Other religions are lagging behind but still following. Secularism doesn't even seem a competitor. Since you can't take religion out of people's lives, the only thing left is to see whether you can interpret religions in such a way as to highlight their potential for peace. It helps in this endeavour, of course, if you believe that religions are more or less generative of human flourishing, as I do.

SHORTT: Sceptics, though, might be forgiven for remaining sceptical when one recalls the sight of bishops giving the fascist salute in mid-twentieth-century Spain, for example, or the outpourings of jihadists across the Middle East and Asia today. And what's more, historical–critical scrutiny of Islamic sacred texts is in its infancy. Even a high Christian view of scriptural authority is modest by comparison with what Muslims believe about the Qur'an.

VOLF: I understand these doubts. I hope I don't have to reiterate here that I deplore the corrupt use to which religion has been put. But sceptics should keep a due sense of proportion. The good often goes unnoticed, especially in our culture, dominated as it is by media that operate under market conditions. I would be very surprised if it turned out that, for the majority of Christians throughout the centuries and in all parts of the globe, their faith was a motivator for evil to a greater extent than it was a motivator for good.

As to historical–critical scrutiny of sacred texts, I employ the method – or rather, a version of it – and have benefited from it. But its significance is often overrated, especially when it comes to religion's authorising of violence. St Francis and Dorothy Day did not need the historical–critical method to be prophets of peace. Neither did my parents or my nanny, to mention some ordinary Christian people. They all drank at the well of the Gospels and Epistles as we have them. On the whole, moreover, it's a mistake to think that the less authority the sacred texts have, the less likely they will be to foster violence. Such a stance is part of the contemporary scepticism about all authority, and unease with religious certainty. But what matters most is the content and interpretation of these texts, not the extent of their formal authority; and more important than the absence of religious certainty is the presence of humility. You also asked about the Qur'an and its extraordinary authority for Muslims. My hope is that the Qur'an can be interpreted in such a way as to foster peace. But such interpretations are for Muslims to undertake, not for me.

SHORTT: Again, though, both liberal Christians and non-believers might take some convincing. They could argue that Christianity has become more tolerant and tolerable on the coat-tails of secular liberalism, as much as through other sources. The Roman Catholic Church condoned slavery until well into the nineteenth century, and didn't even acknowledge the principle of the sovereignty of conscience until the 1960s.

VOLF: Tolerance is one of those big words that say too little and too much at the same time. So some caution is called for. When it comes to intolerance in the history of Christianity, the main problem is not so much with the Christian faith as with its alignment with political power over the centuries. The alliance of throne and altar was uneasy from the beginning, since at its heart the Christian faith is ambivalent towards worldly power. It can't be otherwise, because its main symbol is the powerless God hanging on the cross. I don't think it's surprising, then, to see that democracy owes more to the Christian tradition, in particular to Protestant sectarianism, than to European secularism. I should add that I agree with those historians who see European secularism as a mutation of Christianity and not an independent position. It is in the name of the one Lord that the early Baptists 'democratised' the Church and thereby gave impetus to the democratisation of society. I'm not suggesting that pluralism and democracy are written all over the Bible. I'm saying that faith can be developed in ways that favour political pluralism. The word 'can' is operative. As I've said, I have no interest in exonerating Christianity in the majority of cases; I'd rather repent than defend. My interest is a constructive one – to show that at its heart the Christian faith promotes the flourishing of *society*, as much as of individuals.

I should add that it's narrow-minded and culturally imperialistic to think that pluralism and democracy are universally and unambiguously good. We're guilty of that error these days, given our weakness for sitting in judgement over all previous epochs.

SHORTT: **Doesn't this leave us at something of an impasse, though? The very vexed question of gay clergy in the Anglican Communion shows why. Reinterpreting scriptural references to homosexuality is precisely what liberal Christians would understand by being 'constructive', just as (so it's argued) an earlier generation jettisoned biblical attitudes to slavery. Not so, say conservatives: the traditional ban on gay sex forms a core part of Christian ethics. How do you think theology can establish who's right?**

VOLF: I don't think this leaves us at an impasse, even if it feels like it these days. Rather, this leaves us with arguments to be made and adjudicated. Debates between individuals on weighty matters take time; debates within a tradition as diverse as Christianity on weighty matters take even more time. So I counsel being as hard-nosed about the arguments and as charitable to our opponents as we can possibly be. This is just translating a proper Christian stance toward our enemies into the realm of interpretative disagreements.

SHORTT: **Would you talk more about your approach to Islam now? You have some important qualifications in this area, including your membership of Building Bridges Seminar, the Archbishop of Canterbury's international group for Muslim–Christian dialogue.**

VOLF: I am not an expert on Islam, though I do participate in the

Building Bridges Seminar, and oversee a programme in Muslim–Christian relations at Yale. I come to encounters with Muslims as a Christian theologian. Again, there are two points that I'd want to underline. One concerns the identities of Christianity and Islam. It's not that you have the Christian faith as a self-enclosed entity on one side, and Islam as a self-enclosed entity on the other. They have partly overlapping identities. Second, despite this, it would be a mistake to proceed on the assumption that one faith is reducible to the other, or that both faiths are reducible to a third. Rather, as I've already argued, dialogues should presuppose real though permeable boundaries between the two faiths.

One important way in which we honour overlaps as well as distinctions between Islam and Christianity at the Building Bridges Seminar is by reading each other's Scriptures together as the centrepiece of our encounters. And in my experience, far from closing off the conversation, this exercise serves to stimulate it. After we've read the sacred texts together, I've often had the experience of learning something new, and that includes learning about the Bible and therefore about my own faith. Light comes from an unexpected corner, and I see the whole landscape differently. In this way, the other becomes part of me, in a sense. Under these conditions, even abiding disagreements can be immensely fruitful.

SHORTT: Can you give an example of how the Qur'an has enlarged your view of God?

VOLF: In the famous Surah 112, it is written, 'Say, He is Allah, The One and Only; Allah the Eternal the Absolute; He begetteth not, Nor is He begotten; And there is None Like unto Him.' As I read the text, I could have immediately focused on what looks like a negation of trinitarianism. And no doubt that is also what a Christian theologian needs to do when faced with this Surah. Instead, what struck me in the text was how exalted, unique and absolute Allah is represented as being. In some recent Christian theology God has often been reduced to the status of a companion or buddy, 'who understands and shares our pain'. As I was reading the text I was reminded of how irreverent this kind of talk can be. You might say I did not need the Qur'an to remind me of that; biblical talk of God's holiness and God's dwelling in 'inapproachable light' could have done the same. And yet it *was* the Qur'an that reminded me of the absolute uniqueness of the God whom I worship as a Christian.

SHORTT: How much mileage do you get from the notion of the seeds of the Word in other faiths? As John's Gospel puts it, Moses and

Abraham knew Christ, even though they obviously weren't Christians and had never heard of Jesus. Thus the phrase from John 14:6, 'No one comes to the Father, but by me', often seen as a proof text for Christian exclusivism, can or should be interpreted as meaning that no one comes to the Father except through the Word, who enlightens the hearts of all humankind.

VOLF: I don't think Justin Martyr, who developed the idea of the 'seeds of the Word' in his *Second Apology*,[7] intended to drive a wedge between the Word and Jesus Christ, and therefore between John 1, where the Word is said to enlighten everyone, and John 14, where we read that no one comes to the Father except by Jesus Christ. According to Justin, the relationship between the seeds of the Word and Christ is between scattered parts of the Word and the whole Word. I am pretty sure some form of exclusivism is unavoidable, or at least I have not seen a coherent position that avoids it. Pluralism, as an account of the relations between religions, is just exclusivism expanded: you include major world religions, you manage even to squeeze in Marxism, but you exclude Branch Davidians or Satanists. So the central question is what kind of exclusivist you are going to be. And that takes us back to the concrete forms of faiths and how they advocate relating to respective non-believers. Even though I hold that there is no other Word but that revealed in Jesus Christ, I do believe that God's Spirit is at work in all humanity, whether religious or not. So I have a stake in commonalities between different people's faiths.

SHORTT: What made you an Anglican?

VOLF: I first encountered Anglicanism practically when I arrived in the US to study, and was soon in flight from bad preaching. In Protestant churches of whatever stripe, it was hard for me to find good preaching. And by 'good preaching', I don't necessarily mean rhetorically polished preaching, though that's wonderful, or intellectually challenging preaching, though that's even better. I simply mean the kind of preaching that has the nerve to be unabashedly and joyfully Christian, rather than an ersatz version of something else, such as psychology or sociology, or some common-sense wisdom gleaned from ubiquitous self-help books. Equally unsatisfying, I've found many 'conservative' churches that have retreated into fortresses built with the hard stone of rigid orthodoxy and lost Jesus Christ in the process. The Book of Common Prayer has been a great refuge for me. If the rector delivers a good sermon, I'm very happy. But if the sermon is disappointing, at least I have access to the genuine content of the Christian gospel expressed in the beautiful cadences of Renaissance prose.

SHORTT: Lastly, I'd be grateful if you'd lift the lid on the wider domain of Evangelical scholarship. This book draws together a sizeable body of opinion. But you and your fellow contributors all have, or have had, posts in élite universities, while in the US, for instance, at least 70 per cent of theological students are formed outside Ivy League or comparable institutions. You, however, have worked in both systems.

VOLF: And we should not forget the Third World, too, where most theological training colleges among Protestants are Evangelical. As far as the future of Protestant Christianity is concerned, these institutions are much more important than anything going on in the Western world, whether Evangelical or not. Many Evangelical places I know are intellectually vibrant. Fuller is a case in point: its current President, the moral philosopher Richard Mouw, combines intellectual sophistication with deep Evangelical commitment. Though I don't care for labels, I have the impression that these days there is more intellectual vibrancy and creativity on the more conservative side of the theological spectrum than on the more liberal one.

SHORTT: So someone who is dismayed by the intellectual thinness of Billy Graham, for example, can be reassured that there's a richer diet available close at hand.

VOLF: Billy Graham's intellectual thinness is studied. He is an evangelist who seeks to appeal to the masses and intentionally preaches with the vocabulary of an eight-year-old. It takes extraordinary skill to do that. This is not how I, or many of my former colleagues at Fuller, like our sermons. And many of them would question not just Billy Graham's delivery, but also the theology that informs his evangelistic message. My former colleagues are serving their students a diet that should produce good pastor-theologians. After all, many of them were trained at places like Harvard or Yale and Oxford or Cambridge – not that that's a prerequisite for being a good theologian – and they think deeply and seriously about their faith.

But the source of American Evangelical vibrancy is not the institutions that train its leaders. It is found, I think, in the character of Evangelicalism as democratised religion. Anybody can set up shop and sell his or her religious goods. They don't need to be trained in any particular way or certified by any examining body. The consequence is both a deep conviction on the part of preachers, and the extraordinary cultural closeness of their message to the culture of their audience. The upside of this closeness is the ability of American Evangelicals to mediate faith well; the downside is that often the gospel they proclaim is captive to a given culture. A bit of training from places like Fuller would be of great benefit to many American popular preachers.

SHORTT: **How does this grassroots vibrancy translate into relations between various Christian groups?**

VOLF: Old-style ecumenism, built on relations between representatives of various denominations, undergirded by the work of theological commissions, and aimed at visible unity, is in serious trouble today. When we look at the situation globally, more new churches are founded every day than can come together in the above fashion in a century, even assuming the best intentions, hard work, and ecumenical enthusiasm on all sides. But the situation is far more positive at grassroots level. Old denominational barriers are being broken down. To me, that is very significant. New divisions are being created too, of course. The most troubling to me is the widening divide between Western and in particular American Christians, especially of the Protestant kind, and their co-religionists in other parts of the world. We need to pay much more attention to what non-Western Christians tell us, not only about the character of faith, but also about what it has to say about the neediest of this world. In any case, the future of Christianity belongs primarily to them, not to us.

13
J. Kameron Carter

Black Theology

SHORTT: The reclaiming of tradition seen in other branches of theology over the past two decades has also occurred in your own field: African American religious studies. I'm struck by two things in particular about your writings. First, you endorse the aims of many older black theologians, and respect their achievements. You accept that although the struggle for racial equality is not complete, the civil rights movement has nevertheless achieved a great deal, and was carried forward by more or less religiously inclined figures such as W. E. B. Du Bois, Howard Thurmans, James Cone, Deotis Roberts and Charles Long. Second, though, you've queried the approaches of some of these pioneers, and warn that black theology needs to be vigilant about the language it borrows from secular disciplines if it's to remain authentically theological.

We get a clear view of the terrain in your essay[1] on Jim Perkinson, a white American theologian seeking to apply what he sees as some of black theology's most important insights. You sum up his definition of the subject as being a means of awakening whites (especially white males) 'to the way in which whiteness continues to leverage power and secure privilege in contemporary life'. For him, black theology 'is anything but a mere memory to be consigned to the twilight of the twentieth century. Rather, it is, in the Gramscian sense, counter-hegemonic', and must identify what is at stake in the refusal of whites 'to come to terms with the message ... of black theology and, particularly, with its re-evaluation of ... white and black theology alike'.

As I've indicated, you feel it's quite possible to hold that anti-racism belongs at the heart of Christian discipleship, but to have doubts about the terms in which the problem is cast. For a start, one can discuss race in a way that feeds fantasies about the fundamental innocence of one group or another. Just as some feminist theorists need reminding that men are not automatically oppressors by dint of their maleness, nor heterosexuals oppressors of homosexuals by dint of their orientation, it can also be necessary to point out that whites are not racist by definition, and the corollary of this – that sin can't be confined to a particular structural condition.

So the problem is that Perkinson's characterisation risks feeding an equal and opposite sense of the pre-eminence of race (with the associated antagonisms to which this can give rise), when the point, for a Christian, should be that there is a weightier category than being black or white, and that is being human – or, more importantly, being *created*.

CARTER: Exactly. I'm trying to dig deeper. If you give talk of our shared humanity the theological twist that you just outlined – that's to say, if you invoke the category of creation – then you're saying something more than that we're all in this boat together. Creation prompts the question of how the creature, who is not God, nevertheless reflects and intones God. I think that this is what's lost in much modern racial reasoning.

Here's another way of putting it. If we define the problem as being about the recuperation of my blackness, as if blackness is sufficient to tell me who I am, doesn't this just give me the photo-negative of the discourse of race as it was framed in the first place? The unspoken move of whiteness is to say that my whiteness tells me who I am. It defines me as over and against the black. The black becomes the mirror image that tells me who I am. I want to suggest that that's just another species of the problem.

Stuart Hall says in one of his essays[2] that identity comes at the end of the paradigm, not the beginning. The error of modern racial reasoning is to assume that it comes at the beginning, and that I know who I am apart from being told who I am – that I can name myself rather than be named; that I can define myself without God, who names me through my encounter with the neighbour. The neighbour is a more fundamental category for the Christian than the other. I might have near neighbours and I might have distant neighbours, but we're all neighbours. And I need the neighbour in some sense to know who I am. And so there's this 'ecstatic' structure to existence through which identity comes to me. There's a sense in which I must be beyond myself to receive myself. We are in ourselves as we are exterior to ourselves. But it's not as though exterior and interior are opposites: von Balthasar says it like this – 'our "instasy" is our ecstasy'.[3] And we're most interior to ourselves as we're most open and exposed beyond ourselves. It's precisely in that gesture that we know ourselves. I want to claim that what modern racial reasoning does is to disband that way of looking at the world.

SHORTT: Secular reasoning – and also some ostensibly theological reasoning that's unduly influenced by secular models?

CARTER: Yes. As I've said, it wants to claim that we know who we are, and I want to say, No, that's the problem. Knowing who you are in the sense described can all too easily metastasise into nationalism, or forms of inverted chauvinism. It applies to gender, for example. The response to patriarchy can't be, 'I know who I am because I'm a woman', because that can take you down the road of demonising men. My own research, at least in these initial stages, has really been asking the following question: What is the true arc of our sinfulness? My answer is that it springs from not questioning the assumption that we know who we are. And the reason we begin with the assumption that we know this is because in some basic sense we function from within the broadly modern story of what Ralph Waldo Emerson – who was much admired by Nietzsche – called 'the self-made man', and what Kant and much of German idealism following him spoke of as self-constituting subjectivity. This, broadly speaking, is the narrative that says identity begins with the 'I', and it is the I that dictates the sense of who I take myself to be. To employ scriptural language, one might say that in this sense the self-constituting 'I' attempts to appropriate the prerogatives of the divine 'I'.

SHORTT: Two other ingredients in the creation of modernity that you see as both important and neglected are Christian anti-Judaism and what's been called 'Christian supersessionism'. Could you describe them now?

CARTER: As a way into that, let me first set out why I think that a corrupted theology underlies a good deal of racial thinking. One of the arguments I voice against the way in which black theology has developed is this. We talk loosely about how white theology is a problem, but what is it that makes white theology 'white'? How does the adjective 'white' operate? What are the movements that make it white?

And what I try to do in my work is to say, If we look at a figure like Kant and at some of the people he was in conversation with in Enlightenment circles, including Christian Wilhelm von Dohm, who was Frederick II's Minister of War, and the racial thinker, orientalist and biblical scholar at the University of Göttingen, Johann David Michaelis, we begin to discover that Enlightenment discourse was becoming preoccupied by the so-called *Judenfrage*, the Jewish question. How do we make sense of these Jews? These Jews, they were saying, are a drag on the economy. They are unfit for German citizenship, for military service, and so forth. People were reading Adam Smith's *The Wealth of Nations*, and getting the idea that a community, a state, advances itself out of the productivity of its people. And when a large labour drag arose in Prussia and elsewhere, people started blaming the problem on the Jews. What one starts to get at this time are philosophies that account for indolence in particular people groups. And commentators begin to try to theorise the so-called laziness of the Jew.

Their next move, in order to understand this alleged laziness, is to begin to position the Jew as a human person within a kind of hierarchy of human beings. And so inside the *Judenfrage* another move develops, which I call the *Rassenfrage*, the question of race. The question of race emerges inside the Jewish question and it's given a theological complexion. In his *Anthropology from a Pragmatic Point of View*, Kant says that one of the reasons you get this problem around the Jews, why they're cheaters, why they have all these moral deficiencies, is that they don't legislate morality for themselves. Their legislator is heteronomous: they have an exterior God. Christian morality, by contrast, is inscribed on the heart.

Moreover, one must recognise that inside all of this there is a racialising of Jesus. I argue in my book *Race: A Theological Account*[4] that Kant should be considered in tandem with Michaelis, who sees a clear distinction between Jesus and the Jewish people from which he emerges. Kant echoes this distinction. In his unpublished anthropology notes, he claims that the significance of Jesus is that he presented 'occidental' wisdom in 'oriental' garb. Christians grasp this, he wants to say, but Jews don't, and if they ever did begin to get this, they'd recognise that it entailed, according to his 1798 *Conflict of the Faculties*, the 'euthanasia of Judaism'. It is worth noting that in all of this we see connections between the question of race, the Jews, orientalism and, importantly, colonialism. What holds these connections together is the following question: How are we to understand the meaning, the theo-political significance, of Jewish faith, given an emerging vision of the social world which we now call, broadly speaking, modernity? To what extent is Jewish faith assimilable to modernity? This question presupposes another important question: How are we to understand the on-the-ground meaning of Christianity in relationship to modern, Western civilisation? Is it heteronomous, that is, subject to external law, like Jewish faith? Are its practitioners a heteronomous rather than an autonomous people, as is the case with the Jew and other racial 'others'? But this, alas, leads to a final, important question: How should Christianity understand its relationship to its Jewish inheritance? Answering this helps us get to the heart of the matter.

SHORTT: And supersessionism is on this view a critical component of modern morality?

CARTER: Right. To ask the question of Christian supersessionism is to ask the question of modernity, and in both instances it is to ask the question of theology as just laid out. Furthermore, it is to recognise that inside this series of questions another question emerges, the race question. The question of race emerges to buttress Kant's universalist claims. And so now you need a taxonomy, a hierarchy of human beings, within which to position the problem around Jews. And this is where the African becomes identified as the lowest figure on the totem pole.

SHORTT: There are plenty of people who wouldn't disagree with a word you've just said, but who'd see it precisely as a sign that religion is harmful. Many of Kant's non-Christian heirs are as dismissive of his views about the Jews as you yourself, and embrace tolerant but secular value systems. Tolerant *because* secular, many would say. Would another way into the question of *ressourcement* be to ask what you find defective in the world view of secular humanists, and what difference your vision makes?

CARTER: There are two ways in which I want to approach this vital question: the first, somewhat more theoretically oriented; the latter, more rooted in a historical example. Reflecting on the work of a great thinker – a historian, sociologist, and cultural anthropologist – like W. E. B. Du Bois, himself a humanist, helps one to frame a theoretical response. His work can be seen as entailing a struggle to make democracy true to its best ideals. And if it's true to its best ideals, it will invite and recognise the need for all cultures and groups to sit at the table of 'the kingdom of culture', as he says in *Souls of Black Folk*,[5] the work for which he is probably best known.

This imagery parodies the biblical and eschatological language of the Kingdom of God. It is this imagery, and what Du Bois makes it signify in relationship to a discourse of democracy, that moves him with uncanny eloquence to say – I quote him roughly – that 'I sit with

Shakespeare and wince not; across from me sit Balzac and Dumas.' It is a radically humanist vision in which all contribute to the realisation of human culture. But, as a vision, it's bigger than simply the fact that all *can* contribute to it. Du Bois wants more: the realisation of such a 'kingdom' is contingent on the fact that all *must* contribute. Insofar as this is the case, one can say that Du Bois's vision of a kingdom of culture is itself quasi-Catholic. In fact, at one point Du Bois himself invokes such language to capture what he is after.

Now let me be clear: I am not out to make Du Bois a theologian. He wasn't. But what is the case, and needs to be argued for, given that it is not a commonplace in current scholarship on Du Bois, is that he was a religious thinker; his humanism was deeply informed by religion. This can be argued persuasively from *Souls*, to say nothing of his other works. What we have, then, with Du Bois is (black) secular humanism that is unwilling to jettison the religious dimension. Why is this so?

The hypothesis I'm seeking to test can be stated thus: in the name of the humanism it's pursuing and hoping to realise, black intellectual life has remained implicitly religious, even in its resistance to religion. It has done so because it has kept backing up against the fact that modernity itself, and much of the secularism it champions, calls for a kind of faith commitment, a commitment that is akin to what religions call for. And the corollary of this is that secularism's vision cannot be realised by secular means alone. We are *homo religiosus*.

The secular vision of social good gives you a lot. But what it doesn't yield – as Augustine pointed out in his discussion of Cicero in *The City of God* – is a 'commonwealth'. That is, it doesn't give you the kind of sociality, to say nothing of the politics, in which we do more than just tolerate or put up with one another without killing each other. It is precisely this, a mode of sociality that exceeds tolerance, because it is eucharistic, communal, Christological and finally trinitarian, that Augustine seeks to articulate. He wants to show how Christian existence anticipates this kind of sociality, even if it does so sinfully and falteringly. It is a vision of existence in which we are bound to each other, that you contribute to me and I contribute to you.

SHORTT: A vision not just of co-operation, but communion.

CARTER: Right. More than tolerance, we need communion. And without a theological vision of the sort that I'm trying to articulate, the best we can get from and give to each other is putting up with each other. But if that's all we can hope for, it might put us on a slippery slope, as indeed it did with Kant and many of his heirs. Hierarchies can emerge, and some people become more tolerated than others. Stated differently, tolerance doesn't prevent you from having a hierarchy of order by which American military life, for example, is considered more valuable than Iraqi life, or Palestinian life.

SHORTT: That can happen from time to time, but it doesn't follow necessarily. Many people would probably reply to you that secular constitutions across the world speak of the dignity and equality of all. In a world where much violence *derives* from religion – especially where Islamic terrorism is concerned – how can you convince the sceptic that faith offers the securest foundations for promoting peace and the common good?

CARTER: I'd want to argue that the secular vision sounds good in principle, but there are historical examples that should serve as a warning to us. And just as the violence of Christian and other religious societies must be acknowledged, so, too, must the historical instances of where Christianity has proved pivotal to the advancement of justice and equality. Take the American constitution, which speaks of the equality of all, even though the reality has fallen far short of the ideal. Was it the constitution as such that compelled the nation to make civil rights a de facto and not simply a de jure reality? Was it the constitution that prompted the civil rights movement as a remedy to the injustices of the South and the indifference of the liberal North?

To answer this I want to draw on the brilliant scholarship of the historian David L. Chappell.[6] One of the core questions he has asked is why it was that liberals of the Democratic Party, who were at the zenith of their power in the 1930s and into the 1940s, were unable to deliver civil rights legislation and in this way address at the level of law the problem of American racism generally and anti-black racism in particular? Part of the answer, Chappell says, involved the way in which they reacted to religion. In their resistance to the religious and social conservatism of the Republicans, liberal Democrats effectively took religion off the table. That is to say, the liberal response to the problematic deployment of religion was no religion at all; their response to the troublesome deployment of theology was no theology at all. Using the language of my previous response to your question: the posture was to be post-religious and post-theological.

However, Chappell also reports that many liberal progressives recognised that they needed more than reason and rationality to galvanise their constituencies to work for causes that would bring about the transformation of American society, like civil rights, economic justice and so forth. He documents what he calls a liberal hunger for something more in several thinkers of the New Deal decade: people like John Dewey, William James, Thurman Arnold, Malcolm Ross, Walter Lippmann and Lionel Trilling. According to Chappell, all of these New Deal thinkers, their many differences notwithstanding, evinced a yearning for a secular 'faith' that could do among their ranks work akin to what religious faith tended to do in church ranks; namely, galvanising people around a cause bigger than themselves, even to sacrifice themselves, if need be, for that cause. The cause, in this instance, was a radicalised understanding and enactment of democracy and democratic ideals. With this rudder of faith missing, liberalism moved about somewhat aimlessly. In the end, as Chappell tells the story, despite its faith in the institutions and constitution of democracy, liberalism remained hungry for what was needed to make civil rights move.

Through a deft engagement with numerous historical documents and the lives of a number of people – Martin Luther King Jr, Bayard Rustin, Fannie Lou Hamer, Modjeska Simpkins and many others – Chappell shows how black prophetic religion generally, and black prophetic Christianity in particular, finally gave feet to American civil rights. But the transformation of American politics also required a transformation of the way religion, which was upholding the status quo, functioned. So Christianity proved central to bringing about what neither liberal progressivism nor Republican conservatism could bring about. The American civil rights movement was a potent example of lived theology arising from black Christian faith. Black Christians thereby revived a principle of classical dogmatic theology – that the discourse of theology is always rooted in the grammar of lives that make it intelligible. So understood, the practice of black Christian faith has formed a kind of *ressourcement*.

SHORTT: A *ressourcement* that long predates the civil rights movement, and extends back into the slave era?

CARTER: Right. What I'm trying to do is to seize on and inhabit more richly what I take to be ways in which Christianity was actually received by my forebears, my foremothers and forefathers, people of African descent in the New World. How did these bound and enslaved people receive the religion of the master, and how did they continue to inhabit this religion, but without distortion? How did they effect Christian counternarrative distinguishable from white Christianity?

Here again I must quickly add this point in order to head off possible misunderstandings: New World black folks received Christianity in such a way that one can trace a link connecting their expression of the faith back with the great traditions of Christian life and reflection that were discarded in the modern evolution of racial discourse. My claim is not that the link was intentional. It occurred in most instances unwittingly. But even here I do want to account for people like the black political writer and activist Maria Stewart (1803–79), whose writings[7] engage in important scriptural–exegetical work as part of her political activism, and whose writings actually invoke ideas deriving from figures such as Julian of Norwich. As a matter of history, to say nothing of its theological implications, this sort of awareness needs far more attention than it has received in the past.

Stewart's case is not an isolated one, because if you study the record of the periods in question, you can see that Christianity was received in such a way that black life, even in its bondage and in its enslavement, became theophanic. It became an iconic representation of the nearness of God to slaves, despite their abject condition. This nearness of God to the slaves was the basis of liberation, the ground of freedom. I would instance people like Briton Hammon, who tries to chronicle in his 1760 narrative what it means to be black in the New World situation, fleeing his master. He uses the events of Christ's life as a template for an account of his own.[8] Indeed, he states that he became free on December 25th 1747. I argue in *Race: A Theological Account* that this is more than a mere literary device. I make a case for its being a theological statement. Black life is made free in the economy of the man Jesus of Nazareth, and, through his economy, within the economy of the Trinity.

Here, then, is the dogmatic theological breakthrough: the moment of the birth of the Word is perpetual. It occurs throughout time. Christian dogmatics at various points in its history has made this point. One need only think of Irenaeus' claims in Book III of his *Against the Heresies*, or of Bonaventure, or even of that most trinitarian and Christological of thinkers, Pseudo-Dionysius. The breakthrough, the amplification and clarification, which black Christianity makes through its unique performance of the Christian faith, however, is this: to inhabit the time and history of the Word, Jesus Christ, is to live in the eternal freedom that the Word is and that the Word effects – now, in time. Therefore, it is to live within an economy that transfigures every other economy, most significantly, economies of violence and bondage. Black existence, then, given the theological implications of Hammon's story, is 'a' word of God, just to the extent that it is an articulation of 'the' Word of God. It is a 'word' within the 'Word'. The move to interpret black life within the horizon of the Word embodied by Jesus of Nazareth becomes a way through which Hammon can renarrate his whole life beyond the social arrangement of slavery, and locate his life in a context in which all creation is seen as the gift of the triune God. So understood, black life becomes situated within an economy of the gift – and gift, theologically understood, means freedom.

This trope of narrating black life in its freedom through the freedom of Jesus of Nazareth is picked up by Frederick Douglass, who in his autobiographical narrative of 1845[9] constantly sees his life against the grid of Scripture, countering the exegesis of white Christians who justified black enslavement through theories of the curse of Ham. He's out to tell a different story of what it means to be black, to be free, to be dignified. At the culmination of his story, we find an account of his struggle with the slave master refracted through the three holy days of Easter: he invokes the language of the Triduum and says, upon defeating the slave breaker, Edward Covey, 'I arose.' And then there's Jarena Lee. In her 1836 and 1849 spiritual writings[10] she tells the story of what it means for her not just to be black and free, but of what it means to be a black, female and free. This is a move that Douglass, for reasons that need not detain us here, does not make. Lee accomplishes her move, importantly for modern theology, by framing herself through the scriptural narrative of Pentecost. Here is the basis for a different kind of feminism or womanism – the term employed by many black women with feminist concerns. It gestures towards a genuinely theological feminism.

SHORTT: **To recapitulate then, early black Christians in America can be positioned within a great tradition of faith, even if they didn't consciously see their practice in such terms. And this means among other things that the ground of black Christianity can't be reduced to resistance to white oppression.**

CARTER: That's right, because the tradition I'm talking about recognised that neither blackness nor whiteness has any substance in itself. As I've said, the lie propagated by racism in the modern world is that our substance – the ground of all meaning as regards who we are, individually and collectively – resides in ourselves. When this lie is believed, the result is often nationalism. And tragically, of course, Christianity and theology have regularly been conscripted by nationalism at various stages of history. How can theology make amends? This is not just a question for the black religious academy; it is a question for the religious and theological academy as such. How ought the work of Christian dogmatic theology go forward, given the situation just described?

SHORTT: Let's turn to theology, or dogmatics, more generally. To ask about a 'black Christology' or a 'black systematics' would obviously entail a deep misunderstanding of much that you've been talking about so far. Nevertheless, your arguments do offer hints about how discussion of core doctrines can be enriched by the contribution of black thinkers. Could you say some more about this?

CARTER: You are right to see me as wanting to resist attempts at a 'black Christology' or a 'black systematics' and so forth, at least not in the way they may be typically thought about. I would want to point in another direction. But before I indicate that direction, allow me to say a word more about why I think this is not the way to respond to the problem that 'white theology' represents.

Given the things that I've already said about how black life can be read and heard as 'a' word of God, a word that is an inflection and so an articulation of the eternal Word, you might expect me to want to engage in the practice of theology in either of two ways: either from 'below', and therefore from the vantage point of black life and culture, or from 'above', and therefore from a safe, metaphysical point that is perched above the fray of actual embodied life. This opposition maps onto the age-old battles over how to understand the person and work of Jesus Christ. Is his life to be rendered intelligible from the vantage of his divinity, or is it to be understood from the vantage of his humanity? The former, many say, is the position that won out at the Council of Chalcedon in 451 and thus became the classical position; while the latter, often described as the Antiochene position, is the one that lost out in patristic times, though it is generally held to have undergone a revival during the past two centuries.

One can say that though dogmatic questions were notionally settled at Chalcedon, the underlying issues never really subsided, for they emerged again, perhaps most poignantly in the entire history of Christian theology, in the fifteenth- and especially the sixteenth-century debates surrounding the relationship between nature and grace. The debates were a mainly Roman Catholic affair, but they made their way into Protestant theology as well. At the heart of these discussions was the question of whether created natures are intelligible on their own and, relatedly, whether they have a purely natural meaning and end that runs parallel to, and therefore is independent of, a separate supernatural end effected by grace alone. To my mind, the theologian who has thought about this more insightfully and carefully than anyone else is Henri de Lubac. He wanted to ask why nature and grace came to be contrasted, given that this had not been so in earlier eras. De Lubac worked out the main lines of this thesis in his book *The Mystery of the Supernatural* and further developed it in *Augustinianism and Modern Theology*. He argued that unless the gap between grace and nature were bridged through a reinstatement of pre-modern models, theology would soon become anthropology.

Now why do I bring this up here, speaking as a black Baptist? Because, on the one hand, de Lubac's thesis can be read as an extended working out of a dogmatic Christology. And on other hand, it can help me articulate why formulating a 'black Christology' or a 'black systematics', at least as typically conceived, is problematic. Put succinctly, it risks replicating the very procedures of 'white theology', namely, of operating out of a notion of 'pure nature' as culturally inflected through the notion of 'whiteness'. The problem of white theology, like the problems I've been talking about throughout this interview – problems centring on the troublesome nexus that has occurred between the construction of notions of race in the modern world and the modern construction of 'religion', coupled with the uses to which theology has been put to undergird these developments – all of this could be said to have arisen from the bifurcation of so-called pure nature and supernatural grace.

De Lubac's call essentially was for theology to do its work by following the lead of a more classically oriented dogmatic Christology, in which in Christ there is no break between his humanity and divinity. The reason this is so in Jesus is because he bears the Holy Spirit in fullness, and as such he shows what it means to be human: to be a bearer of the Spirit so as to be raised beyond oneself in order to realise one's supernatural end in God. Given this, what makes white theology the problem that it is is that it is insufficiently Christological in the sense just outlined. And being insufficiently Christological it is insufficiently pneumatological or Pentecostal. White theology has too often functioned from a position of pure nature, a nature that is so pure that white theology need not name itself as 'white', for it is 'natural', indicative of the 'true' state and proper order of things.

It should be evident from much that I've said so far that, to formulate a 'black Christology' or a 'black systematics' as typically conceived, is to risk replicating this procedure, where 'black' comes to function in an essentialised or 'pure' manner. This, I should say, is the risk of many theologies of resistance and many theologies of culture, where culture – that is, being black or female or Hispanic, and so forth – is the site from which the counterattack is to be mounted. The oppressed, therefore, must be very careful about getting stuck in the familiar cultural grooves. The category of culture must be baptised – by full immersion, I would say! – before systematics makes use of it. My hesitancy about formulating a 'black Christology' or a 'black systematics' arises from the fact that I don't believe this purifying work has been sufficiently done.

Nevertheless, I still think there is a way in which one might engage in a kind of black Christology or systematics. What I want to suggest would be more akin to what de Lubac sought to articulate, following theologians like Augustine, though I would want to have his insights do their work against the backdrop of the 'fictive realities', as it were, of race and the work that race does to supplement and often to legitimate the socio-political and economic order of things. The challenge is to conceive of culture in Christological terms, to think no longer of the many ways in which nature commodifies itself as spectacle, as mass-produced entertainment to be bought and sold. To begin to sense the gravity of the issue, one need only think of how quickly hip hop, for example, as a musical expression of black culture, came to be commodified, and put, one might say, back on the auctioneer's block to be bought and sold. This is to say nothing of the commodification of religion. I would suggest that many contemporary theologians influenced by *ressourcement* thinkers from whom I continue to learn a lot, are not making some of these connections, and theology is the poorer for it. It also gives ammunition to hostile observers who think that theology is meaningless.

One final comment. Theology generally, and Christology especial-ly, cannot forsake their link to Israel, for Israel, as the scriptural record would have it, is a nation without analogy, a nation like no other, inso-far as its calling is to be a non-nationalistic nation. Theologically speaking, it is not a 'pure nation' or a 'pure culture'. It is constituted purely through the call of another, Yahweh, and through the law of this other, the Torah. This task is consummated, so Christian thought declares, in the Jew Jesus of Nazareth. I could add more, but will stop by saying simply that systematics and dogmatic Christology – and certainly the black Christology that I'm interested in – necessarily pre-suppose a Christian theology of Israel as a means of staving off the problem of nationalism.

SHORTT: As you know, there is no chapter in this book specifically devoted to Latin American liberation theology. But I'm not thereby trying to sideline an important subject: like interfaith dialogue, it's an area that can be viewed in passing from a variety of angles. One cannot, for example, do serious work in the fields of black and feminist theology without paying attention to names such as Gutiérrez and Segundo and Sobrino. Nevertheless, controversy still surrounds the liberationists' recourse to Marxism – both because it is now widely discredited as an economic theory, and because (as you've already pointed out in the racial context) many have doubts about the principle of giving secular categories a commanding role in theological discourse. How great is your own debt to liberation theology, and what is your assessment of it?

CARTER: I both have and have not been influenced by Latin American liberation theology, though I think that the latter – having not been influenced by it – is more determinative. What I mean by this is that, on the one hand, Latin American liberation theology is important, as I see it, because of its refusal of any theology that it regards as unable to engage the material conditions and problems that call forth liberation concerns in the first place. Indeed, it refuses a theology that is blind to and therefore complicit with structures of oppression. Latin American liberation theology, therefore, represented for me when I first encountered it a kind of bombshell for much of late twentieth-century theology. In its own way it pointed out the impotence and almost irrelevance of theologies that function from the standpoint of 'supernaturalism', as if the 'supernatural' is to be strictly cordoned off from 'nature', to invoke the terms I used earlier in relationship to de Lubac's theology.

But this move also represented its Achilles' heel, as I discovered from John Milbank, one of my teachers. What I learnt from his *Theology and Social Theory* was just how much liberation theology, in its own way, is based on a notion of 'pure nature', one might say, with religious experience being made reducible to and intelligible within the confines of socio-cultural and material processes. Within such a framework, religious experience and the concrete religions themselves signify or point to the capacity of the subject to be free and thereby to be an agent. Faith names this power and capacity for self-transcendent agency, this subjective power of freedom. Indeed, freedom, so understood, is that towards which the immanent human capacity for faith tends. Faith is the experience of removing inhibitions to self-fulfilment, to the realisation of freedom. Theology is one way to talk about this liberating experience of faith.

Here's the problem, though. When theology takes faith as its object and proceeds to talk about it as a signifier of freedom but under the formal and historical categories it has for naming this otherwise immanent experience, theology, in the liberationist view, proves itself necessarily inadequate to the task of making a historically effective, material difference. For just this reason, it is claimed,[11] theology requires social theory and the social sciences, which theorise about the fundamental social and material processes of our world, a task, according to a number of Latin American liberation theologians, that theology cannot do on its own. In Heideggerian terms, theology is only an 'ontic' or regional science, whereas social theory, which now acquires the status of philosophy, is more fundamental: a science that theorises the 'pure nature' of the social world.

What's ultimately wrong with this, one might ask? Two things, the first of which I learned from a comment Milbank makes about this in light of the theology of Thomas Aquinas. It takes faith as the object of theology, when in fact it isn't. God is the formal object of theology, and materially everything else is as well, insofar as everything else relates to theology's formal object. Society, therefore, need not be imagined as left to itself. Theology is a material discourse. Milbank's comment, however, leads me to my own second observation about what is wrong with Latin American liberation theology's approach to the problem of oppression. It is this: the social order can be imagined and performed differently, even at the so-called fundamental or structural level. Latin American liberation theology takes this possibility off the table, and to the extent that it does it remains captive to what I would like to call the tyranny of the present order of things. One might ask: Well, isn't Christian theology, even of the sort you would champion, in the same predicament, trapped within the constraints of the present? I want to say, Ultimately, no. The cogency of this response, however, depends on and indeed requires an ecclesiology in which the Church is understood eschatologically (and not merely teleologically, that is, as the culmination of a natural process), and also in terms of a theology of the mystical body of Christ. For eschatologically understood, Christian theology takes it that God has already enacted *and* is yet bringing to pass a different *ordo*, a different social arrangement, the *ordo* that is the trinitarian life within the economy of creation. But it must also be understood in terms of the mystical body of Christ, for the Church understood in terms of the mystery that is Jesus of Nazareth and the social arrangement he has enacted means that the Church bears within itself the ongoing mystery of Jesus, and indeed, by the grace of the Holy Spirit, *is* this mystery. I make these points because it strikes me that what may be the most misguided aspect of Latin American liberation theology is its neglect of ecclesiology. The same could be said of other liberation theologies as well.

Now I must say that I make these criticisms with a bit of trepidation because, again, it's one thing to point out how and/or why one thinks Latin American liberation theology is theologically off mark (and this must be done), but it's quite another to put theological proposals forward that speak deeply, even if finally differently, to the problems that called forth a liberationist outlook, particularly in the interest of the oppressed in the first place.

SHORTT: Well, you've at least supplied some helpful pointers! In the space that remains, could you say something about life at Mount Level Baptist Church in Durham, North Carolina, where you are associate minister?

CARTER: Our pastor is the Revd Dr William C. Turner Jr, who also happens to be a colleague of mine on the Duke University faculty. He teaches theology and homiletics. What strikes me most about Mount Level is that it's a model of what I call pastoral intelligence: it's a place where theology is always being worked out, expressed on the ground, making us more transparent to God in Christ. And that transparency emerges through ministries where we go to prisons, for example, and we talk to men and women about the faith, and try to supply some of their very tangible, material needs.

As I've made clear, the modern *ressourcement* movements within Roman Catholicism, and other movements such as Radical Orthodoxy and some of the Yale School of Theology, have all provided me with a rich vocabulary as a black theologian for which I feel nothing but appreciation. But that by itself – a vocabulary, that is – still isn't enough, because it is possible to talk the language of theological orthodoxy and still have one's discourse yoked to problematic social structures and social performances. Theological discourse, no matter what its orientation, will always have its deepest witness in the lives it is able to produce. Consequently, spirituality is the final and ultimate test of theology. If they neglect this, even *ressourcement* theologies will run the risk of becoming species of gnosticism: insider discourses of the intelligentsia. They will become testaments to our own alienation.

This, perhaps, is what contemporary postmodernism points to – the alienation of intellectual elites. And what form does this alienation take in the case of Christian theology? I'd contend that it's alienation from church communities, from the people of God – those for whom our work should matter even if they do not always form the main audience for our writings. In attending Mount Level Church I am in communion with a people who see, broadly speaking, that theology matters. They hear it being worked out in Sunday homilies. They participate in its being worked out through the various ministries and services our church provides. And so being at Mount Level Church has taught me to always bear in mind the communities for whom I write, and the connections between these communities. This lesson is also critical for modern theology generally.

14
Oliver O'Donovan and
Joan Lockwood O'Donovan

Political Theology

SHORTT: When Rowan Williams was appointed Archbishop of Canterbury, Oliver, you saluted the choice of a theologian who does not think it the business of theology 'to make Christian faith less offensive to modern man, but rather to expand modern man's imagination to the dimension of Trinitarian faith'.[1] This remark could serve as a compendium to your writings and Joan's, which probe fundamental questions at the boundary between Christianity and secular reason.

A slightly longer abstract of your joint project might run as follows. You believe that biblical models of corporate life remain relevant, despite being embedded in very different forms of society. You are therefore critics of liberal self-sufficiency and of the way liberal writers tend to bracket off two millennia of Christian thought. You do not accept that circles can be progressively squared from within liberalism's own resources: liberal enlightenment is, after all, a form of universalism and, like Christian and Islamic universalism, it is supersessionist and inclined to suppose that it has subsumed whatever good there was in the past. As David Martin has argued, 'The virtue of universalism always harbours the vice of imperialism, but whereas liberal enlightenment sees that very clearly with regard to religious universalism, it is less clear about its own imperialism.'[2] You expose what you call the monist potential of secular enlightenment and its self-appointed role of referee rather than contestant; and you point to the ways in which religious principles can regain relevance after periods of eclipse. For example, the international dimension of European Catholicism was devalued by the Reformation and the

Enlightenment, but re-emerged after 1945 in the reconstruction of Europe and the founding of what became the EU.

You are therefore unabashed in commending the active acknowledgement by society of the lordship of Christ over political institutions. And unlike many liberation theologians, whose use of the Bible you see as highly selective and yoked to alien political vocabulary, you are happy to deploy scriptural models more comprehensively. In your major work *The Desire of the Nations*,[3] you follow the core images of God's rule as found in the Hebrew Bible to analyse the essential moments of political authority: 'salvation' (*yeshua* – God's rule that brings victory, vindication and peace to his people); 'judgement' (*mishpat* – God's rule that distinguishes between the just and the unjust); 'possession' (*nahala/torah* – God's rule that provides particular space and structure for the life of his people); and 'praise' (*epainos* – God's rule that is acknowledged by his people as they gather for worship).

The German moral theologian Bernd Wannenwetsch, among others, has hailed these features as constituting 'a pattern of political authority from where a faithful witness can be expected and judged'.[4] For your more critical reviewers, of course, the problem lies precisely with the scale of your ambition, and what they see as an enthusiasm to restore some idea of 'Christendom'. Let's begin with your own accounts of what you're doing.

OLIVER O'DONOVAN: Thank you for that. The best way of describing how I understand my political work is with Anselm's famous programme, 'faith seeking understanding'. It is not only faith's primary object, God, that needs understanding, but the world in which we have to live. I find myself set down in the late-modern world, looking around and trying to find my way. But the late-modern world is in various respects incomprehensible, which is another way of saying that its secular reason is not wholly reasonable. It doesn't reason *far enough* to satisfy those who have to live in it. It presents us with a series of assumptions that create practical contradictions. And so, as a believer, I look to the Christian faith to shed light on what is going on. I am not interested in the restoration of Christendom. It is a *post*-Christendom politics that my faith has to engage with, to make sense of late modernity as the cultural setting in which I am given to live. That means looking deeper into the soul of modernity than its own superficial self-presentation would encourage. I explore these questions as someone who finds living in the modern world a conceptual and practical challenge.

And that is why the phrase 'practical reason' crops up a good deal in what I write and say these days. If there is any programme of recovery in my work, it is the recovery of practical reasoning, which has been lost in theology, as also in philosophy and the social sciences. My teacher, Paul Ramsey, subtitled one of his books, *How Shall Modern War Be Conducted Justly?*[5] – stressing the word '*shall*', not as a future of prediction, but of deliberation. How are we to *think* about how to act? And how are we to think, especially, about how to act in political contexts, in our human solidarities? How are we to think of ourselves as citizens – but what is a citizen? – of nation-states – but what is a nation-state? Where are we to find an intelligible account of the non-self-interpreting forms and structures through which we have to pick our way? I am a political *theologian* because, as a thinker, I can only address these questions with reference to the illuminating power of the Christian faith. I am a *political* theologian, because, as a believer, I need to be able to put one foot after the next.

SHORTT: Would you say more about your grounds for thinking that secular reason isn't reasonable enough?

OLIVER O'DONOVAN: Reasoning has become addicted to abstract schemas. It picks out certain forms and totalises them, ignoring other aspects of reality. A simple example is what we commonly say about democracy. Democracies announce themselves as constituted by a choice of government by the people or, even more immodestly, by the actual government of the people. No one who has performed the humble duty of casting a vote can find that description remotely transparent. The person whose name I marked will not (chances are) get into Parliament; if she does, she will not form part of the government; and to crown it all, I know hardly the first thing about her. The self-description of democracy is a wholly abstract one, and to bring it into contact with reality we must first treat all the key terms – 'people', 'choose', 'government' – as terms-of-art in need of extensive theoretical development.

Why do we describe ourselves in ways that conflict so directly with our surface experience? Why do we talk about ourselves in conventional ways we don't really believe in? Is there a bad faith written into the heart of late-modern culture, or have we got into a position where we simply don't know what we are doing? What has happened, I think, is that in the attempt to negotiate practicalities, the late-modern world has slimmed its practical political reason down to a minimum. It lives off a starvation-kit in which only a few limited and fragmentary thoughts are left over from what was once a more nourishing understanding of society and government – a theological one. So a theologian may be of help, but not, of course, simply by fitting old answers to new questions, but by recovering resources for new answers. The answers we need now have to be sought out and prayed for, won from engagement with these bewildering contradictions.

SHORTT: I've heard your work described as very cautious as well as ambitious: cautious in the sense that you're often reluctant to commit yourself on an issue that doesn't have clear theological underpinnings.

OLIVER O'DONOVAN: I think both those judgements are right in different ways. I'm cautious about promoting political programmes, even those that I look favourably on. Programmes are the work we pay our politicians for. It is the work of a political thinker to clarify what is being done when such programmes are made, what they are good for, what their risks and dangers are, and so on, and to help us conceive more clearly the wider coherence within which we and our politicians act. And that is where the ambition comes in. I am not among the postmodernists: in principle I admire grand narratives, seductive as they may sometimes be, and want to set things in their broader framework. At the beginning of *The Desire of the Nations* I said that we stand in need of 'Christian political concepts'. Those you mention are drawn from a number of important biblical terms that I selected in order to open up the discussion. They are expansive concepts, but not unhelpfully vague. And they are genuinely political.

Within the framework, however, those who have to act, must act. The thinker cannot and should not try to devise everybody's actions for them. The thinker can and should show what the shape of any given action is. So there is a moment of proper restraint in political thinking, but also a moment of assertive interpretation.

SHORTT: I'd like to put the verdicts of some of your critics to you later. But to continue for the time being with setting out your stall: Joan, you've done a good deal of work on the critique of secular liberalism. You see idolatry lurking in this civil creed, because of its hostility to what you've termed 'communities and institutions embodying transcendently given and permanently binding constraints on human action'.[6] Could you describe your position, and, perhaps, explain how you have come to hold it?

JOAN O'DONOVAN: May I begin by describing my critique of secular liberalism as one phase of an abiding concern to understand the spiritual, intellectual and practical failures of our time in their historical distinctiveness. Broadly, I am convinced that these failures reveal a distinctive manner of human oblivion to transcending goods and rights. In recent years I have consistently identified secular liberalism with (what I take to be) the prevailing modern strand of libertarian and contractarian thought which, I have argued, takes as its starting point the self-centred, self-owning and self-creating subject, and claims to be able to get from that sovereign individual will to an ordered political community, largely through the mechanism of collective contract, of binding collective agreement. But it never really does arrive at political community, because political community presupposes a shared communicating in a wide range of spiritual goods from the beginning – and that's just what liberalism denies.

In my youth, I was fortunate enough to come under the influence of two political philosophers who profoundly understood this failure of modern liberalism, and conveyed it in their writings with riveting luminosity: namely, George Grant and Leo Strauss. I encountered these thinkers as a graduate student, having come out of an undergraduate background in psychology and sociology that had left me wholly unconvinced by the approaches and arguments in these 'disciplines' and, as a Christian with some theological learning, suspecting both of serious intellectual depravity; but I then lacked any clear understanding of how they fitted into the larger liberal picture, historically and theoretically, and what the philosophical alternatives to them might be.

Strauss, the Jewish Aristotelian, and Grant, the Christian Platonist (who was himself indebted to Strauss), furnished me with both a comprehensive philosophical critique of modern liberalism and the social sciences, and two compelling intellectual alternatives to them.[7] As importantly, Grant took up the question posed by Strauss of what role biblical Christianity had played in the coming to be of the modern liberal belief that humans are 'historical' beings who, individually and collectively, create their future out of their own open-ended choices.[8] Grant's answer – that the unique biblical narrative of 'history' had degenerated into an intra-mundane 'historicism' – hinted that there was already something problematic about the biblical narrative. And I suppose that my subsequent career has been a sustained attempt to rescue biblical theology in its political aspects from this implicit charge.

For me this has meant quite simply returning to pre-modern theological articulations of political authority and order which situate it within a dynamic conception of humankind as created, fallen, redeemed and sanctified. Historically, so much of the liberal derailing of Christian political thought has involved a letting go of the biblical doctrines of: firstly, created moral structures to human community, in which love and justice, law and freedom, righteousness and communal right are united, and which are prior to and presupposed by every political order; secondly, humankind's solidarity in sin, as the condition of God's providential establishment of human political authority to be an external, communal remedy; and thirdly, the perfecting of redeemed moral community in the coming Kingdom of Christ, eschatologically present in the universal communion of the visible and invisible Church. When political authority is no longer circumscribed by these doctrines, it has forgotten its proper purposes and limitations, and becomes idolatrously overweening and engineering, as the egalitarian welfare state is today.

SHORTT: And your alarm over what you see as the authoritarian drift of secular liberalism is matched by concern about the complacency with which this is viewed by many people, including many Christians, who suppose that life today is broadly continuous with the political and legal inheritance of our Christian past.

JOAN O'DONOVAN: Yes. They are not reckoning with the evidence that we are living through an eclipse of our Western political and legal traditions. To my mind, a telling piece of evidence for this eclipse is the destructive impact that post-war human rights legislation has had and is having on particular legal and political cultures in Europe and elsewhere. It is clear that rights legislation (especially where it is constitutional and linked to judicial review) is revolutionary and supersessionist in theory and practice, its purpose being to challenge all existing legislation expressing common social, moral and religious judgements deemed by liberals to interfere with the individual's indeterminate freedom of choice. The legal individualism of human rights law (regardless of its inbuilt social qualifications) breeds contempt for a legal past in which both legislators and the legal profession, for the most part, assumed a cultural, moral and religious horizon for public law. As a native Canadian, I have been deeply distressed (but not in the least surprised) at the scandalous judicial attacks on public religious freedom that have been conducted under the 1982 Canadian Charter of Rights and Freedom, and other federal and provincial rights legislation. So when I hear from English judges and lawyers about the revolution in legal education that Britain's Human Rights Act of 1998/2000 is bringing in, I am none too sanguine. While the history of British jurisprudence is scarcely represented in today's legal curriculum, it is inundated with courses on European rights jurisprudence.

SHORTT: In his contribution to this book Christopher Insole outlines his reasons for rejecting the anti-liberal narrative of thinkers like yourselves.[9] How would you defend your work against his criticisms?

JOAN O'DONOVAN: I would say that Christopher Insole's presentation of our anti-liberal historical narrative – that there is a 'modern turn' in the late Middle Ages that is 'supposed to come to fruition around the seventeenth century' – does not do justice to our appreciation of late-medieval and early-modern political thought. While I do see such thinkers as Marsiglio, Ockham and Gerson as background (and in some sense, seminal) figures for an increasingly voluntarist and subjectivist strand of natural rights theory, I also see them as presenting important theoretical alternatives to later developments. This is clear in various of my articles of the last five years. Indeed, I have tried to return contemporary thought about rights to the theological formulations of Ockham and Hooker most particularly. At the same time, I have maintained unequivocally that Christian political thought is better off without the concept of human rights, which always deflects attention from God's right, God's law and God's justice.

Curiously, Christopher Insole's reading of our historical narrative conceals the likeness of his theoretical aspiration and our own: namely, to recover a 'forgotten tradition of liberalism' that is 'theologically informed and motivated'. This, I would suggest, is what Oliver set out to do in the penultimate chapter of *The Desire of the Nations*. Central to this tradition for both Oliver and myself is the theory of government as responsible and limited, as giving judgement under law, and as legitimated by its judicial function.

Having said that, there are aspects of Christopher Insole's liberal agenda that I cannot endorse, chiefly his focus on the preservation of individual liberties. Rather, I would propose that political liberalism that recollects its biblical foundations seeks to preserve individual and collective freedom (that is, moral agency and action) in their interdependence and manifold theological dimensions.

SHORTT: Thank you. Let's stick with broader threads for the time being by discussing your attitude to Christendom. Perhaps you could start, Oliver, since you've hinted that this part of your work has been misinterpreted. Faced with talk of a civil life where citizens and rulers alike are attentive to God's rule, the natural liberal response, encapsulated by a theologian such as John Kent, is that it's all very well in a country where the great majority of the population are religious believers. But it won't do, notwithstanding forecasts of a swing in the pendulum, in a highly secularised country like Britain.

OLIVER O'DONOVAN: Some reviewers have suspected my interest in Christendom as carrying a hint of reactionary conservatism about it. As I say, I have no agenda for the restoration of Christendom, and cannot even conceive what such an agenda might look like if I were to have it. I hoped I had made that clear in *The Desire of the Nations*, but it was not heard, perhaps because secretly people really *want* an agenda for the restoration of Christendom. But I do intend to listen to the Christian tradition on political as well as other subjects, and that is why I am so often caught reading old books when I ought, no doubt, to be keeping abreast of the latest thinking. Those who listen sensitively to the past understand their own present better. It can liberate us from the implausible prejudice that our modernity downstream of the French Revolution has made us more Christian than previous ages could be – 'better Christians than the apostles', as Kierkegaard liked to say, scornfully.

In *The Desire of the Nations* I took issue with the late John Howard Yoder, a man dearly loved and much admired for the best of reasons. Yoder became an important voice for the Anabaptist communities of America, which had not been noted for producing theological reflection. He broke through a certain taboo in bringing their traditions into discourse at a serious intellectual level with other Protestant and Catholic theologians. Nevertheless, in his determination to give the Anabaptist account of things a voice in the public realm, he seriously falsified Christian history in reading it as a capitulation by the Church to the attractions of power. In doing so he encouraged a generation of American Christians to swear their fealty to the First Amendment. Some of the Yoderian rhetoric, though with more nuance and some important safeguards, was taken up by my friend Stanley Hauerwas, for whom the term 'Christendom' acquired a wider use, referring to a religious epistemology that relies excessively on an appeal to public plausibility.

It was in response to this trend that Joan and I compiled our bulky reader, *From Irenaeus to Grotius*,[10] to put in the hands of English-speaking readers a wide selection of political texts from the missing 1200 years. In these texts you can watch the discussion go forward, and ask yourself: Are these people arguing like Christians? How are they using Scripture? Are they critical of themselves and one another? Do they understand the judgement of God against proud princes? Do their voices ever resonate with ours? My favourite example of that concerns the Devil's offer to Jesus of all the kingdoms of this world. I know of only two interpreters who have said that the Devil could make this offer because the kingdoms of the world were diabolical. One was John Yoder, the other Pope Gregory Hildebrand – not the most obvious bedfellows!

SHORTT: **So Christendom has something to teach the modern Christian.**

OLIVER O'DONOVAN: Yes. We late-modern post-Christendom Christians will not be capable of authentic Christian witness unless we have learned from Christendom. Take, for example, the question of how law relates to morality. A generation ago it seemed as if this question was settled beyond dispute in favour of the view that law had to proceed independently of morality, with no interest in *virtues* or *ideals* but concerning itself only with *harms*. Today we are caught up in a fervour of re-moralising legislation. The earnestness of the human rights movement, with its missionary zeal and indifference to all the deep problems in the concept of rights, is one sign of that. But it goes beyond human rights. The hunting controversy in England and Wales may have a historical significance greater than its marginal substantial interest would ever warrant, as the moment when the pursuit of a new public morality overleaped the traditional liberal hedges of rights and harms. Once again we heard arguments in which the vice of 'cruelty' was alleged as a sufficient reason for invoking the criminal law, without any reference to human rights or harms. Christian theology has a long and discriminating legacy of discussing law, one which puts deep tap-roots down into its understanding of God, human nature and salvation. Had the theological tradition been more vitally present to us in this period, it would have warned us both against the sub-moral and the super-moral ideals of law.

SHORTT: **Joan, I imagine Oliver's arguments form part of the rationale for your endorsement of church establishment.**

JOAN O'DONOVAN: Yes. Establishment is probably more under threat now than it ever has been. However, in my opinion, the Church of England will deserve to be disestablished unless its bishops, clergy and laity become less absorbed with the pastoral implications of establishment and more theologically serious about its political and legal implications. It is safe to say that the vast majority of the Church of England clergy and laity today, including members and ex-members of the legal profession, have never had occasion to reflect (theologically or in any other way) on the role that the established Church has played, and, indeed, continues to play, in the British constitution. The fact that, for example, the historical and contemporary statutes of the Church of England are 'primary' public legislation is of little significance to them. But these statutes (which concern doctrinal, liturgical and disciplinary, and not just administrative, matters) have something to say about the political community of Great Britain and its common goods, about the past and present evils that assail just and right human relationships within that community, and the parameters of an appropriate political response to them, and, most fundamentally, about the authority of the British government and its legislation. Moreover, I think that the greatest obstacle to a renewal of public interest in the theological resources of English church establishment for understanding our political community and its law is not the presence of other religious communities or some supposedly secularist consensus of the general population, but the accumulated failure of theological education and evangelical nerve in the established Church itself.

SHORTT: Could you, Oliver, address another criticism now, in a way allied to that of John Kent, and in another way at odds with it. This cavil is summed up by David Martin, who is on the side of seeing high theological ambition in your writings, and yet wants to query how much your contribution to political debate is specifically Christian and outside the range of an independent secular formulation. You've already answered this at one level by saying that we're all sitting on the shoulders of Christian giants, whether we're aware of it or not. But David Martin would want to take a crucial example like the Christian attitude towards the use of force,[11] and say, If you're not a pacifist, it doesn't really matter what Christian lens you employ as the focus of argument, because you are going to end up in the same boat as everybody else: assessing likely scenarios within a tiny range of real options. In other words, just-war theory might have theological origins, but the arguments are entirely available to secular reason, with little or no reference to theology.

OLIVER O'DONOVAN: The plausibility of this objection, it seems to me, arises from a trick of perspective. Moral reasoning proceeds, as we know, from the broadest, most wide-ranging convictions about God, the world and human action down to the detailed points on which concrete practical decisions turn. But concrete decisions present themselves as binary alternatives: we can turn left, or we can turn right; we can say yes, or we can say no. That is simply how we organise possibilities to make them digestible, as it were, for decision. Now, the objection goes: if Christian moral premises make any difference at all, it must be seen in concrete decisions at the end of a chain of reasoning. We must expect to find Christians and only Christians saying yes, where non-Christians and only non-Christians say no.

But such cases rarely, if ever, occur. Christians are actors in the same world as everyone else; they face the same binary choices, and therefore participate in the same common calculative reason surrounding those choices. Those who in 2002 believed as a factual proposition that Iraq was close to acquiring, but had not yet acquired, a WMD capacity, were more likely to judge the case for war favourably than those who believed either that it already had such weapons ready to use, or that it was nowhere near acquiring them. But Christians as such had no reason to hold to one account of these facts rather than another. So if they were not pacifists, the prudential question was likely to sway them as it swayed others, depending on what they took the facts of the situation to be.

The trick of perspective here is to make us focus our attention on the most concrete levels of political reasoning, as though they were the only levels that mattered, and moral thinking were merely a circuitous preparatory journey to bring us to a pre-arranged crossroads of decision. It has forgotten Eliot: 'The last temptation is the greatest treason, to do the right deed for the wrong reason.' Although moves *at that level* of thinking are furthest removed from theological first principles, and so most likely to be common to believer and non-believer, no living, thinking human being confines his or her practical reasoning to deciding things. Not even public bodies do so: the practice of politics requires policy, not only decision. And differences in policy determine the kind of circumstances that present themselves as needing decision. Once you have identified a given public decision and described it, you may find it difficult to see how Christians could respond to it very differently from other people. But by that time the interesting part is all over: identification and description of decisions is the essential intellectual work. Why did WMDs become the sticking point with Iraq? Because of the UN Convention on WMDs. Why was there a UN Convention? Because of huge revulsion at the Western and Soviet policy of massive deterrence, a revulsion focused in very considerable measure within the Christian Churches. Why were the Christian Churches interested? Because they had a long-standing, if partially eclipsed, tradition that asserted the importance of discriminate conduct in warfare. What was the basis of this tradition? The belief that international conflict, though it lay outside the scope of human law, did not lie outside the scope of divine judgement, and that guilt and innocence therefore mattered in war, too.

Can non-Christians not embrace the tradition of discrimination without embracing the belief about God? Well, certainly some do so. There is a jackdaw quality about how most people acquire their moral convictions, that allows them to fill their nests with such fragments of Christian or other moral thinking as seem to meet their needs. Just-war thinking has been popular recently, precisely because it speaks to pressing contemporary problems. But it was not always popular: total warfare was at one point the dominant strategic wisdom of the West. So if discrimination in warfare is a humane insight of some importance which can be lost, we should ask what were in fact the conditions for its recovery in the West and the conditions that need to be met if we are to hand it on to future generations with some semblance of moral coherence. Then, it seems to me, the significance of the theological train of thought will be quite apparent.

JOAN O'DONOVAN: As to how a theological perspective can make a practical difference, I would like briefly to shift the conversation to the area of economic practice. Over four centuries, the liberal economic tradition (which, admittedly, has Catholic neo-scholastic as well as Protestant roots) has emancipated the capitalist free-market from most of the moral restraints imposed on economic conduct within medieval Christendom. While too many Christians over the generations have been found either actively promoting or passively acquiescing in capitalist economic vice and its scientific rationalisations in the modern pseudo-science of economics (can there be a human science that eschews moral judgements?), there has always been Christian proclamation and practice of a more demanding economic ethic, ruled by principles and models of love and justice drawn from the Old and New Testaments. And over the last century, the Roman Catholic magisterium has done more than any other Western institution to demonstrate the continuing relevance of key principles and concepts of scholastic economic ethics developed from classical, biblical and patristic sources. In our day, we need only look at the strong Christian initiative and involvement in movements and organisations for just international trade and debt relief to poor countries, more conscientious consumption habits in the rich nations, and the development and use of technologies throughout the world that are socially, culturally and environmentally beneficial, rather than destructive.

SHORTT: I'm sure that at one level your argument could be multiplied many times over. As is well known, Old Testament Judaism is often described as having evolved into 'ethical monotheism', with the

implication that its novelty partly consisted in the harnessing of
morality with religious belief. It is also generally accepted that
Christian virtues such as humility and compassion were quite
foreign to the ethos of many pagan societies. But this doesn't necessarily stop the advocates of Niebuhrian realism from feeling
hemmed in. David Martin has summed it up thus: 'In a global and
plural situation it is virtually inconceivable that any society might be
so uniformly Christian as to be governed by some version of
Christian sharia, as even the Poles made brutally clear after 1989.
More fundamentally ... Christianity is not a religion amenable to
that kind of translation, partly because the very attempt is subverted
by its own inwardness and suspicion of legal externality, and partly
because gospel precepts lie outside any conceivable structure of
political action.'[12] I wonder if you could use this comment to put
further flesh on your argument.

OLIVER O'DONOVAN: I agree with what David Martin *asserts:* a
Christian form of sharia is unthinkable, not least because the
Christian understanding of the gospel does not permit such a
thought. But I disagree with what he appears to conclude. It is an odd
alternative: either sharia or nothing. The excluded middle, it seems to
me, is a form of legality that reflects the Christian refusal to absolutise
written statute. The gospel transcends all earthly politics, yet it makes
possible an earthly politics unlike what we might otherwise have had.
Christianity has had its own legal traditions very different from
sharia, traditions that insist on the principle of equity, the importance
of precedent and the relevance of customary practice. For this, as a
glance at a writing like Perkins's *Treatise on Equitie* makes clear, it has
the most directly evangelical reasons.

Consider, for example, the attitude towards the death penalty in
the West. Christians were making anxious noises about this in the
fourth century, when it caused them much more heart-searching than
just war ever did. For a period in the Middle Ages these concerns were
suppressed in the face of the more urgent priority of establishing the
idea of a law-state. But they revived again, because they were part of
an ongoing theo-political quest: an attempt to find a point where the
dynamic requirements of earthly justice could be qualified by a turn
towards mercy in response to the mercy of God. Remember *Measure
for Measure* and *The Merchant of Venice*.

David Martin is right to preserve a certain realism about the possibilities open to any political actor, especially in the face of the strong
temptation in a democracy, born of fear, to credit its leaders with infi-

nite power and infinite malice at the same time. But when everything necessary has been said along those lines, there are still some real decisions that major political actors will have to make, and those decisions will carry a large moral, and implicitly religious, freight. It is never the case that there is only one possible course of action unfolding inevitably. The course of events may sometimes assume a kind of inexorability, but even then the *manner* in which realities are faced can be honest or dishonest, courageous or timid, compassionate or ruthless. From the most restricted room to manoeuvre we may still win one or two hard nuggets of well-made decision – or we may fail to win them.

SHORTT: I suggest we talk later about the war on terror, and deal first with the just war, as Oliver, in particular, has done a lot of work in this area. Given what you've said, it seems clear that you can't countenance the bracketing of Christian just-war thinking with general moral theory.

OLIVER O'DONOVAN: That depends on what 'general moral theory' is supposed to be. If general moral theory is a distillation of the practical casuistry of a formerly Christian civilisation, something like the just-war ideal will be part of general moral theory simply because general moral theory derives from Christian reasoning. But if general moral theory is what anyone must subscribe to to be rational, it seems clear to me – in opposition to my friends John Finnis and Germain Grisez – that you don't rationally need to think in just-war terms. Most of the civilisations of the world would not have been rational on those conditions. Islam, with its own well-developed logic of law and war, does not think in such terms. Its thoughts often present the most interesting alternatives to Christian just-war categories, for example, in the role played by the notion of a sacred territory, the *dar al-Islam*, in authorising conflict. For Christian tradition no territorial consideration is an authorising factor as such; the only authorising factor is a concrete *injury* perpetrated by one side against the other.

But not only is it wrong to say that the just-war idea is simple rationality; it is not even the simple rationality of the West, for just-war theory has had its high tides and low tides in the history of Western thinking. One can, I believe, search the debates of the Second World War without finding any extensive moral scruple about non-combatant casualties. Even Bishop George Bell of Chichester mounted his great defiance of the wartime spirit of vengeance not primarily on the issue of non-combatant Germans but on the issue of non-Nazi Germans. In the second half of the twentieth century, driven by concerns over the policy of mutually assured destruction, the category of non-combatant immunity seemed suddenly to recover its relevance. Paul Ramsey stressed that, while the restraints imposed by the principle of proportionate harm are elastic, the principle of non-combatant immunity from direct attack is absolute. Non-combatants are caught up in a war collaterally, of course, and may suffer gravely; yet to make them the deliberate object of attack is an unqualified sin. It was on this basis that the massive destruction strategies of the 1950s and 1960s were exposed to consistent criticism from Christian sources.

And so today the climate is different. During the war in Afghanistan in late 2001, we were told, a controversy arose in the USA because commanders in the field were expected to have every potential target cleared by lawyers in the Pentagon for risk of excessive collateral non-combatant damage. A set of moral factors had come into our thinking that weren't there when the Second World War was fought. They can be intelligently or unintelligently applied. But I cannot regret they are there.

SHORTT: Do you detect an American Evangelical influence behind this change?

OLIVER O'DONOVAN: Roman Catholic, actually. The Roman Catholics led the recovery of the tradition, and Protestants took it up later. Paul Ramsey was of course the most influential Protestant advocate, but the Roman Catholics led the way.

SHORTT: I think you believe that Jimmy Carter played a creditable role in this process because of his demand for armaments that could be used more discriminately – for example, tactical nuclear weapons that could be targeted on silos, not cities. You're critical of the peace movement on this point, because the Campaign for Nuclear Disarmament and others opposed the newer generation of missiles, describing them as first-strike weapons designed to make a nuclear war winnable.

OLIVER O'DONOVAN: Nuclear deterrence was the first great moral disgrace of the West after the Second World War. Jimmy Carter, despite the low rating that his Presidency gets in the USA, even from Democrats, deserves some honour for having turned the development of American weaponry away from the morally unusable towards the morally usable. I was very cross with the peace movement in the 1980s, which got into the self-contradictory position of obstructing every attempt at nuclear disarmament. While Moscow and Washington were gingerly trying to trade disarmament moves, the peace movement found nothing better to do than complain that each new disarmament package made nuclear war more possible. But who ever thought that nuclear war *wasn't* entirely possible as things stood? Only the true believers in nuclear deterrence! So the great lie at the heart of deterrence, the idea that you could make your weapons so destructive that they would prevent war breaking out, was swallowed hook, line and sinker by the peace activists. You see why political theology has to exist: to prevent those who love peace from scoring own goals.

SHORTT: I think that's an important argument, though one might add that the peace movement was motivated by additional concerns that can't be dismissed on this basis. Given the rigorous principles you've spelt out, I imagine you'd be among the first to question the war on terror, on the grounds that it is impossible to wage war on an abstraction.

OLIVER O'DONOVAN: That's absolutely right. There are, of course, two possible levels of questioning: we may ask whether the various acts – the invasion of Afghanistan, the invasion of Iraq and a variety of actions below the level of warfare – were justified on their own terms; but over and beyond that we have to ask whether the enterprise has been correctly *conceived* by this umbrella-notion of a war against terror. Conceiving an action rightly is nine-tenths of its justification – and misconceiving it nine-tenths of its corruption.

I've argued that it's not the task of a theologian to pronounce judgement on particular government policies. The theologian is a citizen, too, of course, and forms views on policy like any other citizen. Yet it is not those views that theology is in business to promote, but the categories and criteria that are relevant for forming them. Paul Ramsey's book *Who Speaks for the Church?* was very critical of the freedom with which the churches habitually pronounced on international policy, but he thought highly of the formula used by Archbishop Michael Ramsey in 1965, addressing Harold Wilson on armed action against rebel Rhodesia: 'If [the Prime Minister] and his government think it necessary to use force for the perpetuation of our existing obligations in Rhodesia, then a great body of Christian opinion in this country would support him in so doing.' The judgement is the government's to make; but the terms of the question are not the government's to set. The 'great body of Christian opinion in this country' wants to know something more than what the government has decided; it wants to know whether the government has asked the right questions.

Public discourse around a war is very depressing, because everyone wants to cry Yes or No more loudly than the next person, and nobody elucidates the *shape* of the decision to be taken. If in the period before the invasion of Iraq the moral analysis had been done with more care, the implications of the sequel would have been clearer to everybody afterwards. Instead of all that 'pro-war', 'anti-war' posturing, we should have asked: What might it take to justify such an enterprise? Then it would not have been so easy for governments to shrug their shoulders when WMD were not discovered. The dishonesty of all that was a result of the chaotic character of the earlier debates, in which the Churches, especially, could have done much better than they did.

SHORTT: **Are you clear that Iraq should not have been invaded?**

OLIVER O'DONOVAN: Good things have come from it, I've no doubt. Whether the suffering will in the end appear to have been worth it, it would be impudent for a Westerner at the present juncture to say. We shall have to wait for the Iraqis to tell us, when they have put these terrible decades behind them. Yet even the good is best attributed to the providence of God. It can hardly be a matter for self-congratulation, since the Western policy has proved so ill-judged. If you make it the centrepiece of your *causa belli* that Iraq possesses concealed WMD and it turns out that it doesn't, the moral ground on which you stood falls away beneath your feet. The British and US governments may not have known the truth in early 2003, but in acting so decisively upon a false hypothesis, they were gravely imprudent. Grave imprudence is a species of practical immorality. On that ground alone the British Cabinet should, for the sake of constitutional integrity, have resigned as a whole, and been reappointed, perhaps in a different form, to complete the work of reconstruction in Iraq. That would have fittingly acknowledged a major blunder, putting us in a better position to help Iraq recover. You don't have to think that a blunder is worse than a crime to know that a blunder can be pretty bad.

When all that has been said, however, I must add a general point about judgements on the past, judgements of the form, 'should have' and 'shouldn't have'. It is a central point of Christian moral thought in general, as well as more specifically of just-war thinking, that we cannot and must not *rest* in such judgements. 'Judge not, that you be not judged.' We cannot indulge ourselves by building our moral postures on other people's mistakes – it is one of the things that the Christian tradition has identified as 'hypocrisy'. We notice mistakes as they are made, and learn from them – but always and only en route to the next challenge. The goal of just-war thinking, as of all moral thinking, is *deliberation*. That is to say: 'how *shall* war be conducted justly?', now or next time.

SHORTT: Would you both devote part of the remaining time to talking a bit more personally about your formation and broader theological outlook. One of several points that have struck me is that you are Evangelicals who would like to see Catholic principles reinstated or promoted in our public life.

OLIVER O'DONOVAN: I am the first Anglican in my family. My relatives were Roman Catholic on one side, and on the other side Methodist. I found my way into the Church of England as a child more or less on my own, and received my catechesis there in an Evangelical context for which I can never be sufficiently grateful. Half a century ago the Evangelicals in the Church of England were doing very well with young people; as a result many Christians passed through their hands who afterwards put a greater or lesser distance between themselves and the Evangelical tradition. I never underwent such a break. Formal theological study confirmed me in a strong commitment to the Scriptures as the norm of all theology, a central emphasis on the atoning death of Christ, and (less strongly present in my theological work, perhaps, but occupying me more at present) a belief that God's reality is inward as well as outward.

I am deeply thankful to have been born in a generation of ecumenical progress. My time in Canada in the late seventies and early eighties exposed me for the first time to intensive interaction with Roman Catholic theologians, and I discovered not only new things I needed to think about – especially in ecclesiology – but also to what a surprising extent the theological concerns I brought with me evoked an echo from them. I like to say, exaggerating only a little, that I learned how to read Karl Barth from a Jesuit. So although I think of myself as an Anglican and as an heir of the Reformation, I regard my Christian heritage as broader than that. The grounding in patristics that one used to get in the undergraduate theological syllabus at Oxford has always been important to me. And my early research on Augustine, of all the Church Fathers the one who speaks most eloquently both to Catholic and Protestant concerns, has been a guiding light to me ever since.

JOAN O'DONOVAN: My Catholic leanings are towards a medieval tradition of Christocentric Platonic 'realism' (in the schoolmen's sense), with which I would regard the Reformation emphasis on the body of Christ as a community of participation in Christ's real benefits (epistemological and soteriological) as continuous in important respects. So the trajectory that I have followed in recent years is from

Bonaventure and Wycliffe to Luther and Calvin. At the same time, I am thoroughly with the Reformers in viewing in a wholly negative light the juridicalising of the body of Christ and of salvation that dominated (but by no means exhausted) late-medieval papalist ecclesiology and penitential theology.

Indeed, it seems to me that, on the one hand, the juridical individualism of the medieval penitential discipline, with its spiritual economy of graded sins and punishments, satisfactions and assigned merits, was the seed bed of the late medieval development of 'subjective rights', understood as individual moral powers and entitlements. Of course, it must be remembered that late medieval 'rights' were embedded in a framework of divine and natural law that was not radically dismantled until the seventeenth century, when the full impact of Renaissance humanism and science had been absorbed – mainly by Protestants. Still, there was a medieval anticipation of the excessively self-conscious, calculating moral subject. On the other hand, the theory of the pope's supreme jurisdictional powers in the Church, extended even beyond this world (into purgatory), involved a most unfortunate positivising and juridicalising of the theological concept of law, that anticipated the secularising of this tendency in Renaissance legal humanism and republicanism, and its Protestant successors.

In so far as contemporary Protestant and Catholic political thought persists in these individualistic and juridical orientations, they shed insufficient theological light on, and offer insufficient theological hope to, our over-legislated, litigiously minded, and ideological polities. There needs to be a more wholehearted return to the traditional Christian political concepts of obligation, obedience, law and justice, which dwells on their social–relational and transcendent–divine meanings, and thereby opens up human political thought and action to the unity of love and justice, grace and law, in God's work of creation and salvation.

I would add, however, that contemporary Roman Catholicism has the unequalled pedagogical tool of the papal encyclical for renewing the theological framework of political thought. Papal social encyclicals over the last century have offered much that is worthy of universal Christian attention, and deserve to be used more extensively by other Churches than they have been. Christian political thought would be considerably more theologically robust today if its practitioners had all made a careful study of the encyclicals of Pope Leo XIII, particularly his 1888 encyclical on human liberty.

SHORTT: You've spoken warmly of Augustine, Oliver. Is he your greatest intellectual influence?

OLIVER O'DONOVAN: Yes. Augustine's is a complex, courageous, painfully honest and extremely well-balanced Christian mind, which gets some things wrong but more things right. I can sympathise with what he gets wrong as well as with what he gets right. He is a crucial focus for Western ecumenism, since, as I've said, his influence has been so great both on Catholics and Protestants. I received a precise but important influence from the reading of Karl Barth, who taught me how the theological endeavour had to understand its intellectual responsibilities and its authority. At one stage I was in danger of being branded a Barthian by well-meaning English colleagues who used the term to characterise anything that struck them as tending to enthusiasm. But in my view a moralist can never follow Barth in his approach to ethics, and it was to Paul Ramsey that I looked for my understanding of how Christian ethics should proceed. Although he was no historian himself, he pointed me back to the sources of just-war theory in the political theology of the late Renaissance. Through him I discovered Hugo Grotius, whom I have read with an enthusiasm that strikes many people as rather eccentric – but that is because they know him only through secondary sources, not first hand. It was Joan who introduced me both to more contemporary political philosophy and to the political legacy of the Middle Ages.

SHORTT: Early on in this conversation, Oliver, you defined your role as being to do with spelling out principles rather than recommending concrete courses of action. I'd like to return to this subject now, because it leaves some observers feeling that there's a top-down quality to your work. They might want to start with thinking about the experiences of communities rather than with questions about authority, for example. They would perhaps want to begin with their experience of visiting people in prison rather than abstract theorising about penal policy. Could you say something about your approach in relation to communitarianism and some of its prominent advocates, such as Rowan Williams and Duncan Forrester?

OLIVER O'DONOVAN: The term 'communitarian' is a fairly loose one, and these two colleagues' work is rather contrasted, sharing, perhaps, only the absence of a doctrinal character that mine may sometimes display, and a preference for questions that arise 'from below', namely from society rather than from government.

The clue that I find helpful in understanding Rowan Williams is to see him as an apologist. His famous Kierkegaardian tag about 'making Christianity difficult', i.e. deliberately inverting the project of the rationalising apologist who attempts to facilitate faith by ridding it of difficult features, doesn't mean that he turns from apologetics, as Barth does, to dogmatics. He makes our difficulty an apologetic opportunity. He uses it to appeal to an experience of the world that is more broken and less ordered than we usually like to acknowledge. He seizes on awkward and unassimilable fragments that will open the way to the mysterious, those that defy smoothing out, just as faith itself does. I heard him very memorably the other day on the practice of kneeling. Rowan can be quite difficult for the proverbial 'plain man'. Paradox and unexpected reversal is the essence of a Williams train of thought; the Kingdom of God is always slipping its hand surreptitiously into the doubter's back pocket and replacing the wallet and credit cards with a better funded set. His engagements with ethics and politics tend to be night-time raiding parties, less interested in knowing how they work than in finding out where they break down, and not with any idea of repairing them, either. Now, if you think back to what I said at the beginning of this discussion, you will see that I have learned something from the apologetics of fracture, perhaps under Rowan's influence. But I don't want to stay my eye on that cracked glass, but through it pass and then the heaven espy. I remember once, when we were young colleagues, complimenting Rowan on a fine sermon, and then adding tentatively, 'I just wonder whether you could have mentioned …' 'Judgement!' he interrupted – correctly.

Duncan Forrester, on the other hand, is a plain man's theologian. I feel almost mystical beside him. I find it hard to think of him as the pupil of Leo Strauss that he was. He has a naturally dialogical style and interdisciplinary curiosity. He has taken the trouble to be well informed about the social situations he has attended to, making the fullest use of social-scientific material without any of my nervousness about the philosophical *Tendenz* of empiricism. He has therefore brought a dense texture of social observation to the bar of theological and moral judgements that are, essentially, those of the plain man – or at any rate, the plain Scotsman. This is theology as pursued in the medieval mould as a practical science of church-direction – if the word did not carry a rather narrow, unsympathetic sense, one could say 'management'. John of Paris or Giles of Rome would have resonated with the kind of man Duncan Forrester is, even if they would not have understood the questions he has had to answer. The reward we all reap from his way of doing things is that the Church he has served so well, the Church of Scotland, has for a quarter of a century had a splendidly clear view on what has been going on around it. But does he incur a cost? Simply, perhaps, the cost of high contextualisation. How will the experiences of Scotland at the end of the twentieth century illuminate a theologian growing up in Shanghai in fifty years' time – which is where the theologians are going to be then, if there are any? I suspect a more theoretical approach could prove more exportable.

But, after all, why should the olive tree leave its rich oil, the fig tree its sweet fruit, or the vine its new wine? What I do, I do better than they could; and what they do, they do better than I could. Yet I hope we have learned something from one another's writing, as we have also enjoyed one another's conversation and company.

JOAN O'DONOVAN: I'd like to connect this point with Oliver's earlier remarks about the subversion of practical reason by the abstracting, totalising forms of liberal intellectual culture. Today people are constantly imbibing such abstractions as liberal democracy, the free-market, individual self-determination, historical progress, equal rights, and struggling to account reflectively for their ordinary experience with these inadequate grand concepts. So, for example, parents now feel obliged to reflect on their relationship with their children as one of reciprocal rights, and children are being liberated to think in these terms as well. But this schema does nothing to illuminate, but rather obscures, the emotional and moral texture of the parent–child relationship, and the concrete emotional and moral challenges for both sides. Right across the board, the reigning ideology into which our populations are increasingly indoctrinated by various public authorities (formal and informal) obscures the concrete moral bonds active in different situations, which people recognise, but cannot adequately express, because they lack an adequate common conceptuality. That is why ordinary people need an alternative, broad theoretical account of the moral world that helps unify their experience without suppressing vital aspects of it.

OLIVER O'DONOVAN: And we draw on experience in our work, too, of course, though our experiences are no doubt much less impressive than some that other people can speak about. But the question is: How does one use experience in theology? And what service can theology render experience? Theology is only one of the Christian services it is good to engage in; it cannot substitute for all the others. Nor can it substitute for the more humdrum experiences of social life, like being the parents of a child growing up. Without such experiences we would never be able to make use of what theology has to give us. But theology has something more to offer than simply repeating our experience back to us: it helps us to assess it and evaluate it. And since any one person can only have a very limited range of first-hand experiences, it can widen our horizons beyond the limits of the first-hand, and integrate our own experience into a universe of other people's experiences.

SHORTT: Perhaps the fundamental point is whether it's possible or right to separate principle from practice so clearly. Let's take the distinction between prison visiting and theology. I think others, especially those on the Church's radical wing, would want to say, Prison visiting *can* be theology, and to deny this presupposes a view of theology as a cognitive enterprise divorced from commitment. More broadly, I think there are many Christians from both sides of the political spectrum who think that a citizen must recommend alternatives to policies with which he or she disagrees. Criticism in itself isn't enough. This view is summed up by R. H. Tawney in *The Attack and Other Papers*, where he says that 'to state a principle without its application is irresponsible', and leaves the principle at too much of a level of generality.[13] It's evident that we're not dealing with an exact science here, because a number of your arguments, for example about the war on terror, do indeed seem to have very practical ramifications. But would you accept that there can be some dangers in the approach you've adopted?

OLIVER O'DONOVAN: Nobody understands what a principle means without understanding what it might be like to apply it. Principles without practical imagination fail the first test of practical thought. But the whole point about a principle is that it is susceptible of multiple applications, and practical reasoning involves keeping the whole range of possible applications in play. If I commit myself irreversibly at the beginning to one of the possible applications, I shall fail to realise the practical potentiality of my principle. A moralist is inevitably a better judge of principle than of detailed policy – that is simply a vocational point, and moralists who claim otherwise have a dangerously inflated sense of their powers. In *The Just War Revisited*[14] I tried to clarify the point in relation to proposals for a standing war crimes tribunal, as follows: the moralist does not have to answer for a proposal's being *practicable,* but does have to answer for its being *realistic.* If I make a good argument for a standing body to try war crimes, it is not a valid objection to say that the USA and Russia will never agree to it – even if, indeed, it is unlikely that they will. It is worth a debate, at any rate. The practical constraints that face a diplomat do not face a moralist; the moralist does not need to be on the winning side of every argument. But if someone objects to my plan that it requires leaders of states locked in armed conflict to behave in ways that are more impartial and self-denying than is reasonable to expect, then I have made myself foolish.

My record for going into practical detail is not all that bad, if you include the two little war books and throw in *The Ways of Judgment*,[15] which is written as a 'political ethics' to complement the 'political theology' of *The Desire of the Nations*. But I have a feeling it still won't satisfy those who want prison visiting to be theology. Theology can learn from prison visiting, as it can learn from diplomacy and politics, and, indeed, it should learn. But theology cannot claim the patron's role over every valuable thing Christians may do in the service of God; it can only offer such activities assistance on the conceptual front. Is it simple theological imperialism that makes people want to fuse these enterprises? I think, rather, that prison visiting is being used as a weapon in an intra-theological dispute about whether Scripture or experience provides the theological norms by which one judges. And in that dispute I am uncompromising. The authority of normative biblical concepts is the guarantee of our freedom in encountering experience. It gives us the words to talk about whatever we experience without question-begging. To make experience provide the normative concepts is to rob it of the open exploratory character proper to it. Experience is to be interrogated, enquired into, spoken about, testified to, enjoyed, praised, in short, to *be experienced*. It cannot be sold on the market to yield a return in epistemology, controlling what we shall think.

SHORTT: **Could you give a brief summary of** *The Ways of Judgment*, **a work that has been much anticipated?**

OLIVER O'DONOVAN: I think of the two books as two phases in a single extended train of thought. They were originally conceived as one, but what has now become *The Ways of Judgment* was postponed when *Desire* began to sprawl out of control. The second book continues the exploration which the first began into how theological and political concepts correspond; but it approaches the correspondence much more from the political side, and so takes on some more concrete political questions, though not at a level of particularity that will satisfy those who expect a commentary on current events. I develop the distinction made in *Desire* between political act and political institutions. The political act is judgement, but political institutions are formed by representation, which is a function of tradition. In the tensions generated here we can situate most of the perplexities and contradictions of political activity. There is some reflection about the character of law, international as well as domestic, and about the character of political constitution. There is also an attempt to establish clearly the connection between 'political' questions of government and 'social' questions of community, and to approach from a new angle questions broached in *Desire* about the relation of civil society to church and that of community to individual.

Notes

Preface
1. Bryan Magee, *Men of Ideas: Some Creators of Contemporary Philosophy* (Oxford University Press, 1978), p. vii.
2. Cormac Murphy-O'Connor, quoted in *The Tablet*, 27 July 2002.
3. Christoph Schwöbel, for example, defends the priority of positive (cataphatic) over negative (apophatic) theology, and criticises the prevalence of apophatic thinking, p.96.
4. Antony Flew, *God and Philosophy* (Prometheus Books, 2005), with a new introduction by the author.
5. Martin Heidegger, *Introduction to Metaphysics*, tr. Ralph Mannheim (Yale University Press, 1959), p.203. For a lucid overview of the subject, see John Macquarrie, *Heidegger and Christianity* (SCM Press, 1994).

1. ROWAN WILLIAMS: Belief and Theology: Some Core Questions
1. Rowan Williams, 'Redeeming Sorrows', in D. Z. Phillips (ed.), *Religion and Morality* (Macmillan, 1996), p.147, in response to Marilyn McCord Adams, 'Evil and the God-Who-Does-Nothing-In-Particular', pp.107ff. in the same volume.
2. Revelation 21:4.
3. James Wood, *The Broken Estate* (Jonathan Cape, 1999; Pimlico edition, 2000), p.311.
4. Williams, 'Redeeming Sorrows', p.132.
5. Rowan Williams, 'Barth on the Triune God' in *Karl Barth: Studies in his Theological Method* (Clarendon Press, 1979).
6. Rowan Williams, 'Balthasar and Rahner', in John Riches (ed.), *The Analogy of Beauty* (T&T Clark, 1986).
7. Andrew Shanks, *Hegel's Political Theology* (Cambridge University Press, 1991), and *God and Modernity* (Routledge, 2000).
8. Rowan Williams, 'What Does Love Know? St Thomas on the Trinity', published in *New Blackfriars* (June 2001).
9. St Thomas Aquinas, *Summa Theologiae* (Eyre and Spottiswoode, 1964–74), I.xxvi.
10. Williams, 'What Does Love Know?', p.263.
11. *ibid.*, p.272.

2. JANET MARTIN SOSKICE: Philosophical Theology
1. Janet Martin Soskice, *Metaphor and Religious Language* (Oxford University Press, 1985).
2. Janet Martin Soskice, *Naming God*, scheduled for publication in 2006.
3. See 'Theology and Falsification', in Anthony Flew and Alasdair MacIntyre (eds), *New Essays in Philosophical Theology* (SCM Press, 1955).
4. Gregory of Nyssa, 'Against Eunomius', in *Nicene and Post-Nicene Fathers* (London and Oxford, 1892).
5. Janet Martin Soskice, 'Love and Attention', in Michael McGhee (ed.), *Philosophy, Religion and the Spiritual Life* (Cambridge University Press, 1992); reprinted in Pamela Sue Anderson and Beverley Clack (eds), *Feminist Philosophy of Religion: Critical Readings* (Routledge, 2003).
6. Gregory of Nyssa, *The Life of Moses* (Paulist Press, 1978).

3. ALVIN PLANTINGA AND CHRISTOPHER J. INSOLE: The Philosophy of Religion
1. John Henry Newman, *A Grammar of Assent* (Oxford University Press, 1985), pp.191ff.

2. Alvin Plantinga, *God and Other Minds: A Study of the Rational Justification of Belief in God* (Cornell University Press, reprinted 1990).
3. Alvin Plantinga, 'The Ontological Argument', in James F. Sennett (ed.), *The Analytic Theist: An Alvin Plantinga Reader* (Eerdmans, 1998).
4. J. L. Mackie in Basil Mitchell (ed.), *The Philosophy of Religion* (Oxford University Press, 1971), pp.100–101.
5. See p.10.
6. Plantinga, 'The Free Will Defense', in *The Analytic Theist*.
7. James Beilby (ed.), *Naturalism Defeated? Essays on Plantinga's Evolutionary Argument Against Naturalism* (Cornell University Press, 2002).
8. *ibid.*, pp.1ff.
9. Christopher J. Insole, *The Politics of Human Frailty: A Theological Defence of Political Liberalism* (SCM Press, 2004), p.4.
10. Lord Acton, 'Study of History', in *Essays on Freedom and Power* (The Beacon Press, 1988), p.28.
11. John Locke in P. Laslett (ed.), *Two Treatises on Government* (Cambridge University Press, 1988), Bk II, section 155 (p.370) and section 240.8 (p.427).
12. Christopher J. Insole, *The Realist Hope: A Critique of Anti-Realist Approaches to Philosophical Theology* (Ashgate, 2005).
13. See p.116.
14. See p.116.
15. See p.124.

4. SARAH COAKLEY: New Paths in Systematic Theology

1. Volume 1, *God, Sexuality and the Self: An Essay on the Trinity* (Cambridge University Press, forthcoming).
2. *Christ Without Absolutes: A Study of the Christology of Ernst Troeltsch* (Oxford University Press, 1988).
3. See Colin E. Gunton, *The Christian Faith: An Introduction to Christian Doctrine* (Blackwell, 2002); Robert W. Jenson, *Systematic Theology Volume I: The Triune God* (Oxford University Press, 2001); and Kathryn Tanner's *Jesus, Humanity and the Trinity: A Brief Systematic Theology* (T&T Clark, 2001), which is intended as a prelude to a larger project. Miroslav Volf is working on a general introduction to Christian theology.
4. Judith Butler, *Gender Trouble: Feminism and the Subversion of Identity* (Routledge, 1990).
5. See Luce Irigaray, *Sexes and Genealogies* (Columbia University Press, 1993).
6. For more on Gregory of Nyssa and gender in relation to his doctrinal thought, see Sarah Coakley, *Powers and Submissions: Spirituality, Philosophy and Gender* (Blackwell, 2002), chapters 7–9; and Sarah Coakley (ed.), *Rethinking Gregory of Nyssa* (Blackwell, 2003), pp.1ff.
7. Elizabeth Stuart *et al.*, *Religion is a Queer Thing: A Guide to the Christian Faith for Lesbian, Gay, Bisexual, and Transgendered People* (Cassell, 1997).

5. CHRISTOPH SCHWÖBEL: The Triune God

1. Rowan Williams, '*Sapientia* and the Trinity: reflections on the *de Trinitate*': a paper delivered to a conference on Augustine and the Trinity at Lancaster University, 1990. See also A. de Halleux, 'Personalisme ou Essentialisme Trinitaire chez les Pères Cappadociens?', in *Patrologie et Oecumenisme* (Leuven: Peeters, 1990), pp.215ff.
2. Williams, '*Sapientia* and the Trinity'.
3. Richard of St Victor, *The 12 Patriarchs, The Mystical Ark*, and *Book 3 of The Trinity* (Paulist Press, 1979).

4. St Thomas Aquinas, *Summa Theologiae*, III.xxiii.2.

5. Robert W. Jenson, *Systematic Theology Volume 1: The Triune God* (Oxford University Press, 2001).

6. JOHN MILBANK AND SIMON OLIVER: Radical Orthodoxy

1. John Milbank, 'Knowledge: The Theological Critique of Philosophy in Hamann and Jacobi', in John Milbank, Catherine Pickstock and Graham Ward (eds), *Radical Orthodoxy: A New Theology* (Routledge, 1999), p.24.

2. John Milbank, *Theology and Social Theory* (Blackwell, 1992).

3. See p.97.

4. Catherine Pickstock, 'Reply to David Ford and Guy Collins', *The Scottish Journal of Theology* 54.3 (2001), pp.405ff.; and 'Modernity and Scholasticism: A Critique of Recent Invocations of Univocity', *Antonianum* 78.1 (2003), pp.3ff.

5. See, for example, Duns Scotus, Opus oxoniense I, distinction III, Questions i and iii, available in Allan Wolter (ed.), *Philosophical Writings* (Hackett, 1987), pp.4–8, 14–33.

6. Rowan Williams, in an unpublished interview.

7. John Henry Newman, *A Grammar of Assent* (Oxford University Press, 1985), chapter 8, 'Inference'.

8. Fergus Kerr OP, 'A Catholic Response to the Programme of Radical Orthodoxy', in Laurence Paul Hemming (ed.), *Radical Orthodoxy – A Catholic Enquiry* (Ashgate, 2000), pp.57ff.

9. The 'Illuminations' series (forthcoming) will be published by Blackwell.

7. DAVID BURRELL: The New Aquinas

1. Roger Scruton, *An Intelligent Person's Guide to Philosophy* (Duckworth, 1996), pp.49–50.

2. Fergus Kerr OP, *After Aquinas: Versions of Thomism* (Blackwell, 2002), p.31.

3. This conception should be distinguished from that of Descartes, under which God is invoked to exorcise the ghost of epistemological scepticism.

4. Josef Pieper, 'The Negative Element in the Philosophy of St Thomas', in *Silence of St Thomas* (St Augustine's Press, 1999), pp.47ff.

5. John Henry Newman, *A Grammar of Assent* (Oxford University Press, 1985), chapter 8.

6. Kerr, *After Aquinas*, p.60; St Thomas Aquinas, *Summa Theologiae*, I.ii.1.

7. Timothy McDermott (ed.), *Summa Theologiae: A Concise Translation* (Ave Maria Press, 1989).

8. David Burrell, *Knowing the Unknowable God: Ibn-Sina, Maimonides, Aquinas* (University of Notre Dame Press, 1987).

9. David Burrell, *Freedom and Creation in the Three Traditions* (University of Notre Dame Press, 1994).

10. David Burrell, *Aquinas: God and Action* (Routledge, 1979).

11. David Burrell, *Faith and Freedom: An Interfaith Perspective* (Blackwell, 2004).

12. Anthony Kenny, *Aquinas* (Oxford University Press, 1980), p.60.

13. Timothy McDermott, in an unpublished interview.

14. John Milbank and Catherine Pickstock, *Truth in Aquinas* (Routledge, 2000).

8. JEAN-LUC MARION: God and the Gift: A Continental Perspective

1. See p. ix.

2. John Macquarrie, *Twentieth-Century Religious Thought* (SCM Press, 1963), p.203.

3. Jean-Luc Marion, *The Idol and Distance* (Fordham University Press, 2001).

4. Jean-Luc Marion, *God Without Being* (University of Chicago Press, 1995).

5. St Thomas Aquinas, *Summa Theologiae*, I.xiii.5.

6. St Augustine, *Confessions* (Oxford University Press, 1991), XII.vii.(7).
7. See pp.137–8.
8. Jean-Luc Marion, *Reduction and Givenness: Investigations of Husserl, Heidegger and Phenomenology* (Northwestern University Press, 1998).
9. Paul Ricoeur, 'Toward a Hermeneutic of the Idea of Revelation', in Lewis S. Mudge (ed.), *Essays on Biblical Interpretation* (SPCK, 1981).
10. Jean-Luc Marion, *The Erotic Phenomenon* (University of Chicago Press, 2005).

9. DAVID MARTIN: Christianity and Society

1. David Martin, *Christian Language in the Secular City* (Ashgate, 2002).
2. David Martin, *Christian Language and its Mutations* (Ashgate, 2002).
3. David Martin, *Pentecostalism: The World Their Parish* (Blackwell, 2002).
4. David Martin, *Does Christianity Cause War?* (Oxford University Press, 1997).
5. John Cornwell, *Hitler's Pope: The Secret History of Pius XII* (Viking, 1999), chapters 7, 8 and 9.
6. David Martin, *The Times Literary Supplement*, 24 and 31 December 2004.
7. David Martin, *The Times Literary Supplement*, 7 February 2003.
8. John Milbank, *Theology and Social Theory* (Blackwell, 1992).
9. Charles Taylor, *Sources of the Self: Making of the Modern Identity* (Cambridge University Press, 1992).
10. David Martin, *The Times Literary Supplement*, 7 February 2003.
11. David Martin, *A General Theory of Secularization* (Blackwell, 1978).
12. David Martin, *Reflections on Theology and Society* (Oxford University Press, 1997).
13. See, for example, Robert Putnam (ed.), *Democracies in Flux: The Evolution of Social Capital in Contemporary Society* (Oxford University Press, 2004).

10. STANLEY HAUERWAS and SAMUEL WELLS: Theological Ethics

1. Stanley Hauerwas, *With the Grain of the Universe: The Church's Witness and Natural Theology* (SCM Press, 2002).
2. Stanley Hauerwas and Samuel Wells (eds), *The Blackwell Companion to Christian Ethics* (Blackwell, 2004).
3. See Alasdair MacIntyre, *After Virtue* (Duckworth, 1985), especially chapter 15.
4. See Jeffrey Stout, *Democracy and Tradition* (Princeton University Press, 2004).
5. See Stanley Hauerwas, *The Peaceable Kingdom* (SCM Press, 1983).
6. See Stanley Hauerwas, *Performing the Faith* (SPCK, 2004), pp.135ff.
7. See Samuel Wells, *Improvisation: The Drama of Christian Ethics* (SPCK, 2004), chapter 2.
8. See John Milbank, *Being Reconciled: Ontology and Pardon* (Routledge, 2003).
9. See Reinhold Niebuhr, *The Nature and Destiny of Man: A Christian Interpretation* (John Knox Press, 1996).
10. Stanley Hauerwas, *After Christendom?* (Abingdon, 1991).
11. See Stanley Hauerwas, *Suffering Presence: Theological Reflections on Medicine, the Mentally Handicapped, and the Church* (T&T Clark, 1986).

11. TINA BEATTIE: Feminist Theology

1. Natalie K. Watson, *Feminist Theology* (Eerdmans, 2003), p.27.
2. Elizabeth A. Johnson, *She Who Is: The Mystery of God in Feminist Theological Discourse* (Crossroad, 1992), Part III.
3. Rosemary Radford Ruether, *Sexism and God-Talk: Towards a Feminist Theology* (SCM Press, 1992).
4. Sarah Coakley, 'The Eschatological Body: Gender, Transformation and God', in *Powers and Submissions: Spirituality, Philosophy and Gender* (Blackwell, 2002).

5. Mary McClintock Fulkerson, *Changing the Subject: Women's Discourses and Feminist Theology* (Fortress Press, 1994).

6. Jean Bethke Elshtain, 'The Power and Powerlessness of Women', in Gisela Bock and Susan James (eds), *Beyond Equality and Difference: Citizenship, Feminist Politics and Female Subjectivity* (Routledge, 1992).

7. Valerie Saiving, 'The Human Situation: A Feminine View', in Carol P. Christ and Judith Plaskow (eds), *Womanspirit Rising: A Feminist Reader in Religion* (HarperSanFrancisco, 1992).

8. Carol Gilligan, *In a Different Voice: Psychological Theory and Women's Development* (Harvard University Press, 1982).

9. Tina Beattie, *Woman* (Continuum, 2003), reviewed by Susan Dowell in the *Church Times*, 3 September 2004.

10. Jane Williams, *The Times Literary Supplement*, October, 2004.

11. Charlene Spretnak, *Missing Mary: The Queen of Heaven and Her Re-Emergence in the Modern Church* (Palgrave Macmillan, 2004).

12. Sarah Jane Boss, *Mary* (Continuum, 2003).

13. Coakley, 'Kenosis and Subversion: On the Repression of "Vulnerability" in Christian Feminist Writing', in *Powers and Submissions: Spirituality, Philosophy and Gender* (Blackwell, 2002).

14. See, for example, Luce Irigaray, *Speculum of the Other Woman* (Cornell University Press, 1985).

15. See, for example, Hans Urs von Balthasar, 'The Conquest of the Bride', in *Heart of the World* (Ignatius Press, 1991), pp.189ff.; and 'Casta Meretrix', in *Explorations in Theology II: Spouse of the Word* (Ignatius Press, 1991), pp.193ff.

16. Hans Urs von Balthasar, 'Woman's Answer', in *Theo-Drama III: The Dramatis Personae: The Person in Christ* (Ignatius Press, 1992), pp.283ff.

17. Michele M. Schumacher (ed.), *Women in Christ: Toward a New Feminism* (Eerdmans, 2004).

18. Grace M. Jantzen, *Becoming Divine: Towards a Feminist Philosophy of Religion* (Manchester University Press, 1998).

19. Janet Martin Soskice, 'Blood and Defilement', in Soskice and Diana Lipton (eds), *Oxford Readings in Feminism* (Oxford University Press, 2003).

12. MIROSLAV VOLF: Faith and Reconciliation: A Personal Journey

1. Miroslav Volf, *After Our Likeness: The Church as the Image of the Trinity* (Eerdmans, 1998).

2. Miroslav Volf, *Exclusion and Embrace: A Theological Exploration of Identity, Otherness, and Reconciliation* (Abingdon, 1996).

3. See pp.100–102.

4. See p157.

5. Oliver O'Donovan, *The Just War Revisited* (Cambridge University Press, 2003), p.5.

6. *ibid.*, p.21.

7. Justin Martyr, *The Second Apology*, in Volume 1 of *The Ante-Nicene Fathers* (Eerdmans, 1969).

13. J. KAMERON CARTER: Black Theology

1. J. Kameron Carter, 'Christology, or Redeeming Whiteness: A Response to Jim Perkinson's Appropriation of Black Theology', *Theology Today* 60/43 (2004).

2. Stuart G. Hall, 'Subjects in Black History: Making Diasporic Identities in Wahneema Lubiano (ed.), *The House that Race Built: Black Americans, US Terrain* (Pantheon, 1997).

3. See Hans Urs von Balthasar, *The Glory of the Lord: A Theological Aesthetics*, 7 vols.

(Ignatius Press, 1982–89), and *Theo-Drama: Theological Dramatic Theory*, 5 vols. (Ignatius Press, 1988–98).

4. Forthcoming from Oxford University Press.

5. W. E. B. Du Bois, 'The Souls of Black Folk', in Nathan I. Huggins (ed.), *Dawn of Dusk: Essays and Articles* (The Library of America, 1986).

6. David L. Chappell, *A Stone of Hope: Prophetic Religion and The Death of Jim Crow* (University of North Carolina Press, 2004).

7. See Maria W. Stewart, 'Productions of Mrs Maria W. Stewart', in Henry Louis Gates (ed.), *The Schomburg Library of Nineteenth Century Black Women Writers* (Oxford University Press, 1988).

8. Briton Hammon, *A Narrative of the Uncommon Suffering, and Surprizing Deliverance of Briton Hammon, a Negro Man, a Servant of General Winslow, of Marshfield, in New-England; Who Returned to Boston, after Having Been Absent Almost Thirteen Years* (Green & Russell, 1760).

9. Frederick Douglass, 'Narrative of the Life of Frederick Douglass, an American Slave', in Henry Louis Gates (ed.), *Autobiographies: Frederick Douglass* (The Library of America; Penguin, 1994).

10. Jarena Lee's 1836 text is carried in Catherine L. Albanese and Stephen J. Stein (eds), *Religion in North America* (Indiana University Press, 1986). Her 1849 text is in *The Schomburg Library of Nineteenth Century Black Women Writers*.

11. See, for example, Clodovis Boff, *Theology and Praxis: Epistemological Foundations* (Orbis, 1978), and Juan Luis Segundo, *Liberation of Theology* (Orbis, 1976).

14. OLIVER O'DONOVAN AND JOAN LOCKWOOD O'DONOVAN: Political Theology

1. Oliver O'Donovan, 'Rowan Williams, The New Archbishop of Canterbury. A Symposium', *Pro Ecclesia*, Vol. XII, No. 1.

2. David Martin, *The Times Literary Supplement*, 24 and 31 December 2004.

3. Oliver O'Donovan, *The Desire of the Nations: Rediscovering the Roots of Political Theology* (Cambridge University Press, 1996).

4. Bernd Wannenwetsch, *Modern Theology* (July 1998), pp.463ff.

5. Paul Ramsey, *War and the Christian Conscience: How Shall War be Waged Justly?* (Duke University Press, 1961).

6. Oliver O'Donovan and Joan Lockwood O'Donovan, *Bonds of Imperfection: Christian Politics, Past and Present* (Eerdmans, 2004).

7. See, for example, Leo Strauss, *Natural Right and History* (University of Chicago Press, 1950); and *What is Political Philosophy?* (The Free Press of Glencoe, 1959).

8. See, for example, George Grant, *Technology and Empire: Perspectives on North America* (House of Anansi, 1969); *Time as History* (Canadian Broadcasting Corporation, 1969); and *English-Speaking Justice* (House of Anansi, 1985).

9. See pp.61ff.

10. Oliver O'Donovan and Joan Lockwood O'Donovan, *From Irenaeus to Grotius: A Sourcebook of Christian Political Thought* (Eerdmans, 1999).

11. David Martin, *The Times Literary Supplement*, 24 and 31 December 2004.

12. *ibid.*

13. R. H. Tawney, *The Attack and Other Papers* (Allen and Unwin, 1953), p.178.

14. Cambridge University Press, 2003.

15. Forthcoming from Eerdmans.

Index of Names

Index